D0024973

GORE
VIDAL

Photo of Gore Vidal by Jane Bown. Courtesy of William Morris Agency, Inc.

GORE VIDAL

A Critical Companion

Susan Baker and Curtis S. Gibson

CRITICAL COMPANIONS TO POPULAR CONTEMPORARY WRITERS
Kathleen Gregory Klein, Series Editor

Greenwood Press
Westport, Connecticut • London

For Audrey and Nona

Library of Congress Cataloging-in-Publication Data

Baker, Susan, 1945–
    Gore Vidal : a critical companion / Susan Baker and Curtis S.
Gibson.
        p.   cm.—(Critical companions to popular contemporary
writers, ISSN 1082–4979)
    Includes bibliographical references and index.
    ISBN 0–313–29579–4 (alk. paper)
    1. Vidal, Gore, 1925– —Criticism and interpretation.
I. Gibson, Curtis S., 1945– .   II. Title.   III. Series.
PS3543.I26Z53   1997
818'.5409—dc20   96–26809

British Library Cataloguing in Publication Data is available.

Library of Congress Catalog Card Number: 96–26809
ISBN: 0–313–29579–4
ISSN: 1082–4979

First published in 1997

Greenwood Press, 88 Post Road West, Westport, CT 06881
An imprint of Greenwood Publishing Group, Inc.

Printed in the United States of America

The paper used in this book complies with the
Permanent Paper Standard issued by the National
Information Standards Organization (Z39.48–1984).

10 9 8 7 6 5 4 3 2 1

ADVISORY BOARD

Contents

Contents

VIDAL'S INVENTIONS

Series Foreword

The authors who appear in the series Critical Companions to Popular Contemporary Writers are all best-selling writers. They do not have only one successful novel, but a string of them. Fans, critics, and specialist readers eagerly anticipate their next book. For some, high cash advances and breakthrough sales figures are automatic; movie deals often follow. Some writers become household names, recognized by almost everyone.

But novels are read one by one. Each reader chooses to start and, more importantly, to finish a book because of what she or he finds there. The real test of a novel is in the satisfaction its readers experience. This series acknowledges the extraordinary involvement of readers and writers in creating a best-seller.

The authors included in this series were chosen by an Advisory Board composed of high school English teachers and high school and public librarians. They ranked a list of best-selling writers according to their popularity among different groups of readers. Writers in the top-ranked group who had not received book-length, academic literary analysis (or none in at least the past ten years) were chosen for the series. Because of this selection method, Critical Companions to Popular Contemporary Writers meets a need that is not addressed elsewhere.

The volumes in the series are written by scholars with particular expertise in analyzing popular fiction. These specialists add an academic focus to the popular success that the best-selling writers already enjoy.

The series is designed to appeal to a wide range of readers. The general reading public will find explanations for the appeal of these well-known writers. Fans will find biographical and fictional questions answered. Students will find literary analysis, discussions of fictional genres, carefully organized introductions to new ways of reading the novels, and bibliographies for additional research. Students will also be able to apply what they have learned from this book to their readings of future novels by these best-selling writers.

Each volume begins with a biographical chapter drawing on published information, autobiographies or memoirs, prior interviews, and, in some caes, interviews given especially for this series. A chapter on literary history and genres describes how the author's work fits into a larger literary context. The following chapters analyze the writer's most important, most popular, and most recent novels in detail. Each chapter focuses on a single novel. This approach, suggested by the Advisory Board as the most useful to student research, allows for an in-depth analysis of the writer's fiction. Close and careful readings with numerous examples show readers exactly how the novels work. These chapters are organized around three central elements: plot development (how the story line moves forward), character development (what the reader knows about the important figures), and theme (the significant ideas of the novel). Chapters may also include sections on generic conventions (how the novel is similar to or different from others in its same category of science fiction, fantasy, thriller, etc.), narrative point of view (who tells the story and how), symbols and literary language, and historical or social context. Each chapter ends with an "alternative reading" of the novel. The volume concludes with a primary and secondary bibliography, including reviews.

The Alternative Readings are a unique feature of this series. By demonstrating a particular way of reading each novel, they provide a clear example of how a specific perspective can reveal important aspects of the book. In each alternative reading section, one contemporary literary theory—such as feminist criticism, Marxism, new historicism, deconstruction, or Jungian psychological critique—is defined in brief, easily comprehensible language. That definition is then applied to the novel to highlight specific features that might go unnoticed or be understood differently in a more general reading of the novel. Each volume defines two or three specific theories, making them part of the reader's understanding of how diverse meanings may be constructed from a single novel.

Taken collectively, the volumes in the Critical Companions to Popular

Contemporary Writers series provide a wide-ranging investigation of the complexities of current best-selling fiction. By treating these novels seriously as both literary works and publishing successes, the series demonstrates the potential of popular literature in contemporary culture.

Kathleen Gregory Klein
Southern Connecticut State University

GORE
VIDAL

1

The Life of Gore Vidal

To date, the career of the American writer Gore Vidal has spanned more than fifty years. He has been both precocious, publishing his first novel at twenty-one, and prodigious. When the definitive Vidal bibliography is published—to the sorrow of his admirers and the relief of his many literary and political sparring partners—it will include thousands of lectures and interviews; several hundred lengthy articles and essays; dozens of stage plays, screenplays, and television scripts; one collection of short stories; and, more to the point of this brief and highly selective biographical sketch, twenty-three novels.

Vidal's life as public gadfly and entertainer-provocateur—as distinct from his literary one—is well known, some would say too well known; he has never been reticent in airing his beliefs or acting on them. He has twice run for national office, once for Congress (New York general election, 1960), and once for the U.S. Senate (California Democratic primary, 1982). In 1968 he actively campaigned for the presidential peace candidate, Eugene McCarthy. His political opponents have consistently dismissed him as a radical leftist, but his insistence on the primacy of first principles (that is, the Constitution and the Bill of Rights) could as easily be seen as the constructionist enthusiasms of an arch-conservative. Vidal himself has rejected both labels, pointing out that the current confusion over political nomenclature renders such easy classifications meaningless.

A category Vidal unarguably does fit, however, and one into which he gained early entry, is that of the American celebrity. The social circumstances of Vidal's family, and the circles he moved in as a child, were exceptional by most standards and uniquely advantageous for a serious writer of his generation. At the very least they seem to have immunized him early on against any awe for the rich and famous. His childhood acquaintances numbered, among others, Amelia Earhart, Eleanor Roosevelt and her cousin Alice Longworth (Teddy Roosevelt's daughter), and members of the U.S. Senate. By his early twenties Vidal was famous (or notorious) in his own right and an intimate of (not to say *with*) Tennessee Williams, Anaïs Nin, André Gide, Truman Capote, and the philosopher George Santayana. Vidal did not, however, confine himself strictly to the literary set. While writing movie scripts in the late 1950s, he and his friend Howard Austen shared a house in Los Angeles with actors Paul Newman and Joanne Woodward. Vidal's recently published memoirs (*Palimpsest*, 1995) provide a gossipy window on those early years and some instructive background for his novelistic career—and, more particularly, his not infrequent social commentary.

Eugene Luther Vidal (he unilaterally assumed the "Gore" when he was fourteen) was born October 3, 1925, at the U.S. Military Academy at West Point, New York, where his father Eugene was an aviation instructor and a former all-American football player. His mother, Nina Gore, was the daughter of U.S. Senator Thomas Gore of Oklahoma, in whose home the young Vidal lived until he was ten. If Vidal is the prototypical autodidact (for all his erudition he has little good to say about his formal schooling), his self-education began in his grandfather's house in the Washington, D.C., enclave of Rock Creek Park. Senator Gore had been blinded in childhood—in two separate accidents, no less—and on his grandson fell the role of reader and sometime amanuensis. In addition to reading the senator a good deal of his official correspondence and frequently guiding him about the Capitol, the young Vidal was encouraged to make use of his grandfather's substantial personal library. As Vidal recollects, he took that encouragement to heart. "I worked my way through a shelf of Scott. I read all of Meredith and Henry James. When I was a bit older I read Flaubert, Proust, and George Eliot. And, of course, I loved Peacock, Huxley, Wodehouse—the satirists. I read Swift . . . and more" ("Interview," Parini 281).

Vidal left the senator's house and library in 1935, when his mother divorced Eugene and married Hugh D. Auchincloss, a wealthy but apparently ineffectual stockbroker. A breathless society writer for *Time* may have overstated the case when he called Auchincloss "the first gentleman of America," but Auchincloss was doubtless a "gentleman" in at least one sense of the word. Vidal is less generous in characterizing his stepfather, but funnier: "Early in life, at Yale, in fact, Hughdie's originality was revealed; *he was unable to do work of any kind.* Since the American ruling class, then and now, likes to give the impression that it is always hard at work, or at least very busy, Hughdie's sloth was something of a breakthrough. The word 'aristocrat' is never used by our rulers, but he acted suspiciously like one; certainly he was inert in a *foreign* way" ("Reflections on Glory," *United States* 1252). In any case, it seems that Vidal, observant youngster that he was, was not ill-served by his mother's second marriage. Although less than industrious, Auchincloss appears to have been intensely social; Merrywood, the Auchincloss house in Washington, was a popular destination for the local lights of the day—powerful politicians, that is—and the adolescent Vidal moved among them at ease. Merrywood, in fact, might be seen as the wellspring for *Washington, D.C.* and the later political novels it spawned. Eventually, Nina Gore Vidal Auchincloss moved on, having given "Hughdie" two children and Vidal a half-sister and a half-brother; Auchincloss himself subsequently married Janet Bouvier, the mother of the future Mrs. John F. Kennedy. Readers of *1876* and *Empire* probably won't be mistaken if they detect resemblances between the Auchincloss clan and the fictional Apgar family.

Vidal's formal education (one suspects it was better than he gives it credit for being) was a private one. He attended St. Albans School in Washington, which he left in 1939, and studied in France until the war intervened. In 1940 he spent an unsatisfactory term at the Los Alamos School in New Mexico, and then enrolled at the Phillips Exeter Academy in New Hampshire. (John Knowles's novel *A Separate Peace* contains a portrait, or caricature, rather, of Vidal at Exeter in the person of Brinker Hadley, as Robert F. Kiernan points out in his excellent critical study, *Gore Vidal* [1982].) It was early on at St. Albans, however, that Vidal fell in love, as he tells us in *Palimpsest*, for the first and last time. The object of his affection, which appears to have been reciprocated, was a classmate named Jimmie Trimble, a star athlete and beautiful adolescent (if his photographs don't lie) who was later killed in battle on Iwo Jima at the age of nineteen. Vidal would go on to commemorate Trimble with varying degrees of transmutation in several novels (notably *The City and the Pillar, The Judgment of Paris,* and *Two Sisters*), but most literally in the partially autobiographical *Washington, D.C.*

In 1943 Vidal graduated from Exeter and enlisted in the army. He was assigned to study engineering at the Virginia Military Institute—a wholly unsuccessful experiment—and was later reassigned to a supply ship in the Aleutians, from which experience came his first published novel, *Williwaw* (1946). Both a critical and commercial success, that story of men at sea propelled him out of his job in a New York publishing house and into the life of a full-time writer. That life, incidentally, might be viewed as "the road not taken" by the enervated protagonist of his next novel, *In a Yellow Wood* (1947).

By 1952 Vidal had lived in Guatemala, traveled in Europe, and bought a house in rural New York. He had also published several more books, one of which was to set his adversarial stance vis-à-vis the critical "establishment" for years to come. *The City and the Pillar* (1948), a sympathetic story of erotic awakening, emphasized the ordinariness of homosexual behavior and thereby earned its author some unsought notoriety and the enmity of the *New York Times*, among others. Feeling himself the target of a boycott, Vidal published three mystery novels under the pseudonym Edgar Box (1952–54) and turned his hand to scriptwriting for television. *Visit to a Small Planet*, perhaps his best original work for that medium, was broadcast in 1955 and expanded into a successful Broadway play in 1957. (A lamentable film version starred Jerry Lewis.) *The Best Man* (1960), a political drama, enjoyed a similar success on Broadway and was made into a movie in 1964. Ultimately, Vidal's forays onto the stage (and screens both small and large) extricated him from a difficult financial situation and provided a storehouse of topical experience for his later fiction, particularly *Myra Breckinridge*.

However lucrative scriptwriting may be, and lucrative it was for Vidal, he has made clear his continuing preference for the novel. "I am not at heart a playwright," he wrote in 1957. "I am a novelist turned temporary adventurer; and I chose to write television, movies, and plays for much the same reason that Henry Morgan selected the Spanish Main for his peculiar—and not dissimilar—sphere of operations" ("Small Planet," *United States* 1160). If not exactly piratical, Vidal's motives were unapologetically mercenary when, under contract to MGM, he went to Italy in 1958 to do background research for the remake of the movie *Ben Hur*. His essay "Who Makes the Movies?" is wryly instructive about that experience (*United States* 1166–79), as is the account in *Palimpsest* (301–307).

Whatever his misgivings about Lew Wallace's novel or the project in general, Vidal's immersion into Imperial Rome gave impetus to the first of his splendid historical fictions. Begun in 1959 and completed in 1964, *Julian* marked Vidal's arrival as a novelist of the first rank. It was also his first published novel since *Messiah* (1954), whose fictional narrator had wanted to write his own novel about the apostate emperor. Initial reviews were mixed; the genre was—with a few notable exceptions—not a distinguished one, and many reviewers didn't know what to make of Vidal's effort. But Julian (known to history as "Apostate") and the milieu of the disintegrating classical world provided the ideal vehicle for the author's artistic strengths and philosophical concerns. The more thoughtful critics discerned the book's merits, and sales were gratifyingly brisk. Remarkably enough, Vidal found time to run for Congress in 1960 as the Democratic candidate in his heavily Republican home district in New York. As expected, he lost the election; he did, however, run stronger than any Democrat in recent memory and served notice that he was no fun to campaign against, especially in the venue of public debate. Vidal's other run for public office came in 1982, when he contested in the California Democratic primary for U.S. senator against former Governor Jerry Brown. Again he lost, though narrowly, and again his opponent had reason to wish that he hadn't run at all, though Brown and Vidal seem to have parted friends.

Such was not the case with Vidal and William F. Buckley Jr., as viewers of their famous conversations at the 1968 Democratic convention in Chicago will remember. While the Chicago police and a dissatisfied citizenry debated the Vietnam War with clubs and rocks outside the convention, Vidal and Buckley demonstrated—rhetorically—a similar regard for each other inside the television studio. Vidal made rude noises about Buckley's rightist politics, and Buckley displayed his literary acumen by intimating that Vidal's recent novel *Myra Breckinridge* was pornographic. An exchange of vituperative essays in *Esquire* magazine followed (Buckley's "On Experiencing Gore Vidal," August 1969; Vidal's "A Distasteful Encounter with William F. Buckley, Jr.," September 1969), and shortly thereafter, lawsuits. That the political issues of the day were much clarified by the Buckley-Vidal showdown is doubtful, but their entertainment value was first-rate. Nielsen's ratings for the convention soared.

The undeniably gamy *Myra Breckinridge* (1968), the novel that so exercised Buckley, further enhanced Vidal's reputation for giving offense. A burlesque of modern French literature, the *auteur* theory of filmmaking, and the movie industry in general, *Myra* did, in fact, offer something to offend most everyone, not only Buckley, but transsexuals and

French film critics as well. It also demonstrated Vidal's considerable comic gifts, which were further developed in a sequel *Myron* (1974), and in *Duluth* (1983), a rambunctious hymn to civil and literary anarchy.

In 1970 Vidal became co-chairman of the dissident (and noisy) People's Party, and in 1972—eager, no doubt, to solidify his position with the establishment—he returned to the stage with his play *An Evening With Richard Nixon*, a production that lampooned the sitting president with dialogue culled from his own speeches. The target, however, may have been too broad or the national mood too grim for a satirical exploration of the Nixon psyche. The play closed after a short run, and Vidal returned to his newly purchased villa in Ravello, Italy, to prepare *Burr* (1973) for publication.

That splendid imagining of the young republic, together with *Washington D.C.* (1967), which ends during the Eisenhower administration, established the historical boundaries for the six installments of Vidal's American histories. Those histories, which have come to be called the "American Chronicles," comprise two centuries of national evolution and expansionism as seen through the eyes of one fictional family, the illegitimate lineage of Aaron Burr. The second of those chronicles, *1876*, was published in the bicentennial year of 1976, and tells of a constitutional crisis that resonates with the Watergate difficulties of Vidal's frequent subject, Richard M. Nixon. *Lincoln* (1984) is a deft and controversial psychological portrait of that president during the Civil War, and *Empire* (1987) is Vidal's jaundiced explication of American internationalism following the Spanish-American War. The latest entry in the series, *Hollywood* (1990), returns to another of Vidal's recurring themes, the unholy alliance between politics and the mass media. This time the movies are recruited by Woodrow Wilson to goad Americans into World War I.

Besides addressing those voluminous and entertaining correctives to his fellow citizens in what he has often called the "United States of Amnesia," Vidal published two other lengthy novels during the same period. Those novels neatly illustrate a few of his central philosophical concerns: the rational ordering of human society and, somewhat paradoxically, the irrelevance of humanity in the infinity of space and time. *Kalki* (1978) is the eerily prescient story of an apocalyptic religious cult, which in some ways foreshadows the Branch Davidian fiasco in Waco, Texas. *Creation* (1981) relates the spiritual quest of a fifth-century B.C. Persian, Cyrus Spitama. As roving ambassador for the Great King, Spitama searches for the meaning of life and man's place in the cosmos.

He finds no ultimate answers but, as Kiernan points out (66), waxes lyrical on the brevity of any man's years:

> When I think of India, gold flares in the darkness behind the lids of these blind eyes. When I think of Cathay, silver gleams and I see again, as if I were really seeing, silver snow fall against silver willows.
> Gold and silver; darkness now. (461)

Or, less elegantly, life is short. Have a go.

And Vidal has indisputably had his go. In 1974 Bernard F. Dick wrote in *The Apostate Angel*:

> Thus far, Gore Vidal has produced an impressive body of work: fiction, essays, television scripts, scenarios, Broadway plays. Obviously, everything he has written is not equally memorable. All one can ask of a writer like Vidal is that he produce something of value in each field he enters. I believe he has. (Dick 6)

More than twenty years later, Dick's assessment is truer than ever; the *enfant terrible* of the late 1940s is rightly acknowledged in the 1990s as a master of American letters. Vidal's most recent novel, the comic and irreverent *Live from Golgotha* (1992), did nothing to undermine his literary stature. Nor did that revisionist account of the crucifixion endear him to the Christian Right, a group whose approbation has never much interested him.

In 1992 Vidal again indulged his taste for unlikely political causes when he wrote several highly pertinent, if wildly underappreciated, campaign speeches for the Democratic presidential aspirant, Jerry Brown. In 1993 he delivered some speeches of his own when he portrayed a U.S. senator in Tim Robbins' film *Bob Roberts*. That role was followed a year later by a part as an acerbic professor of political science in the otherwise mawkish Joe Pesci vehicle, *With Honors*. Credible as he was in both parts, it's doubtful that Vidal could accommodate an acting career in what is, to understate the case, an already busy life. He and Howard Austen, his companion of nearly forty years, continue to divide their time between their residences in Los Angeles and Ravello—the latter having become a popular destination for celebrity movers and shakers in recent years—

and, as ever, Vidal writes. In 1993 he received the National Book Award for his collection of essays *United States*, and in 1995 the first installment of his memoirs, *Palimpsest*, was published. We highly recommend those volumes as companion pieces to the novels discussed in the following chapters.

2

Genre and the Early Novels of Gore Vidal

The years from 1946, the publication date of Vidal's first novel, *Williwaw*, to 1954 (*Messiah*) represent the first period of Gore Vidal's novelistic career. We might say, broadly, that the novels from that period are experiments in genre, or literary form; further, that few if any contemporary American writers have had such public apprenticeships in various genres as has Vidal. The coming-of-age story, for instance, is a genre often accorded serious attention, and examples in the mode are as various as Mark Twain's *Huckleberry Finn* and J. D. Salinger's *Catcher in the Rye*. Several of Vidal's early works are in this vein, and two of those, *The City and the Pillar* (1948) and *The Judgment of Paris* (1952), merit consideration as important American novels.

Other, more "popular" genres include science fiction, historical romances, rousing tales of men pitted against the elements, and futuristic, or prophetic, fiction. But because of the mass appeal of these forms, and because most novels written in them are unremarkable and frankly commercial entertainments, they have, until recently, seldom received academic attention, much less critical acclaim. Vidal, however, was not one to curry favor with the "book establishment," and he tried most of those generic venues, though always with an eye to developing the themes that were to resurface in his mature work of later years. (The detective novels he wrote from 1952 to 1954 under the alias "Edgar Box" are exceptions to that rule. The Box whodunits, quite respectable entertainments in their own right, were written hastily and for money.) Some of Vidal's efforts in popular genres were more artistically successful than others, but none was a resounding financial triumph, and by 1954 he felt that he could no longer support himself—to his own taste, at least—with his fiction. His popular work looked to many to have ended his career as a novelist of any particular distinction, and he spent the next ten years of his life writing for the stage, screen, and television. Vidal's generic efforts, however, laid the technical groundwork for his later, more ambitious, novels; in themselves they demonstrate serious literary intent and an aesthetic sensibility not typical of their forms. In retrospect it looks as though the author was not so much searching for his own "voice," as setting himself the task of mastering various novelistic conventions—prescribing, in fact, his own artistic curriculum. This chapter will follow Vidal's progress and attempt to locate each of his early books in its proper historical and literary niche and relate it to the development of his work from 1964 to the present.

Vidal's first novel, *Williwaw*, was published in 1946, when its precocious author was twenty-one years old. Vidal had begun writing the story two years earlier while serving as first mate on an army freighter in the Aleutian Islands of Alaska. By 1944, the Aleutians had become peripheral to operations in the Pacific Theater, and the U.S. Army was gradually shutting down its bases in the region. That is the premise for *Williwaw*, the story of several ordinary men on a nondescript ship engaged in a routine mission: to deliver a recommendation to close one of those bases. But when nature intervenes in the form of a horrific storm and sexual rivalry results in the death of a crew member, that mission becomes something other than routine.

Critics praised *Williwaw* as one of the best novels to emerge from World War II, and it fits within the genre of war novels, particularly in its depiction of arbitrary boredom punctuated by terror, administrative decisions made without regard for personnel, and a readiness to cover up—even reward—reckless incompetence. *Williwaw* draws on two additional traditions. In its focus on skilled and conscientious performance in the wake of wrong-headed orders, *Williwaw* is also an adventure tale of the "men-at-work" variety. One critic describes the typical characters in popular versions of this genre: "Men, both hero and villain, wearing oil-splattered khakis, rain slickers, or hooded parkas. Men whose high-risk occupations—charter-boat captains, pilots, explorers, smugglers, engineers, and dreamers—are almost story enough" (Bourgeau 191).

(Disaster movies, from *Lifeboat* to *The Towering Inferno* to the spoof *Airplane*, also belong to this narrative genre.)

In another artistic vein, *Williwaw* is also part of a long tradition that presents human beings on a ship in a dangerous sea as a splendid and time-honored metaphor for the human condition at large. Vidal didn't invent this pattern, of course, nor was he the last to use it. Notable examples in the American tradition are as far-ranging as Melville's *Moby Dick* (1851) and Katherine Anne Porter's *Ship of Fools* (1962), but Stephen Crane's short story "The Open Boat," inspired by that writer's experience as a Spanish-American War correspondent, is probably closest, thematically and stylistically, to *Williwaw*. Vidal's prose, like Crane's, is remarkably spare, and the narrative tone is austere and disinterested, befitting the novel's central theme. The universe is physical and unfeeling, utterly indifferent to human affairs; the men who would survive in it had best look to their own interests, particularly in the *extremis* of war. (A useful survey and bibliography can be found in Bender.)

A work's genre suggests particular ways of reading and particular questions. As a war novel of men at sea, *Williwaw* has no single main character; each of the men on board has his own duties. The characters in such novels can sometimes be interpreted as aspects of a composite protagonist whose antagonist is the elements. (The terms "protagonist" and "antagonist" derive from *agon*, Greek for struggle or contest.) Nor is any single character highly developed. Instead, the characters are measured across two scales: competence or incompetence and courage or cowardice. *Williwaw* and similar novels place people in circumstances that make their pasts irrelevant, except insofar as they have been professionally and personally trained to function effectively in a crisis.

Williwaw's bare-bones plot presents the interaction of disparate characters thrown together by chance and the vagaries of war. Major Barkison, a self-important career officer with West Point credentials, has come to the base at Andrefski Bay to assess its viability. His work done, he must return with his report to headquarters at Arunga Island, a short airplane trip but several days away by sea. Bad weather, however, has grounded all air traffic, and though there's no particular urgency, Barkison insists upon going by boat. The only available ship is a dilapidated freighter skippered by the unendearing but capable Mr. Evans, a commercial fisherman by trade, who is marking time till war's end and swilling bourbon on a regular basis to relieve the tedium. The crew includes the first mate, Martin, a professional actor in civilian life and a cynical presence in his military role; the second mate Bervick, a regular army man who contends, inexplicably, for the affections of a local prostitute with Duval, the chief engineer. Besides Barkison, the other passengers are the major's aide, Lieutenant Hughes, and the chaplain, O'Mahoney, a Catholic monk reluctantly drafted from his monastery for the duration of the war. The cast is completed by John Smith, an Aleut Indian who serves in the galley. Smith is a chronic complainer and a stupendously bad cook, the ideal irritant on a less than ideal cruise.

Shortly after the ship leaves Andrefski Bay the barometer begins to fall, an omen of bad weather and the ensuing trouble on board. When the ship stops overnight at the port of Big Harbor to drop off supplies, Duval outbids the jealous Bervick for the favors of a prostitute, precipitating a shipboard crisis that parallels the impending storm. The trip continues the next day, even as the barometer continues to fall and the sea rises. Martin's air of superiority antagonizes Evans, and Barkison, continually dispensing inappropriate platitudes and bald reminders of his own importance, antagonizes everybody else. The well-meaning but ineffectual O'Mahoney alternately vomits and prays, while the jejune Hughes remains unaware of the danger threatening them all. The emotional climate onboard has become as unsettled as the weather, and Evans puts the ship into an uninhabited but protected cove for the night.

The next morning the sea is calm and Evans decides to complete the trip, even though the barometer is still falling. The instrument, Bervick tells him, is probably broken; he's seen it happen before. The ship leaves its haven but, of course, the instrument's reading is correct, and the calm is soon broken by a violent storm, a *williwaw*, as the Aleuts call it. Evan's seamanship pulls the ship through, but Duval is swept overboard and lost at sea while helping Bervick make emergency repairs on deck. Did Bervick murder Duval, or was his death accidental? As the novel ends, a board of inquiry is being organized at headquarters to investigate the matter. The last of the storm clouds dissipates, and as the sun shines down on Arunga the newly promoted Lieutenant Colonel Barkison denounces Evans for attempting the foolhardy voyage.

The disconnectedness from the physical universe that pervades the novel suggests a spiritual condition of anomie (Greek for a state of normlessness and personal isolation) that Vidal will treat at length in the later, and far more accomplished, *Julian* and *Creation*. When *Willowaw* appeared, many reviewers were quick to place it in the tradition of Ernest Hemingway, as was the case, too, with Norman Mailer's contemporaneous *The Naked and the Dead*. The themes of the young Vidal and Mailer, however, probably had more in common with the philosophical branch of existentialism being popularized in postwar France by Jeann Paul Sartre than with the sentimental machismo of Hemingway's war stories (in particular *A Farewell to Arms* and *For Whom the Bell Tolls*). An even more striking departure in artistic and generational concerns can be appreciated by a simultaneous reading of Hemingway's post-World War I novel *The Sun Also Rises* and Vidal's second novel, an examination of the turning point, or coming of age, in one man's life.

In a Yellow Wood (1947) is the first of Vidal's coming-of-age novels, those in which the protagonist—a young man in each case—makes a decision or discovery that will shape the rest of his life. *In a Yellow Wood* compresses its action into a single, critical day. The novel borrows its thematic proposition from Robert Frost's poem "The Road Not Taken" and transports it from northeastern woods to the milieu of post-World War II Wall Street. A young veteran named Robert Holton has taken a beginning position in a brokerage firm, a job that makes no demands on his modest talents but offers him future security and a semblance of direction in his otherwise passive existence. In the course of twenty-four hours this essentially passive character will face various choices (diverging roads, in Frost's metaphor) that force him to examine his complacency. A feeble kind of introspection, however, is the only action his nature will bear. He is offered, in short and somewhat contrived order, freedom, art, and love. All are rejected out of hand and he ultimately chooses the safer (and to his mind, far more respectable) path of advancement in his firm. Lacking, as he does, any robust sense of free agency, Holton makes a singularly unsatisfactory vehicle for the thematic baggage he must carry. Vidal, with characteristic candor, has expressed his own artistic misgivings about the book (*Views From a Window* 87).

Holton and his dilemma will, however, provide a prototype for Philip Warren, the protagonist of Vidal's later and much more successful novel, *The Judgment of Paris* (1952), which will be discussed later in this chapter. Worth noting, too, is the cast of secondary players as they read—or, more to the point, misread—the character of Holton. For the waitress in the diner where Holton eats his lunch and breakfast every day, he is a commanding figure from the mysterious world of high finance and the object of unattainable romantic daydreams. For his co-worker Richard Kuppelton he is a threat, a calculating competitor on the corporate ladder. For Mr. Murphy, the head of his office section, he is a socially connected opportunist making a perfunctory and temporary appearance in the trenches. When Jim Trebling, an old army buddy, arrives and reminds Holton of their plans to go into business in California, he remembers Holton as a carefree soldier and spontaneous seducer of recently liberated European girls. Heywood, the lonely and discontented owner of the firm, sees in Holton what he has forever lost: youth and the limitless golden future. To Carla, the young Italian woman who fell in love with him during the war, he embodies, of all things, freedom. Holton is such a blank page, in effect, that the characters around him reveal themselves by projecting onto him their own anxieties and preoccupations.

Holton's story is finally not about choices made or declined but about the rejection of uncertainty. He rejects Trebling's offer of a business partnership in Los Angeles because "the odds are against you . . . I just mean something might go wrong" (90). (Los Angeles in the late 1940s, it should be remembered, was not a place where the odds were stacked against young entrepreneurs.) Holton's youthful passion was sculpture, but he rejects the notion that he might become an artist as unrealistic and hopelessly romantic. Even Carla, for whom he feels something akin to love, is rejected when she asks him to live with her in Europe. "It just wouldn't," he lamely explains, "be practical" (193). And so he makes his decision, or rather non-decision: "Robert Holton would become a successful broker working in an office" (207).

To be fair, the novel contains some promising writing and anticipates some themes that will drive much better books; it can also be said that *In a Yellow Wood* stumbles into the "fallacy of imitative form." That is, in its meticulous and painstaking depiction of Robert Holton's dreary routine, the novel amasses too many dreary pages. It may be, however, that this exploration of the ordinary and the unremarkable was necessary groundwork for Vidal's next effort, which remains one of the milestones of twentieth-century American fiction.

Published in 1948, *The City and the Pillar*, like *In a Yellow Wood*, tells of a young man's self-discovery. Where the action of *In a Yellow Wood* takes twenty-four hours, however, that of *The City and the Pillar* takes several years. Now acknowledged as a classic of gay fiction, this novel brought its young author wider recognition and an attendant notoriety he claims not to have anticipated. Vidal maintains that the negative reaction to the book (hysterical and homophobic, rather than critical) diverted his career for several years from the literary form he preferred, the novel, to that of scriptwriting. The theater—with its bastard children, the movies and television—has historically depended on homosexual talent. But the world of book publishing in the 1940s was something else altogether—masculine, conservative, and determinedly heterosexual. That the *New*

York Times refused to carry advertising for *The City and the Pillar* speaks volumes for its central theme of sexual repression and its consequences.

That the kind of sexual repression represented in the novel is homosexual is incidental, as Vidal has maintained. Precedents in a heterosexual vein in American literature, after all, are at least as old as Hawthorne's *The Scarlet Letter* (1850), and as recently as the 1960s the subject was still of enough concern to warrant two excellent films, *Splendor in the Grass* (1961, directed by Elia Kazan) and *Rachel, Rachel* (1968), directed by Vidal's friend Paul Newman. The very ordinariness with which the homosexual experience is treated in *The City and the Pillar* may, however, have contributed to the outrage of most of the book's reviewers.

The story begins in a dingy bar in New York City, where a young man named Jim Willard sits in a booth drinking and drawing lines with his fingers through puddles of spilled whiskey on the table. He is very drunk and has no clear memory of how he got there, but he recollects a spring day several years before. His best friend is about to graduate from high school, and Willard feels a sadness both profound and inexplicable. Bob Ford is a year older and, like Willard, an exceptional athlete; unlike Willard, who is widely regarded as shy around the girls, he is a womanizer and something of a rakehell. Ford confides to Willard that he's going to ship out to sea as a merchant marine, but before he leaves, the two boys spend a last weekend together at an old slave cabin on the bank of a nearby river. (That same cabin, incidentally, is drawn directly from Vidal's own childhood and will reappear in his political novel, *Washington, D.C.*) A nude wrestling match on the beach—reminiscent of a scene from D. H. Lawrence's *Women in Love*—culminates in a spontaneous bout of lovemaking, something of a surprise to both boys. To Bob the episode is a forgettable and slightly embarrassing lark, but for Jim it becomes the catalyst for an obsessive infatuation that will set him on an odyssey of painful self-discovery. (For an enlightening discussion of this scene and other aspects of *The City and the Pillar* as gay fiction, see Claude J. Summers' essay in Parini 56–75.)

Willard graduates a year later and hires on as a cabin boy on a cruise ship. The sea, he is told, is a small world where all paths inevitably converge, the place where he will find Bob Ford and effect a reunion with his true other half. His search is temporarily sidetracked, however, when a sexual encounter with a willing, if unappealing, woman occasions a bout of impotence (one of several similar episodes) and, humiliated, he jumps ship. He eventually finds himself in Hollywood, where he takes a job teaching tennis in a resort hotel frequented by the stars and is introduced to the homosexual demimonde of the movie world, a submerged society that both fascinates and repels him. He is, he is sure, not "queer"—a designation that disgusts him—but incomplete, rather, without Bob. Only later, during an extended but ultimately unsatisfactory affair with an older man, the brilliant and self-loathing writer Paul Sullivan, does he begin to understand his real sexual nature. That nascent understanding will prove woefully insufficient to his needs.

Willard joins the army at the onset of World War II but is discharged when a fever leaves him with a mild case of arthritis (this detail replicates Vidal's own experience). Never the initiator of events, he drifts to New York for the duration of the war and lands in a lucrative business deal that transforms a vacant lot into a tennis school with himself as head professional. He spends his evenings cruising the local gay bars and dropping in on parties attended by flamboyant "queens," whom he despises. Nothing if not obtuse, young Jim (several steps behind the reader) has at last recognized his homosexuality, though he imagines his own case somehow unique, romantically fixated as he still is on his memories of Bob Ford.

When Ford finally re-enters Jim's life at the novel's end, their reunion leads to a singularly unsatisfactory—for Willard—and grisly *denouement* (readers should note that the original and revised editions end differently). Bob is engaged to be married and indignant, even revolted, when Jim makes advances to him, and Jim vents his frustration and rage in a final act of symbolic and painful violence. Willard has at last attained his complete self-recognition—his *anagnorisis*—to borrow Aristotle's term—and it is double-edged: His desires are thoroughly homosexual and his idealistic dream has been an illusion. Of the two recognitions, Vidal has himself asserted that the latter is more to the point (*Views From a Window* 88), and, though he has acknowledged the damage that societal pressures can inflict on "homosexualists" (Vidal's coinage), romanticism is a still-greater danger.

It should be noted that *The City and the Pillar*, despite the assumptions of some critics and journalists, is not autobiographical in a literal way. Willard's lower-middle-class background, for example, is quite unlike Vidal's, as are many of Jim's experiences. Further, Jim Willard is, as a character in a later novel/memoir succinctly puts it, "a dumb bunny" (*Two Sisters* 173). Vidal has been called many things, but "dumb bunny" isn't one of them. It is fair, however, to observe that *The City and the Pillar* is emotionally autobiographical, at least to some extent. In his memoir, *Palimpsest* (1995), Vidal returns to his youthful love, never forgotten, for Jimmie Trimble, his classmate at St. Albans. It is easy to imagine *The City and the Pillar* as a cautionary tale, from Vidal to Vidal perhaps, warning against the lure of romanticism.

Romantic sentimentality certainly plays no part in Vidal's next novel, *The Season of Comfort* (1949), nor does the book figure heavily in the author's affections; in fact, he claims to be unable to reread it. Whatever Vidal's feelings about the novel, however, it remains worthwhile and instructive in terms of its psychological insights and as an experimental stage in the writer's artistic development. The subject, less pervasive in American fiction when the book was published (1949) than now, is the disintegration of (in contemporary jargon) a dysfunctional family as seen through the eyes of an abused child. It will come as no surprise to readers of Vidal's recent memoirs, *Palimpsest* (1995), that the central tension of *Season of Comfort* is provided by the mutual loathing between a tyrannical and alcoholic mother and the recording child, her son. An appropriate fictional antecedent, perhaps, is the stormy domestic violence that drives Huckleberry Finn away from his father, the drunken and loutish Pap.

The Season of Comfort also represents Vidal's third refashioning of biographical material in a coming-of-age novel. This is by far the most autobiographical of Vidal's novels, and he seems here to rely more on formal (stylistic) experimentation than on creative reimagining to establish some distance from his narrative. *The Season of Comfort* could well be called a *Bildungsroman*, the German term for "novel of education" or "novel of formation." The *Bildungsroman* focuses as much on how the protagonist becomes what he (rarely she) is as on the moment he moves from adolescence to adulthood. (The male pronoun is appropriate here; only recently has a tradition of female *Bildungsroman* been recognized.) Well-known examples of the *Bildungsroman* include Goethe's *Wilhelm Meister*, Dickens's *David Copperfield*, Samuel Butler's *The Way of All Flesh*, and Thomas Wolfe's *Look Homeward Angel*. An interesting variation, relevant to *The Season of Comfort*, is the *Künstlerroman*, in which the protagonist becomes an artist. *Look Homeward Angel* could be included here, as well as James Joyce's *Portrait of the Artist as a Young Man*. Both the *Bildungsroman* and its subset the *Künstlerroman* invite psychological analysis of the protagonist; other characters, however, tend to matter primarily in their effects on the central figure. Also worth considering in such novels are the relative weights an author places on nature vs. nurture, that is, heredity versus environment, broad socio-historical setting versus a highly particularized family.

The Season of Comfort is organized around a series of passage rites, from birth to leave-taking, in the life of William Hawkins Giraud, each of which triggers a cluster of memories, most of them painful. That extended reminiscence culminates in a barrage of recrimination between parent and child delivered in the high modernist stream-of-consciousness style of James Joyce and Virginia Woolf. That style will later be refined by Vidal to splendid comic effect in *Myra Breckinridge*, and the autobiographical elements will be presented with more detachment in *Washington D.C.*, but the immediacy and corrosive anger that drive *The Season of Comfort* validate this small early novel on its own terms. For purposes of comparison, Philip Wylie's under-appreciated *Finley Wren*, a contemporaneous and more polished variation on the same theme, is highly recommended, as is Jane Smiley's recent *A Thousand Acres*.

For many years after *The Season of Comfort*, Vidal avoided the semi-autobiographical mode. After the rapid appearances of his first four novels, he seemed to embark on deliberate experiments in achieving artistic distance from his experiences. One technique for honing one's craftsmanship while evading the temptations of perpetual self-revelation is to write in the formulaic genres. In John G. Cawelti's definition, "A formula is a conventional system for structuring cultural products." He argues: "We can best define these formulas as principles for the selection of certain plots, characters, and settings, which possess in addition to their basic narrative structure the dimensions of collective ritual, game, and dream" (see Cawelti, in Ashley 88, 92). Vidal's next two novels, *Dark Green, Bright Red* and *A Search for the King*, both published in 1950, lend themselves particularly well to classifications as popular genres, though neither can be dismissed as strictly an entertainment. The former is a thriller, the latter a medieval quest-romance.

Dark Green, Bright Red is very much a thriller of international intrigue, whose hero moves in an exotic world of political conflict, betrayal, and surprising turns of events. Eric Ambler and Alistair MacLean often write in this genre, which is a subset of the espionage thriller. This type of thriller prefigures the ethos of what has come to be known as "the action movie," an ethos we could sum up as "trust no one and reserve your allegiance for the job at hand." *Dark Green, Bright Red* is the story of an American soldier of fortune who has cast his lot with a band of reactionaries bent on overthrowing the leftist government of a Central American republic. The general circumstances will be familiar to readers of Joseph Conrad's novels, particularly *Heart of Darkness*, or the exotic twentieth-century thrillers of Graham Greene (particularly *Our Man in Havana* and *The Comedians*). A marginal and unwitting character from an empire-minded power finds himself enmeshed in Third World intrigue and runs afoul of his own country's subversive machinations. In this case the power involved is the United States, and the field of action, though unnamed, is suspiciously like Guatemala, a country Vidal once lived in. Thinly disguised, too, are the United Fruit Company and the CIA, whose fictional counterparts work together to thwart a land-redistribution scheme proposed by the duly elected government.

Though somewhat formulaic in structure and not the best novel of its type, *Dark Green, Bright Red* is an interestingly dissident period piece. When the book was published the United States was squaring off with Soviet surrogates in Korea, and the CIA was widely held to be a necessary, even crucial, element in the line of defense against the "global" ambitions of the Soviet Union. Agency interference in the internal affairs of Latin American countries was not unknown, of course, but the popular literature of the day was disinclined to cast the organization in the role of villain. (Today, when many in government are questioning the basic competence of the CIA and others are calling for its outright abandonment, Vidal may be forgiven if he feels a twinge of righteous vindication.) The broader theme Vidal was pursuing, however, was that of imperialism and the inevitable moral and political corruption that follow in its wake; that theme will resurface in his "American Chronicles," most explicitly in the aptly titled *Empire*.

A Search for the King followed almost immediately on the heels of *Dark Green, Bright Red*, giving ample evidence of its young author's versatility and his penchant for the kind of historical research that years later would inform both *Julian* and *Creation*. Although *A Search for the King* can be classified as a medieval "quest romance," it is not primarily a love story. Rather, the label refers to modern novels (or movies), often with medieval settings, that employ patterns and conventions of the "chivalric romances" so popular in the fifteenth and sixteenth centuries. In a typical chivalric quest romance, the hero undertakes a search that engages him in a series of adventures fraught with danger and temptation. Through bravery, loyalty, and perseverance—as well as luck or divine providence—he survives these episodes essentially unchanged and is rewarded accordingly. The literary joke of Cervantes' *Don Quixote* is that the title character has read too many romances and confuses them with everyday life. For a quest romance in an updated setting, see the first of the Indiana Jones movies, *Raiders of the Lost Ark*. Among the conventions to remember in reading a quest romance is that the hero is tested, rather than changed or developed, by his encounters. Too, the adventures can occur in just about any order, and episodes may be added or subtracted without substantially altering the narrative. Finally, a quest romance makes no sharp distinctions between real and supernatural events, probably because in the formula's original heyday, people were more likely to accept as real various creatures we now consider fictions of the supernatural: wizards, dragons, unicorns, werewolves, magical swords, to mention a few. *A Search for the King* is beautifully managed in this respect; what its characters would have accepted as real is presented as real. Although working in a formulaic genre, Vidal demonstrates here the historically sympathetic imagination that will inform some of his best novels.

While conforming to the conventions of quest romance, the novel also incorporates elements of fantasy and occasionally conveys the sense of otherworldliness characteristic of the so-called magical realism of Gabriel García Márquez's *A Hundred Years of Solitude*. Although the search in question is not driven by any overt homoerotic yearnings, a case might be made that the seeker, the troubadour Blondel, is a medieval analogue to Jim Willard of *The City and the Pillar*, though Blondel's quest is ultimately a good deal more successful than Willard's.

The king of the novel's title is Richard I of England, who in 1192 is sailing home from Palestine, where he has retaken the ancient city of Acre from the Muslim Saracens. When his fleet puts in at Zara, a small Greek port on the Adriatic, Richard disembarks with a small party of his comrades-in-arms and continues the journey overland, believing that will be the less hazardous route. He is, however, mistaken, and while riding through Austria the travelers are waylaid and captured by Richard's sworn enemy, Leopold, Duke of Vienna. Only Blondel, the king's minstrel, escapes, and it is through his eyes that the story of Richard's ordeal unfolds in a tapestry woven of political history and medieval folklore.

While Blondel, penniless and alone, tramps through the frozen Austrian woods in search of his king, Leopold conspires with King Phillipe Augustus of France, and Henry, the Holy Roman Emperor, to extract a huge ransom for Richard in the plausible guise of a fine. The three monarchs plan to try him for a murder in Palestine, one he probably didn't commit, and for making an unsatisfactory treaty with Saladin, king of the Saracens. Further complicating matters is Richard's brother, the infamous Prince John, who plots to steal the English throne in the king's absence. Meanwhile, their mother, Eleanor of Aquitaine, arrays her own forces to forestall the usurpation until Richard can return to defend his kingdom.

Blondel's journey traverses not only a geographical search for his king but a process of self-discovery, a recurrent theme in Vidal's early novels. Expelled alone into a new and alien world, the minstrel experiences a loss and a fear he's never known before, not even in battle. Richard was the center of his existence, and without him the universe is formless and threatening, particularly when his journey takes him through a magic-infested Germany totally unlike his native France. There he encounters all manner of danger—werewolves, a cannibalistic giant, even a vampire—but eventually emerges, more or less intact, to find Richard. But along the way he finds something he wasn't looking for: an awareness of himself as a momentary consciousness flickering in the immensity of time. (The philosopher-king of *Julian* will have a similar existential awakening when Vidal resumes writing novels after a ten-year hiatus.) In the aftermath of war, Richard and Blondel are reunited on the corpse-littered battlefield of Nottingham, where Richard has routed his brother's army and regained his kingdom. Both men are certainly older, and Blondel, at least, is considerably wiser.

Though written in "popular" form, *A Search for the King* is intended to edify as well as entertain, and succeeds admirably within its generic constraints. In a similar vein—that is to say, mythological swordplay of considerable literary merit—are two recent novels that bear comparison to Vidal's: John Gardner's *Grendel* (the old *Beowulf* saga told from the monster's point of view), and Thomas Berger's rendition of the Camelot legend, *Arthur Rex*. Of course, one of the attractions of ancient myth for these and other modern writers is its malleability; one artist's interpretation may be as good as another's. In his next novel Vidal again appropriates legend, this time from preclassical Greece, and transports it to the twentieth century.

In 1952 Vidal published the most artistically mature and ambitious of his early novels, *The Judgment of Paris*. Here he returns to a story of a young man's coming into adulthood. Compared with this novel, *In a Yellow Wood* and *The Season of Comfort* look thin indeed. The difference is in part one of tone, of the wry angle Vidal takes on his protagonist. For example, *The Judgment of Paris* ostensibly begins as a *Künstlerroman*, but with the engaging twist that the protagonist has no artistic talent whatsoever, despite some dilatory attempts, now abandoned. Too, the novel embeds delicious burlesques of some familiar narrative formulas. While just barely remaining a realistic novel, *The Judgment of Paris* is a harbinger of the extraordinary "inventions" (Vidal's term) to come: *Myra Breckinridge, Myron, Duluth,* and *Live from Golgotha.*

Set in various locales of Western Europe shortly after World War II, *The Judgment of Paris* reworks what is probably a post-Homeric Greek myth that seeks to explain the origins of the Trojan War. As the myth would have it, Eris, the goddess of Strife, arranges—just for the hell of it—a heavenly beauty pageant. Vying for the Miss Olympus title are Hera, queen of all the gods, Athena, goddess of wisdom, and Aphrodite, goddess of love. Conscripted to judge the contest is the unlucky mortal, Paris of Ilium, the handsomest and least enviable of all men. To name a winner, of course, is to incur the divine wrath of the two losers. As it happens, all three contestants attempt to bribe the hapless judge (perhaps things weren't so very different in 1200 B.C.). Hera would grant him worldly power, the governance of all men, should he select her as the winner; Athena would bestow on him sublime wisdom; and Aphrodite, that shrewd navigator of the human heart, offers him the most beautiful of all mortal women. The hapless Paris makes his choice (Aphrodite) and claims his reward (construed as the abduction of Helen); he lives, as Homer tells us, to regret it.

Although Vidal has often been accused of an anti-modernist bias in his literary style and choice of subjects, the grounding of *The Judgment of Paris* in preclassical legend is, in fact, a characteristic technique of the so-called high modernists, most notably employed by James Joyce in his masterworks *Ulysses* and *Finnegans Wake,* and T. S. Eliot in "The Wasteland." Vidal's Paris is Philip Warren, a twenty-eight-year-old American who has allotted himself a year of travel in Europe before returning to the United States to pursue a career in the law. Like the original Paris, Warren is no hero driven to great deeds by an over-riding desire for glory; like Robert Holton (*In a Yellow Wood*), he is a self-absorbed dilettant unable to participate in life except as a dabbler or voyeur. In the course of his *Wanderjahre,* however, life will be forced on him when he meets three women who represent in modern guise the three choices presented to the Paris of ancient legend.

Vidal takes care to place his goddess-analogues and their seemingly chance encounters with Warren in classically appropriate settings. In Rome, Warren meets Regina (Latin for Queen) Durham, the wife of a powerful American politician. Mrs. Durham initiates an affair with Warren and offers him an entree into the world of temporal power. (Why she does so isn't made clear, but it should be remembered that goddesses are often at loose ends and the manipulation of mortal affairs is their traditional pastime.) Later, in Egypt, Warren is taken up by an other-worldly archaeologist, Sophia (Greek for Wisdom) Oliver, an enthusiast of metaphysical knowledge and messianic philosophy. Warren feels no sexual attraction to this latter-day Athena, but finds her compelling in her serene rejection of the modern world. They agree to meet in Paris, where Warren resumes his affair with Regina Durham and begins an-other with the beautiful Anna Morris, young wife of a boorish American industrialist. In a scene reminiscent of the original Helen's abduction, Warren takes Anna to the seashore and in the act of cuckolding the insufferable Morris (read Menelaus) feels something akin to love, if only for himself.

There are echoes here of Jim Willard (*The City and the Pillar*) and Robert Holton (*In a Yellow Wood*), as well as an adumbration of the adolescent Peter Sanford (*Washington, D.C.*). Like those other World War II gradu-ates, Warren is something of a shadow-player on an alien stage; his aim-lessness in the world mirrors an interior disaffection that renders him essentially passive. Only when external events illuminate some unex-pected choices does he recognize his free agency and become the active initiator of his own life. *The Judgment of Paris*, however, is more than a coming-of-age novel with a convenient mythical metaphor as its launch-ing pad. The historical awareness and attention to cultural detail that characterize many of Vidal's later novels—those same qualities that may have led some critics to regard him as "old-fashioned"—are more in evidence here than in his earlier books and represent something of a watershed in his development as a social novelist. His depictions, for instance, of the chaos of postwar Italian politics and the emergence of what would later be called the jet set prefigure the broader canvases of *1876* and *Empire*.

Too, Vidal's gift for knockabout satire—distinctly reminiscent of P. G. Wodehouse in this instance—emerges here in an unlikely subplot. A cabal of elderly and spectacularly inept homosexuals recruits Warren into a series of intrigues to restore the Italian monarchy, establish a pro-letarian dictatorship, and finally, create a new world order centered on the adoration of a deranged hermaphrodite named Augusta. If the manic comedy strikes a discordant, even distracting, note for some readers, it will be used to better effect in later, more purely surreal, novels such as *Duluth* and *Myra Breckinridge*. The next novel Vidal was to write, and his last to be published for ten years, is surreal in its own right, but hardly comic.

With *Messiah* (1954), Vidal drew on two venerable literary traditions, one thematic and the other stylistic. The former tradition, that of utopian literature, dates to 1516, when the Englishman Thomas More published a book about an ideal society on a fictional island he called Utopia. (The word "utopia" was More's invention and his pun, a combination of the Greek noun for place and the prefixes "eu" for happy, or "u" for non-; thus a utopia is at once a happy and a nonexistent place.) In 1932 another Englishman, Aldous Huxley, twisted the form 180 degrees with his novel *Brave New World*, the story of a future society gone terribly wrong. Some critics have used the term "dystopian" to describe novels such as Huxley's, and it is in that category that *Messiah* belongs. (Other notable examples contemporaneous with Vidal's book are Ray Bradbury's *Fahrenheit 451* and George Orwell's *1984*.) The stylistic tradition Vidal employs, the epistolary device of telling a story through letters or memoirs, is as old as the English novel itself; Samuel Richardson's *Pamela* (1740) is probably the most famous example of that eighteenth-century convention.

Set in the near future, Vidal's story is presented as the memoirs of the elderly Eugene Luther, a one-time disciple of the long-dead John Cave (note the initials), founder of a twentieth-century American religious cult that has gained ascendancy in the Western world. Luther, who lives under an assumed name in the ancient Egyptian city of Luxor, was the codifier of Cave's gospel, a fairly simple message that has since been corrupted and transformed into the ideological basis of a corporate theocracy. When a Caveite "communicator," or missionary, arrives in town to spread the word among the Muslims, Luther assumes the man has come to kill him. He, after all, is the only surviving member of the church founders, the one who knows the malignant truth of Cave Inc.'s origins. He begins his journal to set the record straight for posterity, and in the process develops some of the themes that Vidal returns to in the latter part of his novelistic career.

Luther, who once attempted his own novel about the Roman Emperor Julian, might himself be the fictional precursor of that particular apostate. With Vidal they share a distaste for imposed religion and institutional priesthoods, and an appreciation for the insignificance of man in the sea of space and time. Too, like the John Hay of *Empire* or Charles Schuyler of *1876*, Luther is fascinated—though hardly pleased—by the gradual disintegration of his aging body, the corporeal announcement of his own imminent immersion into eternity. And when Luther speaks of the quasi-religions of the mid-twentieth century (i.e., Marxism and Freudianism), or of the American reaction of "nativism," we get a detached view of the forces that Vidal will address with more urgency in his political *roman à clef, Washington, D.C.* (a *roman à clef* is literally a "novel with a key," i.e., a story that incorporates actual persons fictionally, if thinly, disguised). Religion, politics, and mortality are all at issue here, arrayed against the ever-impolite subject of human gullibility. Luther tells us that, when confronted with an epidemic of UFO sightings, the administration in Washington hints,

> as broadly as it dared, that a sizable minority of its citizens were probably subject to delusions and mass hysteria. This cynical view was prevalent inside the administration, though it could not of course propound such a theory publicly since its own tenure was based, more or less solidly, on the franchise of those same hysterics and irresponsibles. (10)

Eugene and Luther, incidentally, are Vidal's own given names.

Readers of Vidal's earlier novels, particularly those before *Judgment of Paris*, may also notice that the young writer of *Messiah* was developing a prose style reminiscent of Henry James's, a style unlike the terse naturalistic mode of most of Vidal's contemporaries. This more elegant syntax proved congenial to Vidal's own authorial voice, and that voice became his dominant one when he returned to the novel in 1964, with *Julian*. Accompanying the new voice is a broader, more external range of concern; *Julian* and the books that follow are social novels, larger in scope and more akin, in spirit and aspiration, to the novels of Balzac and Dickens than to the serious fiction of Vidal's contemporaries. They are stories of the world and the people who move in it, not stories of alienation and personal *angst*; they are full of public life and places. They are also full of ideas, of literary and historical allusion, and cultural detritus, too. Appropriately enough, though in another context, Vidal has quoted the eighteenth-century French encyclopedist, Diderot, who spoke approvingly of his own contemporary, Voltaire: "He knows a great deal and our young poets are ignorant. The work of Voltaire is full of things; their works are empty" ("Edmund Wilson," in *United States* 284). Diderot's cranky aphorism about Voltaire's work could as easily be applied to Vidal's, which is erudite, discursive, and "full of things."

The entertainments Vidal wrote from 1964 to 1992, each of which will be discussed individually, can be separated into two categories: the historical novels and the social satires, which the writer calls "inventions." The next section of this book will deal with his historical fiction, the work for which he's probably best known, and, however grudgingly, most appreciated. Indeed, the classical novel *Julian* and the six installments of Vidal's "American Chronicles" might be said to have revivified the ancient genre for many American readers. The form, of course, is at least as old as the *Iliad*, but when Homer composed his epic about the Trojan War he wasn't inhibited by a documented record of his materials. (In fact, until 1870, when Heinrich Schliemann discovered the ruins of Troy, the great poem was widely regarded as purely imaginative.) Vidal and other serious writers who attempt a historical novel about more recent events, however, are faced with a task of scholarly research that didn't confront the old Greek. That may be one reason that so few serious writers enter the field, and, consequently, the reason that so many literary critics dismiss it as somehow unworthy of serious consideration. And too bad for them. For the reader, however, who approaches Vidal's fictionalized histories with an open mind and no rigid preconceptions as to what constitutes literature, the serious pleasures of narrative entertainment and artfully distilled scholarship are there for the taking.

Vidal's idiosyncratic and funny "inventions" will be discussed at length in later chapters. Roughly speaking, those inventions are satirical, sometimes broadly comic, novels which frequently incorporate generic elements from the author's early experiments in pop fiction. Sci-fi conventions, for example, are crucial to the development of *Duluth* and *Live from Golgotha*, and the dystopic futurism of *Messiah* will reappear in *Kalki*. Even the loony anti-romanticism of *Myra Breckinridge* has an antecedent in the thwarted love story of *The City and the Pillar*, but these and the other "inventions" defy classification. They are, after all, like Vidal himself, *sui generis*.

VIDAL'S HISTORICAL NOVELS

3

Vidal's Historical Novels: An Introduction

Fictional narratives set in the past are as old as literature itself; arguably, *The Iliad* is historical fiction, although as the Russian critic Mikhail Bakhtin points out, such epics are set in an " 'absolute past,' a time of founding fathers and heroes separated by an unbridgeable gap from the real time of the *present day*" (218). (As we shall see, there is something of this quality in much of Vidal's fiction.) Historians of the novel generally agree, however, that the historical novel begins with Sir Walter Scott's tales of a Scottish past. In part, the historical novel as a modern (i.e., postclassical) genre requires a view of history that seeks to represent the past faithfully and accurately. (Earlier views of history stressed history as moral example, in which famous men and women of the past offer positive or negative examples for present conduct.) Historical novels are distinguished by the writer's effort to recreate imaginatively and accurately an earlier time. A novelist may fail in this attempt, certainly, or manage only clumsily the historical details. The genuine concern with accuracy, however, distinguishes the historical novel from the "costume drama" school of heavy breathing, bodice-ripping historical fiction that fakes its history, that presents thoroughly modern people and situations in period clothing, with only an occasional reference or vocabulary item, say, to establish a supposed past.

Like many other forms, historical novels are easier to recognize than to define with any precision. A substantial number of critics, however, would agree with the following criteria:

1. Historical novels must be set in the past. Some critics call for a distinct time span between a novel's temporal setting and its composition; Avrom Fleishman, for example, suggests "an arbitrary number of years, say 40–60 (two generations)" (3). George Dekker argues, sensibly enough, "For a fiction to qualify as 'historical,' what more can be required than that the leading or (more to the point) determinative social and psychological traits it represents clearly belong to a period historically distinct from our own?" (14). (The context indicates that Dekker means by "our own" whatever prevailed at the time of the given novel's writing.)

2. Serious historical fiction strives for fidelity to known history, to what Vidal often calls "the agreed upon facts," reminding us that we know history only through textual records, whose reliability may be subject to doubt (although in varying degrees). Fleishman quotes Mary Renault: "I have never, for any reason, in any historical book of mine, falsified anything deliberately which I knew or believed to be true. Often of course I must have done through ignorance what would horrify me if I could revisit the past" (xii-xiii). (See Vidal's praise of Renault in "The Top Ten Best Sellers," *United States* 80–82, as well as his defense of his own research in the essays about *Lincoln* in that same volume.) The concern for fidelity to facts is perhaps the single most important characteristic of historical fiction. In his recent *The Historical Novel from Scott to Sabatini*, Harold Orel cites the conscientious research of historical novelists as otherwise diverse as Sir Walter Scott (8), Edward Bulwer-Lytton (17–18), Wilkie Collins (21), George Eliot (23–24), Thomas Hardy (26), Charlotte Brontë (30), Charles Dickens (33), Conan Doyle (92), and Rafael Sabatini (154). Certainly, Vidal in both his fiction and his criticism reserves some of his sharpest satire for pseudo-historical novels, those that are written out of ignorance or disdain for historical accuracy.

3. Historical fiction requires the imaginative recreation of a past era in all its material and psychological minutiae. Such imaginative re-creation should provide a coherence so that readers believe events and motives could indeed have been as the author describes.

4. On the model of Sir Walter Scott, historical novels most often depict a clash between two cultures or a critical juncture in a particular culture.

So far, there is general agreement among the various critics who have attempted to define and analyze historical fiction. Two additional characteristics are worth noting as applicable to Vidal, though neither is as widely assumed as the four discussed above.

5. Fleishman argues that a historical novel must include at least one character who existed. "The historical novel is distinguished among novels by the presence of a specific link to history: not merely a real building or a real event but a real person among the fictitious ones" (4). "Must" is a strong word, but Fleishman is persuasive. At any rate, the presence of characters who were once alive is certainly characteristic of Vidal's historical novels.

6. Much historical fiction is self-reflexively concerned with the construction of history. By taking such interests as definitive, Susan L. Mizruchi is able to track a historical consciousness through several American novels not usually considered "historical." Again, whether we take this historiographic orientation as definitive, it is distinctly typical of Vidal. (Historiography is the study of what history is and how it ought be written.)

Mizruchi also argues that scrutiny of historiography works to politicize the novels in which it occurs; not everyone will agree. It is certainly true of Vidal's historical fictions, however, that they are always novels of politics. Vidal's historical novels differ from many in the same genre in that they are also political novels, though in varying degrees. The term "political novel" is most often used for fictions that argue (however implicitly) for or against particular power relations. Thus, novels of protest, antiwar novels, feminist novels, novels by minority or Latin American or South African writers are likely to be referred to as political. The argument has also been made for writers of the modernist avant-garde and, more recently, postmodern fictionists that their refusal to use traditional forms and their experiments with language are politically subversive. (The argument has also been made that at least most modernist and postmodernist novels are politically regressive.) Certainly, Vidal's mature novels display his progressive politics, as do his many essays. His historical novels, however, are political in another sense as well. That is, they depict politics in action; they recount the activity of politics in government. Vidal writes about people who wield power, and he writes about their wielding it. As we recommend using the terms, a "political novel" espouses a political stance; a "novel of politics" examines political processes and a political system. (Obviously, these terms are not mutually exclusive.)

The "novel of politics" in this sense has its own tradition. In England, Benjamin Disraeli (British prime minister in 1868 and 1874–1880) wrote novels of politics, as did Anthony Trollope in his Palliser series. Trollope ran unsuccessfully for Parliament, and, currently, Jeffrey Archer is a member of Parliament who writes fiction about the inside workings of government. In the United States, Robert Penn Warren's *All the King's Men*, Allen Drury's *Advise and Consent*, and the recent anonymous *Primary Colors* are all "novels of politics."

All of Vidal's historical novels are also novels of politics, though to varying degrees. *Julian* is primarily a fictionalized biography of the fourth-century Roman emperor, but Julian's life is necessarily one of political maneuvering. Further, Vidal frames Julian's memoir with letters between two powerful men who knew the emperor and have their own political motives for publishing the story of Julian's life. Vidal's other novel of the ancient world, *Creation*, recounts the life of Cyrus Spitama, a fictitious character in the historically real courts of three Persian emperors: Darius, Xerxes, and Artaxerxes. Here, too, we see politics in action, as various princes compete to inherit the throne. Once Cyrus (who narrates the novel) begins to travel as an ambassador, the novel becomes one of comparative politics, as each place Cyrus visits operates under a different political system. Cyrus stresses the real power exercised by women, despite their being sequestered in a harem, and by the eunuchs who administer the harem and the court. In part, the eunuchs possess power because they control access to the emperor ("Great King") and the information he receives. (Vidal probably would not object to comparisons with the White House staff in recent years.)

Although political description and maneuvering are important in *Julian* and *Creation*, in Vidal's American histories political activity becomes central. These novels include *Burr, Lincoln, 1876, Empire, Hollywood,* and *Washington, D.C.* The overarching theme of these six novels is the development of the United States into an empire. Within each novel, important characters either hold political office or wield political influence through newspapers, magazines, or (later) movies. The workings of government provide the backdrop for their actions and politics provides the arena in which they are tested and measured, both morally and intellectually.

Julian (1964) is set in the fourth century A.D. and *Creation* (1981) in the fifth century B.C. (Both have been called novels of the "classical world," but it is worth noting that the time span between them is approximately the same as that between *A Search for the King* and *Washington, D.C.,* some 800 years.) The other six—*Burr, Lincoln, 1876, Empire, Hollywood,* and *Washington, D.C.*—are known as Vidal's "American Chronicles." As we might expect, Vidal experiments with the artistic possibilities of historical fiction, so no two of these eight novels are formally identical. *Julian, Burr,* and *Lincoln* are all fictionalized biographies of famous men, but Vidal chooses different narrative points of view for each, and these choices affect how intimately we see the central figure. In *Creation, 1876, Empire, Hollywood,* and *Washington, D.C.,* the main characters are fictional, and they interact with figures drawn from history. Although their protagonists are similar in this way, the five novels also combine characteristics of historical fiction with those of differing genres. *Creation* resembles an epic quest, while *1876, Empire,* and *Hollywood,* if read in sequence, resemble the "family saga" variety of bestseller. That is, these three novels chart the adventures of a single familial line (fictional descendants of Aaron Burr) across several generations. Ostensibly, *Washington, D.C.* continues this saga, but it is also very much a personal novel, in which Vidal reworks and achieves artistic distance from the autobiographical materials he used less successfully in *The Season of Comfort.* (From today's vantage point, *Washington, D.C.* could be called the story of a dysfunctional and abusive family, though these are hardly the phrases one would have used in the 1960s when the book appeared.) Whatever the formal differences among Vidal's American histories, however, they all share the same seriousness of purpose and offer the same agreeable accessibility to the general reader. Each of those novels may be enjoyed separately or, better yet, in its chronological order in the overall epic.

Julian
(1964)

In 1964 Vidal published his historical fiction *Julian*, a richly imagined and carefully researched novel about the death throes of paganism in the classical world. Readers of that novel will—perhaps unavoidably—draw parallels between the social and political forces at play in the fourth-century Roman Empire and the various conflicting, and perhaps irreconcilable, interests at stake in twentieth-century America. In the fourth century, as now, an entrenched but embattled society beset by internal factionalism and external pressures both military and economic was faced with an ominously uncertain future. When Vidal began his novel, in 1959, the similarities were even more sharply delineated, if no more profound, than they are today. The Cold War between the West and the Soviet Union embodied many of the elements present in the centuries-old hostility between the Greco-Roman world and the ancient Persian empire on its Asian border. The growing power of Christianity in the fourth century, particularly the insistence of its clergy upon religious and secular privileges, posed constant and intractable problems for the Roman political authorities. These problems had been exacerbated by Julian's uncle, the Emperor Constantine, when he rescinded Diocletian's proscriptions against the Christians with the Edict of Milan in 313 A.D. He further compounded the problem on his deathbed (337 A.D.) when he accepted, or demanded, baptism and thereby effectively established Christianity as the state religion.

The Roman Emperor Flavius Claudius Julianus is known to posterity as Julian the Apostate because he renounced Christianity. He ascended to the imperial throne upon the death of his cousin and predecessor Constantius II in the year 361. His reign ended a scant sixteen months later when he was mortally wounded in a cavalry battle near Ctesiphon, a Persian stronghold on the Tigris River. Fortunately, much of Julian's own writing survives, as do numerous accounts of him by his contemporaries and by later historians. Using those sources as his blueprint, Vidal constructed (to the outrage of some contemporary Christians) his fictional portrait of a pagan hero.

Whatever history lessons a reader is likely to take from *Julian* are valid ones; Vidal's research for the project was methodical and exhaustive (the standard edition of Libanius alone runs to twelve volumes), and the story he tells is compatible with the generally agreed upon facts of Julian's brief reign. It should be noted, however, that *Julian* is not (nor does it claim to be) a scholarly biography. Whereas the novelist may invent dialog and embellish events with imaginary detail, biographers may not. Nor may they impute specific motives to characters or place them, for convenience's sake, where they may not have been. Vidal, of course, in the interests of his story, can and does do all the things a biographer may not, but he exercises his artistic license with restraint. The significant characters in *Julian*, save Macrina, are the people Julian knew, and the military and political crises he describes in his fictive journal are verifiable matters of record.

PLOT DEVELOPMENT

Vidal's telling of the story of Julian the Apostate, last of the great pagans, begins some years after Julian's death with an exchange of letters between two of Julian's old friends and teachers. Libanius of Antioch, the renowned rhetorician, writes to Priscus, the Athenian philosopher, asking for a copy of Julian's memoirs, which came into Priscus's possession during the emperor's fatal campaign in Persia. Libanius's intention is to publish the memoirs with a commentary; his motive is to mount a literary counter-offensive against the Christian clergy. The Athenian agrees but requests anonymity in the project. The Emperor Theodosius, after all, has recently become an enthusiastic convert to Christianity, to which he credits his recovery from a near-fatal illness. After much haggling over the price of copying the documents, a bargain is struck and the personal history of Flavius Claudius Julianus unfolds.

In the year 337, Julian relates, when he is six years old and his brother Gallus a sickly eleven, their father is murdered by his own nephew, the newly elevated Emperor Constantius II. His victim, Constantius wrongly believed, intended to usurp the throne. The two children are spared because they pose no immediate threat to Constantius—Julian is a mere baby and Gallus isn't expected to survive childhood. In constant fear for their lives, the brothers are reared in exile and under continuous surveillance by Constantius's informers, a revolving crew of nominally Christian officials ambitious for their own advancement. Julian's one source of happiness and consolation during his otherwise grim childhood is the tutor Mardonius. Although a Christian himself, Mardonius is also an inspiring teacher of classicism, and under his tutelage Julian hatches a strategy for survival. He will study for the priesthood and in so doing remove himself from the emperor's murderous suspicion. Then, camouflaged in the trappings of Christian piety, he will indulge his newfound passion for pre-Christian antiquity. He will be a philosopher.

The brothers survive their adolescence and, surprisingly, Constantius appoints Gallus to the high office of Caesar (effectively, vice-regent) in the eastern provinces. Julian is allowed to pursue his studies in the university city of Nicomedia; there he is befriended by the physician Oribasius, his conduit to the netherworld of magic and the ancient mysteries, the submerged but still vital link to the old gods of paganism. Sponsored (or duped, as Priscus would have it) by the magician Maximus, Julian is initiated into the rites of the warrior-god Mithras and has a revelation that shapes the rest of his life. He believes that he "was chosen on that steep mountainside to do the great work in which [he is] now engaged: the restoration of the worship of the One God" (84). And so the future emperor discovers his life's mission, soon to be set in motion by events at the imperial court. (A clarification: Julian sees all the pagan deities as different names for a single God. He rejects not Christ but Christianity's claims to exclusive truth and its intolerance toward other religions.)

Gallus proves to be a singularly cruel and depraved tyrant, even by Roman standards. With the eastern half of the empire in near rebellion, Constantius recalls him to Milan, where he is tried for treason and executed. Julian himself is subsequently summoned to the court, where he fully expects to meet the same end. Instead, Constantius appoints him Caesar in Gaul (that region of the empire north of the Alps) and orders him to put down the German tribes encroaching on that province from across the Rhine. The emperor, of course, expects the inexperienced youth to fail and thereby remove himself from the line of succession. To Constantius's chagrin, however, and Julian's own surprise, the novice Caesar proves to be a brilliant general and a capable governor. He subdues the Germans and reorganizes civil administration, and by reducing provincial taxes he cements his personal popularity with the Gauls and thus ensures an eventual confrontation with Constantius, who now faces other difficulties in the East.

In the autumn of 360, the Persian King Sapor captures the Roman stronghold of Amida on the Armenian border and Constantius is forced to raise an army and march from Italy to Asia Minor, where he immediately sets up winter quarters and waits—waits, in fact, for the army of Gaul, which he has ordered Julian to send him. Julian attempts to comply but his troops threaten mutiny and proclaim Julian the new Augustus, rather than serve under Constantius. Various dreams and omens—on which Julian increasingly relies—convince him that his time has come. He advances on Constantius and his own destiny, but before the rivals can meet, Constantius dies and Julian is acclaimed emperor of all the Romans. He is now ready to restore the old religion and fulfill the revelation he received on that steep mountainside near Nicomedia.

Unfortunately for Julian, not everyone shares his vision of the future. By the time of his investiture in Constantinople, the new emperor has acquired an entourage of self-interested soothsayers, philosophers, and disaffected Persians, including Ormisda, Sapor's brother and claimant to the Persian throne. Bad enough to be encumbered by these, the army is also infiltrated by spies and staffed with Galileans (Julian's dismissive term for Christians) who dread a resurgence of paganism. Undeterred, and convinced by the magician Maximus that the goddess Cybele has instilled in him the all-conquering spirit of Alexander the Great, Julian presses Constantius's war against Persia. That campaign proves to be his last and the death knell of the old world.

The denouement of *Julian* is contained in a final correspondence between Libanius and Priscus, who has withheld certain notes the emperor made twenty years before in Persia. We learn of Julian's delusions and the treachery of his enemies. A murderer is revealed and the empire that was Rome fades into the past.

NARRATIVE STRUCTURE AND POINT OF VIEW

Structurally, *Julian* is complex; the story is told by three narrators, each of whom writes from more than one temporal perspective. As noted earlier, the novel is framed by letters between Libanius and Priscus. The epistolary form of narration is at least as old as the use of the heroine's letters in Samuel Richardson's *Pamela* (1740), and Bernard F. Dick notes several parallels in novels about the ancient world (Dick 106). In *Julian* the use of letters as narrative device sets a present time (the year 380) for the fiction. That is, in epistolary narrative readers accept the convention that the letter-writing coincides almost exactly with the events recounted. As observed earlier, Priscus sells to Libanius the memoir written in 363 A.D. by Julian during his ill-fated campaign to conquer Persia. The period covered by this memoir (331–363 A.D.) provides the significant past for the novel. (Note that Libanius wants to use the past—represented by Julian—in his present struggle against total dominance by Christianity. The theme of exploiting the past for a present advantage will recur in Vidal's novels, particularly in *Live from Golgotha*.)

Much of the novel, then, purports to be Julian's memoir, that is, a history of his life as he looks back on it. As a retrospective view, a memoir is written out of memory, always suspect and subject to pressures and distractions in the present. But memoirs are also written with an eye to the future. In accepting the fictional pretense of the novel, readers must assume that Julian constructs his memoir at least partly out of a desire to control how he will be remembered. Julian specifically admits that he is recording his notes as history as well as to amuse himself (361). But by the year 380, Julian no longer controls his manuscript or how the future will see him. We can see this process in action when Priscus inserts his own comments into the memoir, sometimes flatly contradicting—rewriting—Julian's version of events, and not always to Julian's advantage. Priscus also slips in jibes, thinly disguised as flattery, at Libanius, the ostensible audience for these comments; here, Priscus's own intentions replace Julian's. Adding to the structural complexity—and to the fun—are Libanius's responses to the accounts and interpretations offered by both Julian and Priscus. These responses pose as Libanius's notes to himself, sometimes reminders of the biography he plans to write, sometimes expressions of his indignation at Priscus's insults, and sometimes his personal reflections triggered by reading the memoir.

Several critics have discussed the effects of this triple narration, particularly as it keeps the audience at some distance from Julian and prevents us from entirely trusting his version of events. The presentation of multiple viewpoints also works thematically, suggesting that the individual human personality is, finally, unknowable (see Dick 106–7, and Kiernan 57–58). What has not been discussed is that this pattern of memoir with interspersed comments and responses takes us through only the first four-fifths of the novel. The remaining 20 percent is narrated rather differently. In a crucial exchange of letters, Priscus reveals that he has also preserved the notes Julian kept during the Persian campaign. He offers to sell these papers to Libanius, and how shrewdly he does so. First, Priscus claims to be thinking of publishing these notes himself. He next tantalizes Libanius (and the reader) with a claim to know the details of Julian's murder. Only then does Priscus name his price—equal to that Libanius has already paid for the entire memoir—but Libanius agrees. From this point forward, except for the final few pages, the novel consists of Julian's notes or journal, not simply annotated but amplified and (sometimes) deciphered by Priscus. It's important to note that a memoir and a journal or notes-toward-a-memoir differ in their intended audiences. That is, journals and notes are written primarily for oneself and memoirs primarily for a future audience. Thus, a journal can be more cryptic and more revealing, less self-conscious and less concerned with one's image or how one will be remembered. In a sense, a journal can be more honest, more personal, and more straightforward than a memoir. (It should be remembered, however, that journals are not exempt from self-delusion or from desires to present one's self favorably to oneself.) This shift from memoir to journal is a brilliant narrative stroke. As Julian's death draws closer, we are drawn closer to him. That is, readers are allowed more immediate and more intimate glimpses into Julian's thoughts. (More precisely, this is the illusion fostered by the shift from imitated memoir to imitated journal notes.) At the same time, however, we get proportionately fewer of Julian's words and more of Priscus's. Brief journal entries by Julian, at times a single paragraph or a mere list of idiosyncratic abbreviations, will launch Priscus into several pages of his own eyewitness account. This shift in proportion also works to intensify the portrait of Julian: Priscus provides all the information and narrative development we need, so Julian's journal can emphasize emotions.

The final chapters of the novel bring us again to the year 380. Priscus reports his discovery of Julian's murderer, and in a parallel recognition,

Libanius at last acknowledges that "[t]he world Julian wanted to preserve and restore is gone" (458).

CHARACTER DEVELOPMENT

> I sometimes feel that the history of the Roman principate is an interminable pageant of sameness. They are so much alike, these energetic men; only Julian was different.
>
> Priscus, on the Roman emperors (447)

As Vidal's Priscus notes, Julian was indeed different from the general run of men who ruled the Roman Empire. From his writing—much of which survives—and from his actions, he appears to have been less interested in self-aggrandizement than in effecting a radical and (to his mind, at least) beneficent change in the direction of Roman society. He was, after all, a believing pagan at the head of a state whose institutions and forms were already dominated by the Christian church and becoming more so. That alone, however, wouldn't seem to account for the romantic appeal he continues to exert in the historical consciousness of the West. What kind of a man was he, and what was the extraordinary life that shaped him? Ultimately we cannot know, but Vidal's characterization of the apostate emperor is plausible and even endearing, and as literary portraiture, remarkable. Although the novel includes miniature sketches of several figures, the focus never leaves Julian, his life and its aftermath.

In his memoirs, Julian recounts the formative memories of his childhood. His mother dies giving him birth and his father, kindly but distant, entrusts his upbringing to the tutor Mardonius. The teacher introduces the lonely boy to literature and Hellenic cosmology, the twin foundations of his lifelong passion for classical lore. Julian's early years pass uneventfully until he is six, when his father is murdered by the Emperor Constantius, an apparently devoted and publicly pious Christian. As Julian watches the centurions drag his father away to his death, an understandable antipathy toward the church of Jesus is planted in the child's heart. That antipathy hardens in Julian's adolescence as he watches the persecution of the old religion by the functionaries of the new.

The revulsion Julian feels for the Galileans doesn't, however, corrode his essentially benign nature; nor does he stoop to revenge when the opportunity presents itself. Instead, he offers Jesus a place of honor in the Roman pantheon of gods, provided that the Christians extend the same tolerance to worshipers of other deities. By way of contrast, a useful strategy for characterization, Vidal offers the oafish and thoroughly vile elder brother Gallus as a counterpoint to the mild and consistently humane Julian. Were their characters not well documented in history, two such unlikely siblings would strain the reader's credulity. Where Julian is reflective and innately decent, Gallus is impetuous and beastly. Vidal allows the brothers to comment on their own natures. Both brothers recognize a Roman ruler's power to treat other people as he pleases. Gallus acknowledges that, when so inclined, he commits rape and murder. Blithely, he credits God for his own sanguinary lunacy: "What I am, [God] wanted me to be. That is why I am good." He continues to justify himself, "I build churches. I establish religious orders. I stamp out heresy wherever I find it." Then his attention shifts to the understandably nervous Julian. "I can hardly believe," he says with weary exasperation, "[that] you are my brother" (95).

Neither can Julian, who after his own ascension will rebuke himself for the presumptuous sin of splashing his friends in the baths. But Julian understands the temptations of absolute power: "First, the tyrant plays harmless games: splashes senators in the bath, serves wooden food to dinner guests. . . . Then the small jokes begin to pall. One day he finds it amusing to rape another man's wife, as the husband watches, . . . or to kill them" (271). The strategy here is typical. In this novel, secondary characters (i.e., all but Julian) are shrewdly realized sketches, but ones that function above all to highlight aspects of Julian.

Indifferent to money, Julian is generous in an offhand way, and his largess is available for the asking (Priscus berates himself for not asking). Eccentrically humane by the standards of his day, he discovers that he actually enjoys war and is notably courageous in battle, throwing himself into combat in a most un-emperor-like fashion. Worth mentioning, too, is the high degree of personal devotion Julian exhibits toward his friends and colleagues. In a world in which such a trait could be a frivolous and even suicidal extravagance, Julian is almost uniquely loyal. Whether that quality was largely innate or acquired is moot. It did, we know from the historical record, bind together a disparate coterie of warriors and reactionary Hellenes that nearly derailed Christianity. Julian's virtues, then, are many, but the historical figure was human, and so is the fictional construct.

Throughout the course of the novel Vidal establishes less salutary facets of Julian's personality, flaws eventually fatal to Julian, but critical to the story. Events prove that the emperor is willful and superstitious; from his days as a student philosopher he becomes increasingly reliant on dreams, omens, and the pronouncements of oracles to shape his actions. But he cannot accept any interpretations of these phenomena that conflict with his divine agenda, and his willfulness eventually kills him. The seeds of his own destruction germinate in his Hellenic soul and, appropriately enough, flower in a perfectly tragic conclusion. He is a blinkered idealist, a character out of time and place, a heroic anomaly.

Generally, the secondary characters in *Julian* are recognizable types that Vidal furnishes with individual quirks. The eunuch Eusebius, for instance, is a recurring historical type; the self-serving *eminence gris* behind Constantius's throne, he will be instantly recognizable to anyone familiar with the court intrigues of Henry VIII's Cardinal Wolsey or the Czarina Alexandra's Rasputin. Julian's brother Gallus is, quite simply, a monster—one whom our own age would probably classify as a homicidal psychopath. His well-documented excesses, unchecked by moral or statutory constraints, amply demonstrate his regrettable character, though Vidal makes him humanly accessible by depicting him as an unintentionally hilarious dunderhead.

Necessarily more complex are the old Hellenists Priscus and Libanius, who reveal themselves through their letters even as their correspondence provides the narrative frame for Julian's story. Physically infirm and emotionally tortured by the disintegration of the classical world, Libanius is humane and principled; he wishes, he tells Priscus, to provide a historical bridge between the old religion and future generations by publishing Julian's politically sensitive memoirs. Priscus, on the other hand, cares nothing for any religion, though he shares Libanius's passion for the intellectual rigor of fading antiquity. Unlike Libanius, he enjoys rude good health in his eighth decade and is dedicated to enjoying more of it, a dedication that precludes his active participation in publishing the emperor's papers. Priscus will, however, discreetly cheer Libanius on from the sidelines—or more likely, from the Athenian brothels he still frequents. The two elderly philosophers, one earnestly high-minded and committed to the preservation of civilization, the other resigned to civilization's end and committed to the preservation of his own enjoyment of what remains, are ideal and consummately witty foils for each other.

Also witty, but decidedly and vocally anti-intellectual, is the Athenian girl, Macrina, who becomes the great love—to stretch a point—of Julian's life. Macrina is the niece of the renowned orator Prohaeresius, and she affords Vidal the opportunity to develop a purely fictional and surprisingly modern character within the stringent historicity of the novel. When they first meet, in a disreputable student tavern, the handsome young woman fondles the future emperor under the table while refuting, to the horror of the company, the teachings of both Jesus and Aristotle. Contemptuous of received wisdom and unabashedly sexual (had Julian married her and made her empress, she would have styled herself "Macrina the Insatiable"), Macrina resembles Vidal's later creation, the fearless and wanton Myra Breckinridge, horny scourge of the authoritarian *Cahiers du Cinema*. Julian's stay in Athens is lamentably brief, and so is Macrina's active participation in the novel. She does, however, conceive a son by him, and true to her proto-feminist nature, keeps that knowledge—and the child—to herself.

LITERARY DEVICES

Although an obsession with his divine destiny proves fatal to Julian, the novel's frequent references to this trait serve several artistic purposes. A close look at this pattern will suggest how tightly *Julian* interweaves plot, character, and theme. First, these references enhance coherence. *Julian* is a sprawling novel, spanning two continents and nearly fifty years. As fictional autobiography, it runs the risk of all biographical writing—that of being, or appearing, mechanically or routinely episodic, a simple sequence of "this happened, and then this happened, and then this happened," and so on. Despite its size and scope, however, *Julian* is economically written in the important sense that details carry a full share of significance. It is a measure of the novelist's skill that a single recurring motif can work simultaneously to several structural and thematic ends. Although we have room here to discuss only one such motif in detail, the following analysis of a prophetic pattern in the story should indicate the careful construction behind what may at first seem a discursive or digressive novel. As observed earlier, throughout the novel Julian invokes omens, oracles, auguries, visions—the whole repertoire of time-honored techniques for predicting the future. For just a few examples, Julian's future is predicted by soothsayers and magicians, by a decorative wreath that falls to crown him, by an old blind woman in Vienne, by the livers of many sacrificial bulls, by the Delphic oracle, by Etruscan astrology, and in dream-visions of Rome's guardian spirit.

These prophetic moments serve multiple artistic purposes. For example, the various omens and oracles foreshadow events and thus lure us into reading further to see precisely how or whether the predictions come true. Too, the references to such practices as divination by examining an animal's entrails both establish an alien atmosphere and remind us that the fourth-century world differed considerably from our own. (Not that we never try to forecast the future; we just don't do so with animal guts.) From another perspective, Julian's compulsive prognostication might be analyzed psychologically. Julian spends his youth painfully and yet quite reasonably aware that Constantius may order his death at any moment. Such deeply felt vulnerability to the whims or policies of power easily breeds a desire for divinely provided foreknowledge. (Vidal has often commented on the foreknowledge and fear of death as an impulse toward religion. In *Julian*, Priscus expresses this view; see pages 81, 151.)

Julian's dependence upon omens also helps demonstrate his psychological growth. We watch him change from a frightened boy into a man whose confidence derives from his faith that the gods have planned a special role for him to a man at least approaching megalomania or delusions of grandeur. He does, after all, begin to believe he somehow reincarnates Alexander the Great. And as Julian defies the multiple omens that warn him against continuing his Persian campaign, a reader is likely to see him as foolhardy, reckless, bent perhaps on self-destruction. We may begin to sympathize with the skeptical Priscus. Priscus doesn't believe in omens, but as he ponders such disasters as earthquake and fire, even he becomes uneasy. Worse, he tells us, Julian sent to Rome to consult the oracular Sibylline books. Priscus firmly believes these books are "a grab bag of old saws and meaningless epithets." But their message to Julian was plain enough: "Do not go beyond the bounds of the empire this year" (358).

Something odd happens here. The novelist seduces us, his readers, into trusting omens and auguries we'd find laughable outside the imaginative world of this novel. In *Julian*, the old pagan gods tell the truth. Readers, then, are likely to want Julian to heed their warnings and to feel impatient with his contorted decipherings, with his insistence on twisting obvious interpretations to endorse his own intentions. Here a seductive representation of character becomes thematically persuasive. Vidal does not convert his audience into believing in Cybele, Mithras, Helios, or any other avatar of Julian's one god. By manipulating our sympathies, however, he may lead us to feel that something valuable was lost when Christianity overwhelmed older forms of worship and ritual.

THEMATIC ISSUES

When Vidal placed Julian at the vortex of his story of the turbulent fourth century, he chose a man and an epoch particularly well suited to his themes. Those themes transcend thousands of years and the better part of recorded Western history; they also provide the medium in which the narrative line grows. They will not, by any means, be alien to readers today. Certainly the hostility between East and West will strike a familiar chord. The antagonists then were the contending empires of the Mediterranean world, Rome and Persia (present-day Iran, essentially), and the issue of that day was largely territorial. It is this thematic conflict that moves Julian across the ancient landscape and affords him opportunity to muse on the differences between the despotic Asiatic mode and the Western emphasis on individual worth. Those familiar with the recent war against Iraq, Operation Desert Storm, may discern a rhetorical similarity between our own commander-in-chief's style and Julian's. The Roman emperor describes the Persians thus: "They are arrogant and boastful and revel in cruelty. The nobles terrorize the lower classes, . . . torturing and killing them as they please, and there is no law to protect the helpless . . . Their laws are savage" (398). How unlike the Romans they are!

And how unlike Julian are the Christians, and how irreconcilable their perceptions of heaven and the nature of God. This thematic problem lies at the heart of the novel and propels Julian from Nicomedia to the stewardship of Hellenism. The debate between apostate and Christians is theological, but the battleground is the Roman state; the stakes are men's souls and worldly power. In Julian's view the Christians are atheists who worship not gods but a man, and a dead man, at that. That they reject the old pantheon of gods means they reject the one true God who is manifested in the various deities of Hellenism. For the Christians, Julian is the anti-Christ, sent from hell to alienate men from their Savior (and the clergy from their perquisites). Vidal symbolizes the outcome of that debate in a powerfully elegiacal image. As the dying Hellene Libanius hobbles on his crutches from a funeral in a Christian church, his attention is drawn to the bejeweled golden image in the Byzantine dome. Through cataract-clouded eyes, he sees the Christ Pantocrator; to Libanius, it looks like Death.

Thematically, *Julian* argues that the old gods—or more precisely, their rituals and ceremonies—did not die. Rather, they were absorbed, incorporated into Christianity. In a headnote to the novel, Vidal comments on the establishment of Christianity in the fourth century: "For better or worse, we are today very much the result of what they were then" (n.p.). It is worth remembering that during the writing of *Julian* (roughly 1954–1964), the West was defining itself through an absolute contrast and conflict between West (us) and East (them). The West, in this sense, is defined as democratic, Christian, heir to the classical genius of ancient Greece and Rome. The East, in those years, was primarily identified with atheistic and totalitarian Communism, heir to barbaric cruelty and despotism. ("West" and "East" are relative terms whose denotations are more likely to change than their connotations.) *Julian* confounds this sharp bifurcation, in part by reminding us of Christianity's Asiatic roots. For example, Maximus outlines for Julian ways Christianity imitates such pagan religions as Mithraism and Zoroastrianism (77). Julian himself recognizes that his lineage is not Roman at all, but Asiatic; his entry into Constantinople feels to him like a homecoming (274). The novel also makes explicit a historical irony: Some of the seminal figures of early Christianity—Basil the Great, Gregory of Nazianzus, and John Chrysostom—were pupils of Libanius, an unreconstructed pagan.

A NEW HISTORICIST READING OF *JULIAN*

> History is idle gossip about a happening whose truth is lost the instant it has taken place.
>
> Priscus, 397

"New historicism" is a blanket term applied to several current, related approaches to the study of literature. Like many of today's methods of literary criticism, new historicism reverses or overturns some long-standing assumptions and practices. Traditionally, in what would now be called "old historicism," fiction was understood as reflecting its historical context, particularly intellectual and theological theories of its time. Literary scholars could turn to historical documents to explain and to account for a work of literary fiction. Oversimplifying somewhat, we could say that this tradition assumed that history was more reliably clear and unambiguous in its meaning than the fiction that merely reflected it. It is true that new historicists debate theory and methodology among themselves and often disagree about particular points.[1] They do, however, agree in rejecting the basic assumption of old historicism. That is, new historicists argue that every history is a fiction, an account shaped by particular interests and constrained by rules and conventions, much like literature. What we are used to calling history is no more reliable, unequivocal, straightforward, or real than what we usually call fiction. If this is the case, literary scholars cannot rely on recorded history to explain literature directly. Instead, new historicists often set literary and non-literary texts side by side with the goal of understanding the unstated assumptions, the mentality embodied in the practices of a particular culture at a particular time. For example, in the opening of this chapter *Julian* was discussed in connection with the East–West conflict at the forefront of national consciousness during the Cold War. A new historicist might ask whether Vidal's novel sustains or undermines this boundary that has seemed so definitive. As we shall see, moreover, new historicists do not limit themselves to specifically political history any more than they limit themselves to strictly literary texts. Social history, the history of everyday life, can be as informative as the outcome of a battle or the troubles of a monarchy.

It is not easy to reverse long-standing habits of thinking, but the results of new historical inquiries suggest that the effort is worthwhile. Reading Vidal's historical novels is excellent preparation for developing a new historicist perspective. Again and again, these books remind us that what we call history is at best a mixed bag. Data are provided through unreliable memories, partial recollections, and reportage that may be self-serving, dishonest, or simply mistaken. These data are then shaped—some would say bent—into narratives by fallible historians, who may, consciously or not, promote their own views, however unintentionally. Further, it can be argued that as historians organize data into narratives, they inevitably engage the same patterns that shape literature.[2] Indeed, the fictional nature of history is a recurring theme in Vidal's novels, and we shall return to it in later chapters. Here it will be useful to focus on a topic that has fascinated many new historicists: the exercise and maintenance of political power as a form of theater. That is, the workings of drama can illuminate politics as often as political circumstances can account for particular plays. This reading will first outline power–theater associations that pervade *Julian* and then consider what social and cultural conditions between 1954 and 1964 could have provoked this connection. (Vidal began writing *Julian* in 1959, but he was reading and thinking about the apostate much earlier; in *Messiah* the narrator is working on a study of Julian's life.)

Vidal's Julian claims to have been a grown man before attending a theatrical performance, and he admits to a certain priggishness that doesn't quite approve of theater (18). His classical education, however, obviously included the Greek dramatists; he quotes, for instance, the tragedians Aeschylus and Euripides (52) as well as the comic playwright Menander (265). He does enjoy a performance of Aeschylus's *Prometheus* (330), but not Aristophanes's satiric comedy, *The Frogs* (345). Despite his professed distaste for the theater, Julian several times compares himself to an actor, and he feels that others have behaved toward him as if he were destined to be a tragic hero (43). He describes his first encounter with Constantius after Gallus's death: "Like two actors we played our scene impersonally until it was done" (158). Late in the novel, following Julian's account of his brooding fears, suspicions, and despair after he commands his soldiers to return home, Priscus is surprised to discover how skilled an actor Julian indeed was. Priscus admits that he saw nothing of Julian's dark feelings in his confident, even exuberant, performance before the soldiers (431). This is entirely to the point. Julian has grown up to be a master of theatrical displays of power. He seems to learn early that to remain emperor is to remain a master actor, a performer for whom negative reviews could be fatal. In part, he learns from watching his cousin. As represented in the novel, Constantius is something of a dullard. Long after the fact, Julian mocks his lack of oratorical skill and verbal polish. At the same time, however, Julian is impressed by Constantius's mastery of theatrical ceremony. Of particular note is Constantius's ability to perform the role of emperor with his army as his audience. Julian describes Constantius orchestrating the performance of his supporting cast—the army: "The voices rang out as though spontaneous (actually, everything had been carefully rehearsed). Constantius remained very still while they spoke." When the demonstration ends, Constantius answers his troops with imperial solemnity: " 'Your response is enough. I see that I have your approval' " (166). Constantius and Julian inhabit a world in which support of the army is vital in maintaining one's rule; a bit of theatrical expertise is no bad thing.

Julian learns well from Constantius's example. One significant moment occurs in Gaul just before the Battle of Strasbourg. Priscus tells us that Julian wanted to attack immediately, but he knew the army was tired from marching and hot from the noonday heat. Julian makes a speech urging caution and suggesting battle be delayed until morning. Suddenly, a standard-bearer shouts, " 'Forward, Caesar! Follow your star!' " Turning to the legions, he exclaims, " 'We shall free Gaul this day! Hail Caesar!' " (201–202). And so the battle begins.

Later, grinning like a schoolboy, Julian asks whether Priscus enjoyed the standard-bearer's speech. When Priscus assures him that the speech was perfectly apt, Julian boasts that he'd rehearsed the soldier's performance the previous night, "with gestures" (202). In other words, Julian stage-managed the entire episode. Remembering this scene, readers may well wonder about the later moment when Julian's army begins chanting and hailing him as Augustus, in effect proclaiming him emperor (226). Neither historical records nor Vidal's novel tells us with certainty what Julian may have done to orchestrate this demand that he take on the purple mantle of emperor. And in his memoir addressed to future readers, Julian says of the moment, "as if by signal . . . they began to chant" (226). A reader's speculation on Julian's directorial hand in this demonstration is invited by the apostate's own comments on Julius Caesar: "I am sure that Julius Caesar very carefully instructed his friend to offer him the crown in public, simply to see what the reaction might be" (230). It seems reasonable to assume that Julian orchestrated the entire affair. Throughout *Julian*, power is secured through theatrical display. Such display is not the only resource for preserving power, but it is one a Roman emperor required, as do our own politicians and leaders—and they can exploit technologies undreamt of by the Romans. In this sense, *Julian* both reflects its own time and forecasts a future. *Julian*, we could say, encodes as ancient display the increasing influence of television in shaping public life. From a new historicist perspective, a cultural anxiety or present tension plays itself out, in disguised form, on a narrative stage. That is, *Julian* translates a cultural uneasiness over the potential power of a new technology into a comfortingly distanced tale of the ancient world. Note that considering the novel in these terms does not require a belief that either Vidal or his readers in 1964 were consciously fretting over the thought that television might become the central fact of public and political life. Significant anxieties are rarely so well defined. Instead, we can consider the circumstances that could lead to a widespread but not directly articulated anxiety.

Although published statistics vary, the 1950s and early 1960s saw a dazzling increase in the number of television sets in the United States, from 5,000 in 1945 to 15 million in 1951, 41 million in 1958, and 85 million in 1960.[3] Such leaders as Franklin Roosevelt and Winston Churchill had used radio broadcasts to great effect, and Vidal seems to have recognized early the even greater potential of television. (At the time, the triviality of television programming and the fatuousness of commercials were often deplored, but the fears expressed most about the new technology concerned radiation and surveillance rather than the power to mold public opinion and direct the course of public events.)

Even before *Julian, Messiah* (1954, rev. 1965) assessed seriously the power of television to shape events, as opposed to merely recording them. The messiah of the book's title is John Cave, a rather ordinary man with a rather ordinary message. As the narrator observes, however, "Cave certainly had one advantage over his predecessors: modern communications. It took three centuries for Christianity to infect the world. It was to take Cave only three years to conquer Europe and the Americas" (*Messiah* 167). Rulers no doubt have always used theatrical display as a mode of sustaining their power, but advances in the technologies of communication allow for greater dissemination of imperial performances. Set in a not-too-distant future, *Messiah* implies the potential of mass media; set in a distant past, *Julian* represents the theatricality of power in action. Both books now seem prophetic.

NOTES

1. See two anthologies edited by H. Aram Veeser: *The New Historicism* (London: Routledge, 1989) and *The New Historicism Reader* (London: Routledge, 1994).

2. See, for example, two books by historian Hayden White: *Metahistory: The Historical Imagination in Nineteenth-Century Europe* (Baltimore: Johns Hopkins University Press, 1973) and *Tropics of Discourse: Essays in Cultural Criticism* (Baltimore: Johns Hopkins University Press, 1978). For an overview, see Lynn Hunt, ed., *The New Cultural History* (Berkeley and Los Angeles: University of California Press, 1989).

3. Statistics are available in James Trager, *The People's Chronology: A Year-by-Year Account of Human Events from Prehistory to the Present*, rev. edn. (New York: Henry Holt, 1992); and Bernard Grun, *The Timetables of History: A Horizontal Linkage of People and Events*, rev. edn. (New York: Simon and Schuster, 1982).

Creation
(1981)

Regarding Cyrus Spitama, the profoundly curious protagonist of *Creation* (1981), Vidal says, "What he comes to see is that he was asking the wrong questions." That is, he was "hung up on the notion of creation."

Vidal said later, "Western culture is always asking the wrong questions. It's our fatal flaw" ("Interview," Parini 286). Although Vidal calls the quest to know origins wrongheaded, his own novels, in fact, return repeatedly to foundational moments, to inaugural events, to decisive and determining crises. The writer may, in fact, have more in common with Spitama more than he would care to admit.

Set in the fifth century B.C., *Creation* tells the story of one man's quest to understand the beginning of the universe and the enormous journey his search takes him on.

PLOT DEVELOPMENT

Cyrus Spitama is the son of an Ionian Greek woman and the paternal grandson of the Persian Zoroaster. Although Cyrus, his father, and his mother, Lais, are fictional, readers should know that the grandfather is not; Zoroastrianism, which he founded, was the state religion of ancient Persia. It is precisely because of that authorial conceit—Cyrus's Greek-

Persian parentage and his illustrious grandfather—that Vidal can initiate his story.

When Cyrus is a boy he witnesses Zoroaster's murder and hears God speak through the dying man's mouth—an event, needless to say, that makes a lasting impression on the youngster. He is subsequently taken under the protection of Darius, the Great King of the Persian Empire, and brought to the royal court, where he unwittingly becomes enmeshed in a murderous web of palace intrigue. A friendship develops between Cyrus and Xerxes, one of Darius's sons and a leading candidate to inherit the empire. (At this time, Persian kings named their own successors; sibling rivalry in the royal household was frequently homicidal.) In Cyrus, Xerxes finds someone whose religious distinction qualifies him to be a prince's companion but, at the same time, a non-rival in the succession sweepstakes. As Xerxes' loyal friend, Cyrus several times serves as go-between in the efforts of Atossa, Xerxes' mother, to secure her son's position as heir to the throne. Plots and counterplots abound, and—somewhat like Vidal's Julian—Cyrus is often uneasy abut his own chances for survival.

But Cyrus does survive and eventually becomes a kind of roving ambassador for three successive Persian emperors. (His diplomatic missions will give structure to the unavoidably episodic plot and provide the pretext for a vivid travelogue of the ancient world.) Darius sends Cyrus as trade emissary to India, where he has some extraordinary adventures and meets several holy men, including the Buddha. He marries the daughter of a king, and is introduced to Fan Ch'ih, an envoy from Cathay. (In a note Vidal explains that referring to "China" would be erroneous and confusing.)

Cyrus returns to Persia, and his old friend Xerxes ascends to the throne, though not without difficulty. Because of Spitama's association with Fan Ch'ih, Xerxes sends him to Cathay, again as a trade emissary. Along the way he's taken prisoner by and escapes from various Chinese princes who regard him as an exotic curiosity. Those adventures bring him into contact with Confucius and Master Li, the founder of Taoism. Neither will answer Cyrus's questions about creation, but Confucius leaves an indelible impression in his mind as the wisest of all men. Confucius's extended conversations with Spitama give Vidal an opportunity to indulge his own oft-stated enthusiasm for the sage.

Cyrus returns at last to Persia, and he calls the next dozen years the happiest in his life. This pleasant interlude is only briefly summarized in the novel, however, and the business at hand resumes with the assassination of Xerxes. Then under Artaxerxes, Xerxes' son and now Great King, Cyrus lives quietly until summoned to negotiate a treaty with the Athenians. As a living symbol of this treaty, Cyrus is sent to Athens, where he meets a troublesome handyman named Socrates and lives out the remainder of his long and eventful life.

As mentioned before, the plot structure of *Creation* is best described as episodic. That is, the novel achieves its effects cumulatively, adding incident upon incident, like beads on a string. Episodic structure differs from—but is no less valid than—the types of developmental plots in which events arise causally, each resulting from those that precede it and all ultimately revealed as interrelated. (The latter is what people generally mean when they say a novel or movie is tightly or cleverly plotted.) The classical model for a developmental plot, as described by Aristotle, is Sophocles's *Oedipus the King*. This play has its definite beginning, middle, and end, and it builds carefully toward a reversal of fortune that coincides with the moment of recognition, the moment when the play's secret is revealed. The classical model for *Creation*, however, could be Homer's *Odyssey*, a compilation of discrete adventures, most of which are interchangeable, any of which could be omitted, and to which others could be added without damaging the narrative logic.

As a general rule, episodic plots encourage readers to compare scenes or incidents, to seek thematic or tonal links among them rather than to ask what will happen next. (As we shall see, episodic plots also call for particular strategies of characterization.) *Creation* thus encourages readers to compare several different civilizations—Persian, Greek, Indian, and Cathayan—as well as competing principalities within each of these. Much of this novel's pleasure derives from the rich accumulation of exotic details, the particularities of each society Cyrus encounters. Similarly, the novel's themes are grounded in the mix of similarities and differences Cyrus finds in these societies' customs and beliefs.

Episodic plots always risk appearing arbitrary or incoherent. This risk is easily enough overcome through the use of a single strong protagonist throughout otherwise loosely linked episodes. In *Creation* the narrator, Cyrus Spitama, provides continuity. We see the various courts through his eyes, certainly, but also through his biases, preconceptions, and most important, his interests. Because Cyrus is especially curious about the origin of existence and especially alert to religious and political machinations, the reader learns much about these matters.

CHARACTER DEVELOPMENT

In its treatment of character, *Creation* differs from *Julian*, Vidal's other novel set in the ancient world. In *Julian*, the reader learns about the Apostate as a particular human being whose adult personality can be seen as evolving through his formative experiences. Cyrus Spitama, however, remains constant, relatively unchanged so far as we can see, by his remarkable explorations. In part, this effect stems from Cyrus's stance as retrospective narrator, recounting his adventures from the perspective of old age. Unlike the narrator of *Kalki*, for example, Cyrus is not represented as trying to recapture any earlier innocence or ignorance. He speaks securely in the moment of what we would call 445 B.C., as the frequent asides to Democritus and references to then current events remind readers. He is not particularly interested in constructing a coherent autobiography, nor does he have any substantial stake in the present interpretation of past events. Rather, Cyrus is an observer, and a relatively objective one. He is, however, outraged at Herodotus's account of the "Persian Wars," and he insists on referring to the battles of 498 to 449 B.C. as the "Greek Wars," which is the appropriate name from the Persian point of view.

For all *Creation*'s intellectual speculation, Cyrus Spitama closely resembles a folk hero, appropriately enough for an episodic novel recounting a quest. First, Cyrus is remarkable by birth. He is the grandson of Zoroaster, the great prophet of Ahura Mazdah (the Great Lord). Further, at the age of seven, Cyrus witnessed his grandfather's murder and heard for himself the Great Lord's voice. (He had, as he tells us, partaken of the "sacred haoma," a strong, probably hallucinogenic liquor.) This unusual experience does not turn Cyrus into a prophet, a visionary, or even an especially devout believer (see, for example, 30–31). As the last surviving grandson of Zoroaster, he's treated with reverence by some, including Hystaspes, the father of Darius and the satrap (governor) of Bactria, where Cyrus is born. (Darius is a follower of Zoroaster, primarily for political purposes.) Hystaspes's influence preserves Cyrus's life and arranges for his princely education. Thus, Cyrus becomes the boyhood friend of Xerxes, Darius's son and future Great King, and of Mardonius, who will be Darius's greatest general). The priests of his grandfather's religion mostly envy Cyrus, but appearances and protocol demand that they treat him with respect.

When Darius sends Cyrus to India, he orders Cyrus to question local religious functionaries, using his Zoroastrian connection as a pretext for doing so. The point here is that Cyrus's descent from Zoroaster does not so much shape his personality as it supplies opportunities for him to pursue his curiosity about origins, about creation. Cyrus's birth is primarily relevant to his role as archetypal seeker rather than to some sort of psychobiography.

Like others engaged in epic and folktale quests, Cyrus has his patrons: Darius sends him to India, Xerxes to Cathay, Artaxerxes to Athens. He also chances upon helpers as he needs them: Prince Jeta in India or Fan Ch'ih in the Cathayan province of Lu. Cyrus is rewarded as similar heroes often are; his earlier help to Fan Ch'ih is repaid at a time of danger.

Like Odysseus, one of his prototypes, Cyrus is wily. Early on, we see him outwitting a schoolmate (41), and he remains a master of verbal self-preservation. He is also shrewd, frequently understanding the unspoken language of political tacticians. (See, for example, 166, 179, 386). He can resort to shameless flattery when necessary, and more than once he lies outright—despite his frequent assertions that noble Persians do not lie. Cyrus is also patient, as folk heroes often must be. For example, in Cathay Cyrus becomes a slave, first of Huan and then of the eccentric Duke of Sheh. Some sort of subjugation is typical of epic and folk heroes. Heracles must perform labors for King Eurystheus and also disguises himself as a woman. In general, heroes have to bide their time until the moment is ripe to emerge from servitude. Heroes of epic quests lead charmed lives, but they also must patiently endure ordeals.

In addition to Cyrus, *Creation* also includes numerous skillfully rendered secondary and minor characters. (Kiernan considers this portrait gallery the book's greatest strength, 63). Certainly, Cyrus Spitama encounters several formidable women. His mother, Lais, claims to be a witch. She is undoubtedly a master of deadly poisons, equally prepared to poison someone or to take credit for having done so. Lais's lethal craft is exploited by two successive queens of Persia, both of whom are politically powerful despite their sequestration in the harem. The first, Atossa, is the daughter of Cyrus the Great, a chief wife of Darius, and the mother of Xerxes. (Eventually readers learn the secret that enables her to wield so much influence.) A second queen, Amestris, a wife of Xerxes and mother of Artaxerxes, is jealous; thanks to Lais's arcane knowledge, any girl Xerxes finds especially attractive is dead within a month. Other powerful women in the novel include Artemisia of Halicarnassus, who leads her troops into battle, and, last of all, Aspasia, the mistress of Pericles.

Often, the memorable characters Cyrus encounters in India and Cathay are distinguished by a single trait, a literary tactic as old as Aristophanes and as recent as last week's sitcom. Bimbisara, for example, tends to repeat the last phrase spoken to him and then abruptly change the subject (182). Bimbisara's son and heir, Ajatashatru, weeps at the slightest provocation. He becomes Cyrus's father-in-law, as well as a parricide and one of the cruelest rulers in a world of cruel autocracies. One of the most amusing figures is the Duke of Sheh in Cathay; this duke is a Cathayan aristocrat, although there is no such place as Sheh. (The word means "holy ground," 337.) A thorough eccentric, the Duke of Sheh is a reflexive liar (or fantasizer, it's hard to tell which) and an obsessive collector of dragon bones. Nonetheless, he helps Cyrus escape from the brutal Duke of Ch'in. Sheh treats Cyrus as a slave, or perhaps a household pet, but he does take Cyrus to the province of Lu, where Cyrus rejoins an old friend from his days in India.

Despite these and other small, well-wrought portraits, *Creation* is emphatically not a novel of character, like *Julian* or *Lincoln*, in which the nature of the central figure is the central theme. Rather, the novel focuses on questions of religion and on comparing local customs in all their variety. And most of all, *Creation* urges us to compare the multitude of answers Cyrus receives to his queries about the beginning of things.

THEMATIC ISSUES

Religion and politics may be barred from polite conversation, but they have usually been the topics of choice in the old and heated cultural dialogue between East and West. They are also Vidal's topics of choice in *Creation*, and the thematic avenues he takes to explore the validity of knowledge itself. The antagonists this time are the Persian Empire and the Greek city-states, and the man in the middle is the Persian-Greek Cyrus Spitama, a searcher after truth who may be asking the wrong questions.

For all Cyrus's Persian upbringing and biases, which include considerable contempt for Athenians, he is finally quite Greek in his curiosity and his philosophic bent. When Cyrus returns first from India and then from Cathay, no one at the Persian court is particularly interested in his experiences and observations, and certainly not where his information lacks immediately practical value. Darius, it should be noted, had charged Cyrus Spitama with retrieving some specific information about the Indian kingdoms, information relevant first to trade and ultimately to conquest. Xerxes's interests are the same. As Great King, Xerxes likes the idea of opening trade routes to Cathay, but beyond the possibilities of trade or conquest, neither Great King is markedly curious about a wider world. And neither are Cyrus's mother, Lais, or his wary patron, Atossa.

Cyrus has similar experiences on his travels. For example, various holy men he meets are visibly bored when he tries to tell them about Zoroastrianism. (Neither are the Zoroastrian priests interested in all Cyrus has learned of other religions, 494.) The various rulers are equally fatigued whenever Cyrus describes Persian customs—unless, that is, they bear directly on the strength or strategies of Persian imperialism. As he travels across the world, most of the people Cyrus encounters lack curiosity for curiosity's sake. Only Greeks seem to desire knowledge or information independent of any obvious utility. There's no doubt something of a joke in all this; who, after all, is fascinated by anyone else's vacation slides or home videos? But the pattern is unmistakable. In fact, the first person to ask Cyrus Spitama about all he's seen and done is Democritus, his thoroughly Greek nephew. (Not, we should note, Cyrus's Greek mother, who is blissfully self-centered. Nationality is not all.)

Cyrus Spitama's nephew, of course, is not just any Greek youth. He is Democritus, the philosopher and materialist. In the first of his addenda to his uncle's life story, Democritus notes the religious doubts Cyrus had but would not confess. Cyrus insists there must be a beginning and an end, as Zoroaster preached; he rejects the Eastern view of existence as a circle. But he admits to Democritus, "There *is* something missing. Something I could not find anywhere on this earth in the course of a long life" (488, italics in original). Thus the quest of Cyrus was a failure, but a valuable failure. Democritus credits his uncle with enabling his own insights: "[B]y relating to me in such detail his failure, he made it possible for me to understand what he could not—the nature of the universe" (488). Through learning about the world's multiplicity of beliefs and customs, Democritus refuses them all: "Matter is all. All is matter" (488).

Vidal may well share the views of Democritus, but his more immediate concern is with ethics, with questions of how people are to live in this world. In the same interview quoted at the beginning of this chapter, Vidal asserts his admiration for Confucius as offering the sanest way of life ("Interview," Parini 287); Cyrus Spitama feels much the same (419). Although drawing parallels between author and character is risky and presumptuous, Vidal's biographers would do well (we believe) to study his portrait of Confucius. Certainly, one could say of Vidal what Cyrus says of Confucius: "He made himself an expert on the past so that he might be useful in the present" (383).

Like so many of Vidal's novels, *Creation* is set in what we can call a founding moment. Cyrus personally meets the human representatives of four great belief systems, Zoroaster, Buddha, Confucius, Master Li. Zoroaster, as the prophet of Ahura Mazdah, can be taken as a founding father of monotheism; some historians of religion believe the teachings of Zoroaster influenced the Hebrew Bible, and thus Christianity and, later, Islam. It is important to note, however, that Zoroaster preached a dualism, an evenly balanced struggle between good and evil. Orthodox Christianity considers such dualism heresy, but versions of this heresy appear and reappear over Christian history.

Further, Cyrus notes the rise in Athens and elsewhere of various Eastern cults, including those of Orpheus and Mithras. Again, most religious historians believe that the development of Christianity was influenced by such mystery religions. ("Mystery" religions are those that require elaborate initiation rites for their adherents. So far as scholars can determine, these rites are believed to confer immortality in the form of an afterlife.) On this theme, *Creation* pairs well with *Julian*. One novel depicts the variety of religions that preceded Christianity or competed with it. The other marks the triumph of Christianity, the last gasp of the old pagan gods in the Western world.

Another of *Creation*'s central themes is the political exploitation of religion. Most of Vidal's novels remind us that politics has always been a backroom business involving intrigues, compromises, deceptions, and at times downright dishonesty and graft. (Conversely, Vidal's novels also insist that politicians can have strong principles and commitments to worthy actions. Chicanery may be the hallmark of politics, but chicanery can serve either good or bad ends, either good or bad people.) Too, Vidal's religious skepticism is apparent in many of the novels, as well as his essays and other writing. Vidal seems to believe first that religious sentiments arise from the fear of death, specifically death as a return to nothingness. Second, Vidal invariably portrays religious institutions as arenas of political maneuvering and power struggles. More than the other novels, however, *Creation* addresses the uses rulers make of religion. Before Cyrus leaves for India, Darius speaks candidly to him: "Give particular attention to their gods. It has been my policy always to support those religions that are truly popular. Once you pretend to honor the local deity, the priesthood is immediately on your side. Once you have the priests, you don't need much of a garrison to keep order" (124).

In India, the royal chamberlain of Magadha is equally candid about supporting Buddhism: "Any religion that believes that this world is a kind of illness to be got rid of by prayer and by respecting all life and by not wanting earthly possessions is enormously helpful to a ruler. After all, if people don't want material things, they won't want what we've got" (215). (Other references to using religion to exercise secular power appear on 15, 38, 48, 53, 61, 128, 141, 164, 168, 286, 301–02, 306.)

A DECONSTRUCTIVE READING OF *CREATION*

Deconstruction, most famously practiced by the French philosopher Jacques Derrida, is a branch of philosophy that seeks not to demolish literature itself, as some think, but to challenge the assumptions of some other critical schools, most immediately structuralism. Because Cyrus Spitama searches for a single answer to what he discovers is the wrong question, and because deconstruction opposes the structuralist's supposition that a single unifying principle can ultimately be inferred in the universe, our choice of a deconstructive reading for *Creation* seems apt.

Unfortunately, deconstruction can be rough sledding for literary specialists, let alone the generalist or recreational reader. For that reason, and because a detailed discussion of any branch of literary criticism is outside the scope of this book, we will simply mention one area of deconstructionist—structuralist disagreement particularly relevant to *Creation*. Given the binary pair "speech/writing," the structuralist argument implies that speech has precedence, or "priority." Derrida, conversely, argues that the specific claims for the immediacy of speech over writing are specious; he demonstrates that the qualities or characteristics that have traditionally established writing's secondary status are true of speech as well.

Thus, one could say that the definition of writing includes within it, or subsumes, the definition of speech. In this fashion, we can see that the conditions of writing are also the preconditions necessary for a spoken language. From the deconstructionist perspective, speech is a type of writing rather than, as in the usual view, writing being an imitation of speech.

Elsewhere we have mentioned Vidal's interest in founding or inaugurating moments. *Creation* recounts the originating circumstances of several religions: Zoroastrianism, Buddhism, Taoism, Confucianism. *Creation* itself is set in another, related, beginning.

> In the beginning, there was the spoken word. The first narrations concerned the doings of gods and kings, and these stories were passed on from generation to generation, usually as verse in order to make memorizing easier. Then, mysteriously, in the fifth century B.C. all the narratives were written down, and literature began. From Greece to Persia to India to China, there was a great controversy. Could a narrative be possessed that had been committed to writing rather than to memory? Traditionalists said no; modernists said yes. The traditionalists lost. Now, twenty-five hundred years later, there is a similar crisis. Modernists believe that any form of narration and of learning can be transmitted through audiovisual means rather than through the, now, traditional written word. In this controversy I am, for once, a conservative to the point of furious reaction. (*United States* 669)

The above extract is from Vidal's essay, "Lincoln and the Priests of Academe." It could, however, serve as an epigraph to *Creation*, which is set in the century and the places where narratives began to be written rather than spoken from memory.

Creation thus depicts the spread of writing as a founding moment, one on which the modern world entirely depends. Between 513 B.C. (when Cyrus witnesses Zoroaster's murder) and 405 B.C. (the date of Democritus's coda or epilogue to Cyrus's narrative, nearly forty years after the death of Cyrus) writing prevails over the spoken word. In describing his education, Cyrus says, "We learned to read and even to write, if necessary" (55–56). Xerxes read "with some ease" but Cyrus doubts that the future king could write. Darius, for that matter, is better at arithmetic than at reading; reports from his satraps were encoded with a "simplified syntax" (121). By the end of the novel, however, Democritus takes writing for granted as the way to preserve a narrative.

In this context, it is worth remembering that *Creation* opens with an oral reading by Herodotus of his history of the Persian Wars. (Herodotus's history remains today a standard source for classical historians; by and large, people continue to speak of these wars from the Greek perspective.) This one-sided view irritates Cyrus so much that he begins recounting his version of what he calls the "Greek Wars" to his nephew,

Democritus, who writes them down. It is true that Herodotus and Cyrus (before he became blind) could write, but it is equally true that oral presentation apparently remains for them the norm. Indeed, Cyrus at one time believes that "whenever holy words were written down, they lost their religious potency" (223). Even near the end of his life he believes "there is nothing more effective than the human voice when it summons from the recesses of memory the words of Truth" (223). Still, Cyrus has come to accept the necessity of inscribing the words of Zoroaster: "I now want a complete written record of my grandfather's words on the simple grounds that if we survivors do not make it, others will" (223). (Written records can be compared with each other more easily than can spoken ones.)

The much younger Democritus begins his closing passage, "I, Democritus, . . . have organized these recollections of Cyrus Spitama into nine books. I have paid for their transcription, and they can now be read by any Greek" (509). (Note that Democritus's additions are aimed at any audience, while Cyrus's narrative had a particular audience.) Just a few pages earlier, Democritus interpolated a conversation he and Cyrus had, one that Cyrus would not have wanted preserved (486). Such additions, as well as subtractions, substitutions, and other changes, are always possible in the transmission of written texts. In part, Cyrus Spitama hates the writing down of Zoroaster's wisdom for precisely this reason, as if the oral transmission from memory to memory were more authentic, truer to the source, than transmission mediated by the written text. But he comes to accept that this belief in speech's superior magic is an illusion. Whether orally or in writing, priests will inevitably corrupt the words of Zoroaster. Moreover, as Democritus suggests, writing makes certain kinds of knowledge available to "any Greek," any reader. Writing makes possible both the accumulation and dissemination of knowledge, both philosophy and science as we know them.

It is also worth noting that Cyrus believes no one has read his accounts of Eastern geography in the Persian archives. But they are there, awaiting some future reader. One of the greatest differences between written and spoken language is that an oral tradition must be unbroken or be lost entirely. Writing, however, can lie dormant until some reader seeks it out or stumbles over it accidentally. As *Creation* repeatedly suggests, meaning is never fully present in speech alone. It requires an audience. (And there will always be a delay, however brief, between a word's being spoken and its being understood.) In *Creation* this condition (or restriction) is frequently represented in Cyrus's grasp of what is not actually said. Indeed, Cyrus can recognize when he's becoming the medium of communication rather than a participant in it. ("Bimbisara was warning Darius through me," 179). Thus speech is less independent, less fully present than it seems. This pattern is repeated when Cyrus is sent to Athens as the embodiment of a treaty so secret that no one can be told about it. Cyrus serves as (replaces, substitutes for) the document; he becomes himself a text.

At least with reference to an immediate audience, writing is freer and more independent than speech. *Creation* contains at least two images for this freedom. First, there is Cyrus's description of Babylonian cylindrical seals, decorated with beautiful "picture-writings" no one can read (139). But readers know that scholars will eventually decipher cuneiform writing and Babylon will, in a sense, be heard—or read—again. Similarly, although Cyrus has written down the facts of his journeys, they lie unread in the Persian archives. They are not lost, however, only dormant. Writing can wait for a reader; speech has only a brief moment to find a listener.

Creation demonstrates that speech has no inherent advantages over writing. Speech goes no further than writing in guaranteeing truth or accuracy. Both speech and writing are subject to change through transmission, and there is always a delay between the production of a sentence and its reception. What the spoken word can do in the absence of writing is maintain a priestly caste. When only a priest knows, say, all 65,000 names for the gods (85), his authority and power are unique. (There have been times in history when only priests could write, but their texts could always be stolen; you cannot steal someone's memory.) Writing is a technology that enables, but cannot guarantee, democracy. If we look closely at the binary oppositions Derrida deconstructs, we shall find again and again that their hierarchical relation, the subordination of one to the other, ultimately helps maintain inequities of the status quo.

6

The "American Chronicles": An Introduction

By virtue of his circumstances, talents, and consuming interest in American political history, Vidal has been well positioned to write a series of fictionalized histories (or historical fictions) of the United States from the late colonial period through the 1950s. Though the initial entry, *Washington, D.C.* (1967), is chronologically last in the series, something much larger grew out of that semi-autobiographical *roman à clef*. In an interview, Vidal explained how his "American Chronicles" came about.

> I suppose it was during the composition of *Burr* that I realized that a sequence could be made of that material. I had several references to Aaron Burr in *Washington, D.C.*, and of course my stepfather's family was related to Burr. Somewhere along the way I realized I was involved in a family history, that it could all be expanded from there. In *Burr* I focused on the first thirty years of the republic. I wanted to keep going, to see what would happen to these people and their descendants. Eventually, the story spanned two centuries. ("Interview," Parini 286)

That expanded story delineates, in an intricate tableau of literary, intellectual, and cultural Americana, the evolution of the United States from New World backwater to global superpower. The usurpation of republican ideals by imperial opportunism is the underlying theme of the chronicles; the fictional thread that ties them together is the social and political adventurism of the descendants of Aaron Burr.

Enthusiasts of historical fiction will note that less skillful efforts in the genre tend to place the history at the periphery of the accompanying romance. (See the discussion of the historical novel as a genre in Chapter 3.) Vidal's technique, neither unprecedented nor typical, is to fictionalize the historical characters at the heart of each novel's political narrative. Presidents Grant, Wilson, and Harding (or for that matter, William Randolph Hearst and Mark Twain) are accorded fully developed personalities that allow them to function as characters in the novelistic form. Some of that character development is necessarily speculative, but the results of Vidal's method are at once historically credible and artistically satisfying.

Readers of Vidal's "American Chronicles" can feel confident about the history recounted therein. Vidal believes a novelist can be more daring in interpretation—of motive, especially—than can a historian. Such freedom in interpretation, however, as Vidal has repeatedly insisted, in no way licenses any carelessness about facts. His approach is to immerse himself in reading material relevant to the historical moment of the novel he's working on, with a preference for documents from the period itself. In writing *Burr*, for instance, Vidal was fortunate in being able to purchase 200 volumes from the sale of an Aaron Burr collection. Of that novel's Helen Jewett, he says, "I got the story from Philip Hone's diaries. Invaluable for a picture of the 1830s. When I say there was a red moon over the Battery on such and such a night, I have taken it from his diaries" (*Views From a Window* 117). For *1876* his reading included browsing for weeks through old periodicals, the same ones his fictional narrator writes for. Vidal seeks through his research to capture the flavor of an era as well as its facts. Close reading indicates that the cadences of prose as well as turns of phrase and vocabulary vary from novel to novel, in historically appropriate ways. And as Vidal points out, "In my novels, [when] I [introduce] an actual figure [from] history, whatever he says and does is what he actually said and did. The real thing is usually much more interesting than any gloss. You can do whatever you like with the fictional characters" (*Views From a Window* 120; brackets in original). Although Vidal does his own research, his publishers also hire professional historians to double-check the novels for factual accuracy. Certainly, Vidal invents the Schuyler-Sanford lineage, as well as occasional minor characters. Sometimes, as with David Herold in *Lincoln*, he constructs a plausible biography for a factual person about whom little is known. Keeping this degree of poetic license in mind, however, readers can trust Vidal's historical accuracy at least as far as that of television documentaries or college-level textbooks.

A brief overview of the Schuyler-Sanford line as depicted in the six novels may be in order. The American journalist and historian Charles Schermerhorn Schuyler is Burr's bastard son and the narrator of *Burr*, which ends shortly after Schuyler takes up residence in Italy. Schuyler is an elderly man when he re-enters the United States at the onset of *1876*. He is accompanied by his daughter Emma, a titled but impoverished mother of two adolescent sons who remain in France with their deceased father's mother but re-emerge for secondary roles in later installments of the series. Although Schuyler and Emma appear briefly in *Lincoln*, they won't survive *1876*, save in memory. Emma's daughter Caroline will extend their direct lineage through the succeeding novels *Empire* and *Hollywood*. Caroline's half-brother Blaise Sanford and his son Peter will provide the familial coda to the cycle in *Washington, D.C.* It is our suggestion, and the author's, that the "Chronicles" be read in historical order. Any of the six novels, however, stands on its own merits and may be enjoyed separately.

Burr
(1973)

An epic set in the early years of the American republic, *Burr* is in part an effort to rehabilitate Aaron Burr's reputation. As such, the novel becomes the exploration of an enigmatic figure, an oddly self-destructive genius, a would-be emperor with thoroughly democratic sympathies.

PLOT DEVELOPMENT AND POINT OF VIEW

Burr opens with the title character's second marriage, to Madame Jumel in 1833. The novel begins with a newspaper announcement of this marriage, thus presenting for readers the straightforward facts about the life of Aaron Burr. In short order, we learn that Burr was born in 1756. In 1804, while he was vice president, he killed Alexander Hamilton in a duel. In 1807 President Thomas Jefferson had Burr arrested on the charge of treason. Jefferson claimed that Burr had plotted to "break up the United States." He was found "innocent of treason but guilty of the misdemeanor of proposing an invasion of Spanish territory in order to make himself emperor of Mexico" (2).

As the novel will show, there is much more to Aaron Burr than the notorious duel and charges of treason, but they remain the givens any study of Burr—however fictionalized—must take into account. In retrospect, Burr's duel with Hamilton and his western adventures seem dazzling in their self-destructive miscalculation, marks of folly in an otherwise intelligent man. As the novel emphasizes, legend has negotiated this contradiction by demonizing Burr, by representing him as unremittingly wicked. Vidal is looking for a better explanation.

Vidal depicts Burr, his life and times, by juxtaposing two narratives. The framing storyline is recounted by fictional character Charles Schuyler in a journal covering the years 1833 to 1836, with a postscript or epilogue set in 1840. Loosely based on minor novelist Charles Burdett, Schuyler is an aspiring writer and a clerk in Burr's law office. He hates the thought of being a lawyer and hopes to support himself by writing for newspapers and magazines. A newspaper editor commissions Schuyler to prepare a pamphlet exposing presidential contender Martin Van Buren as Burr's illegitimate son. (Public hostility toward Burr is underscored by the editor's conviction that associating Van Buren with Burr will thwart the younger man's presidential ambitions.) In response to Schuyler's apparent interest in his life, Burr gives him notes about the American Revolution and then dictates further memoirs. The novel alternates between Schuyler's diary from 1833 to 1836 and Burr's recollections of the years 1775 through 1808.

As in *Julian*, the strategy of doubled narration serves multiple purposes. Frequently, for instance, just as one storyline reaches a crisis or poses a compelling question, the novel shifts to the other narrator, nudging readers to keep reading. Too, the doubled point of view provides *Burr* with the technical advantages of two distinct modes of narration. Schuyler describes incidents for us almost as they happen, while Burr's memoir is written long after the events it recounts. A general rule of first-person narration is that the more contemporaneous accounts seem to be with occurrences, the more immediacy a reader is likely to feel, reacting with the narrator to things as they happen and sharing the narrator's concern for consequences. In this way, contemporaneous first-person narrative techniques (which can include the representation of letters, other documents, or stream-of-consciousness as well as diaries) enhance the possibilities for suspense. As readers, we can participate in the narrator's anxieties about what may happen. On the other hand, first-person narratives presented as retrospective can create the technical illusion of an increased or enriched perspective. That is, narrators' accounts of their earlier years can indicate reflection upon and analysis of actions and their consequences. (Of course, retrospective narration can also suggest distortion by memory lapses or self-serving impulses.)

The differences between contemporaneous and retrospective narration can be seen vividly in *Burr*. Schuyler's journal invites us to ask questions about plot: Will Schuyler be charged with murder? Will he betray Burr? Conversely, Burr's memoir is likely to provoke questions about theme and motive: Why would a man like Burr fight a duel whose results will be disastrous, win or lose? How different would our country be if Burr had been elected president? The point here is that in giving us two different kinds of narrators, *Burr* allows for more various narrative pleasures and more complex engagement of readers than either mode would be likely to evoke independently. As we shall see, the doubled narrative format of *Burr* also contributes to the development of characters and themes.

CHARACTER DEVELOPMENT

The main character in *Burr* is Aaron Burr. Clearly, Vidal wants readers to think afresh about the man who has been remembered primarily for having killed Alexander Hamilton in a duel. To a considerable extent, the character of Burr emerges through his conflicts with a series of antagonists. Much of the novel turns on a rivalry between Burr and Hamilton that eventually destroys them both. The novel initially links Burr and Hamilton through comments made to Schuyler by various women. First, Burr's new and less than candid wife (Madame Jumel) tells Schuyler of attending George Washington's inauguration in 1789, where she danced with Burr and then Hamilton. She comments, "I admired them both, yet both were tiny and I've always been partial to tall men" (31). A wealthy widow when Burr marries her, Madame (as Schuyler calls her) is rumored to have once worked in a brothel (2), and the next explicit comparison of Burr and his rival also comes from a madam. Mrs. Townsend, proprietor of a brothel Schuyler frequents, reminisces about the relative charms of Burr and Hamilton: "And how [Burr] loved the ladies ... Why he would *talk* to them by the hour, busy as he was. Not like General Hamilton who was always much too busy to talk to anyone who didn't matter" (38, italics in original).

In his memoir, Burr reiterates likenesses and distinctions between Hamilton and himself. As early as the second sentence of the second paragraph in Burr's notes on the American Revolution, we are told: "Unlike Hamilton, I had taken no part in the various debates that precipitated the revolution" (46). That is, Vidal's Burr opens his memoir by comparing himself with Hamilton. This comparison haunts the novel. In part, Hamilton and Burr belong to opposing political factions, and thematically, they represent two very different views of what their young country should become. Most interesting for characterization, however, are the images Burr uses to describe the almost mystical connection between himself and Hamilton, the perpetual fascination and rivalry that will destroy them both: "I suspect that when Hamilton looked at me he saw, in some magical way, himself reflected" (290).

The novel's development of Burr and Hamilton as deadly rivals is complicated by the predictable bias of retrospective first-person accounts. In the memoir, Burr tells us of Hamilton's envy and presents himself as graciously tolerant until he is provoked beyond reason by Hamilton's slanders. Yet in its repeated allusions to Hamilton, the memoir reveals Burr as an old man still ruefully obsessed with the rival of his earlier years. The novel presents this obsession as central to Burr's character, but its interpretation may vary from reader to reader. In *Burr* we witness a man pondering his life and constructing out of his memories a narrative he can live with, or rather, die with. (We are reminded that the memoir is selective when Schuyler consults others about important events or facts Burr omits.) Most readers will grow quite fond of Burr, whether they finally assess him as a charming old rogue, an ill-used hero, a cynical self-server, or all of the above.

Perhaps it is best to accept that personality and motive remain finally mysterious. Whatever their private demons and desires may have been, Burr and Hamilton are linked perpetually in national memory, each in some sense defined by the other. Whatever their contributions to the political and economic histories of this country, as legends Burr and Hamilton need each other. Vidal's novel may reverse the moral partisanship that has dominated legend, but it reiterates a myth of heroic and doomed antagonists. It may be useful here to remember that the literary terms "protagonist" and "antagonist" derive from the Greek *agon*, for struggle, contest, or battle. Burr speculates that he and Hamilton would "have been friends had we not been two young 'heroes' . . . each aware that at the summit there is a place for only one" (69). He comments further on the fact that neither reached the summit: "I hurled Hamilton from the mountain-side, and myself fell" (69). Burr may feel he and Hamilton both lost, but he also casts their rivalry as a battle of Titans.

This mythic struggle is echoed in later events. After Hamilton's death, Burr's primary antagonists are Jamie Wilkinson, with whom he plots to conquer Mexico, and Thomas Jefferson, who has cheated him of the presidency and who charges him with treason. Thus the strategy of characterizing Burr through contrast with his enemies continues, but with a difference. Burr perceives both Wilkinson and Jefferson as his allies up to a point, and he underestimates their capacities for treachery. Burr recognizes Hamilton as a rival from the beginning, but he is betrayed, even duped, by Jefferson and Wilkinson. As depicted by Vidal, Burr is a peculiar mixture of the shrewd and the naïve, an oddly innocent skeptic. One senses that his sustaining grace, and a good deal of his charm, is his tenacious optimism, which is contagious (see 509). This optimism can also be blamed for his misplaced trust in Wilkinson and Jefferson.

If antagonists define aspects of Burr's character, his allies color readers' overall responses. For example, Burr inspires the love of his illegitimate son (Aaron Columbus Burr), the loyalty of Andrew Jackson, and the devotion of numerous mistresses. Particularly telling is Charles's description of a casual moment when Burr buys a taffy apple on the street: "The ordinary people greet him warmly while the respectable folk tend to cut him dead" (3). And of course, readers are strongly influenced by Charles's perspective on Burr. There is not room here to discuss this perspective in detail, but we can sum it up as follows: As the novel progresses, Charles becomes increasingly fond of Burr, moving through fascination to admiration to love. Early on, he calls Burr "the slyest trickster of our time" (24); when Burr dies, Charles goes to pay his respects, and he tells us, "I ran from the room, hot-eyed, wishing that I had the Colonel to talk to one more time" (553). (One does not, however, sense that Charles understands Burr.) The final revelation about Charles's parentage completes the portrait of Burr. Quite simply, Burr has done all he could do to help Charles and asked nothing at all in return.

Of course, Charles is a prominent character in his own right. One might expect that the reader would learn more about Charles than about Burr, because Charles reveals himself in the journal or diary that provides the novel's framing narrative. (Charles's diary is for his own reference, not for the public's amusement). Certainly, Charles readily confides his self-doubts and anxieties within its pages. Most of these doubts are practical ones, turning on his overwhelming desire to support himself by writing. In this one area of his life, Charles is steadfast, even dogged, and he subordinates everything else to his goal. He is determined to write well, often interrupting the narrative to record his chasing after the precise word he needs at the moment. This is a writer's ethic, and Charles embraces it.

In all other matters, Charles seems less scrupulous, or at least less committed. It is not that he is dishonorable or ungentlemanly; he simply comes across as rather passive, malleable, and subject to whims—his own and those of others. His liaison with the prostitute, Helen Jewett, is typical. He risks his reputation to set up housekeeping with her, a bold action in his circumstances. Yet even this daring move seems more to happen to Charles than to result from a deliberate decision. He does take responsibility for Helen, even more so when she becomes pregnant, but this responsibility is expressed as a need to make more money through writing. Charles accepts financial obligations but he resists emotional responsibility, at least insofar as the reader is directly told.

Something of a similar pattern can be seen in Charles's relationship to Burr. To the reader, it seems obvious that of all Charles's benefactors, Burr is the most helpful and the least motivated by self-interest. Employment in Burr's law office supports Charles while he establishes his writing career, and through Burr (one way and another) Charles gathers the material for much of his writing. In part, the narrative structure demands that he attract all sorts of assistance and generosity; only thus can he plausibly take Burr's patronage for granted. Otherwise, readers could tumble to the secret of Charles's parentage too soon and with too much certainty. That is, if the final revelation that Burr is Charles's father is to have its full effect, both Charles and the reader must credit Burr's generosity to Charles's nature rather than to Burr's. (This is not to say that readers may not suspect something of the sort; indeed, such suspicions can heighten narrative interest.)

Burr repays rereading in light of its culminating revelation. Indeed, knowledge of Burr's paternity intensifies the central moral conflict of Charles's narrative. That is, surely Charles is betraying Burr in writing a pamphlet exposing him as Martin Van Buren's biological father. Charles feels an occasional pinch of conscience in this matter, but no loyalty outweighs his determination to earn enough money to live as a writer (and avoid being a lawyer). One could argue that *Burr* is structurally flawed in letting Charles off this moral hook too patly. He is prepared, after all, to sell his scurrilous pamphlet to the highest bidder— his benevolent patron be damned. Conveniently enough, however, the best price is offered by a publisher who will defuse the revelation's political impact: Charles's narrative will be embedded in an attack on Van Buren ghost-written for Davy Crockett and therefore discredited. Vidal's Crockett is a "drunken fat-head" (486), and his "marvellous death" at the Alamo obliterates his "foray into political libel" (548). Thus Charles gets the money he needs without compromising the interests of a man who surely deserves his loyalty and without harming those who will turn out to be his father and half-brother.

What may appear to be ethical hedging can be justified generically. The story of Charles is best read as a romance in the tradition of Henry Fielding's *Tom Jones*, Shakespeare's *Cymbeline*, or the *Star Wars* movies. In such narratives, a kindly providence always seems to protect the hero from committing irreparable transgressions, particularly such transgressions as would be worsened by the revelation of exalted parentage that traditionally concludes a romance. Often the sin barely avoided is incest, whose ascription depends upon an accurate knowledge of one's parentage and kinship ties. In *Burr*, incest is deflected from Charles but not forgotten: Harman Blennerhassett is married to his niece (438); Hamilton's unbearable and unconfirmed slander is that Burr and his daughter were lovers (356); Jefferson's slave mistress is his wife's half-sister, although unacknowledged of course (257). (Additional female characters will be discussed in the final section of this chapter.)

THEMATIC ISSUES

Burr shares several thematic concerns with other Vidal novels: political corruption as inevitable; religious skepticism; founding moments; the fictional aspect of history and the tendency of legend to displace fact even where fact is available. *Burr*, however, breaks some new ground. In this novel, Vidal implies the question that pervades his "American Chronicles": What kind of country should the United States be and how did we become what we are? Contrary to the complaints of some early reviewers, it is more than a gratuitous twist in plot that Aaron Burr is Charles Schuyler's father. *Burr* is very much a novel about fathers and their progeny. Questions about Burr as the biological sire of specific children correspond to questions about the legitimacy of the country's origins. Questions about literal and metaphorical paternity reflect upon each other.

Even the rivalry of Burr and Hamilton casts them as brothers. They compete for the role of favored son and victorious inheritor of a patriarchal line. Hamilton, a bastard, is explicitly asserted to be engaged in a perpetual quest for father figures. According to John Adams, because Hamilton is a bastard, he searches "for fathers and mothers and he picks them up wherever he goes" (217). Burr, on the other hand, descends legitimately from Jonathan Edwards, the fiercest voice of New England Puritanism, and both his father and grandfather were presidents of the College of New Jersey (i.e., Princeton). Still, although the novel does not dwell on the fact, Burr was orphaned at the age of two (84); his lifelong search seems to be for mothers and children. This private quest, however, seems less important than Burr's role as a founding father, the best of whose legacy has been forfeited.

Written during a time of national division and self-doubt, *Burr* works deliberately to demythologize and desentimentalize patriotic legend. Through the eyes of Aaron Burr (and indeed drawing on Burr's own writing) the novel gives us, for example, a George Washington disastrously inept as a general but highly skilled at partisan maneuvering. Burr comments, "History, as usual, has got it all backward" (71). Running similarly counter to hagiographic history, Thomas Jefferson is a vain and humorless hypocrite who, moreover, writes awkwardly. Further, and typically, although Washington is for a strong central government while Jefferson adheres to the right of any state to withdraw from the union at any time, both are dedicated above all to the preservation of property rights. And both decry monarchy while behaving remarkably like kings. (One of Vidal's recurring themes is the desire people have for messiahs. *Burr* and other books of the "American Chronicles" present a similar longing: Ostensibly committed to republicanism, most Americans want their presidents to resemble kings.)

Earlier, we noted that Vidal's "American Chronicles" track the transformation of our founders' republic into an empire. What *Burr* makes clear is that the will to empire and dreams of empire have been with us since the beginning. The men who wrote our Constitution knew their Roman history. As long as that remarkable document is in force, it ensures that we will not be ruled by a single dictator. Unfortunately, our subsequent history demonstrates the possibility of an empire without an emperor. *Burr* introduces the imperial theme in several ways. First, numerous characters in the 1830s sections of the novel seem fascinated with Napoleon, who turned another republic into an empire. Madame Jumel, for instance, boasts of having known Napoleon (14–15), though Burr confides to Schuyler that "Madame has a vivid imagination" (15). More important, the novel presents the imperial aspirations of Burr and Jamie Wilkinson, but also those of Thomas Jefferson (see, for example, 240–241, 418–19).

A FEMINIST READING OF *BURR*

Feminist criticism takes many forms, and feminist critics do not always agree about goals, let alone about the best strategies for achieving them. We can generalize, however, that much feminist literary criticism works to call attention to female figures within a male-dominated literary tradition. Some feminists prefer to focus exclusively on women writers, most of whom have been neglected or undervalued by traditional critics (most of whom have been male). Another branch of feminist literary criticism argues for examining female characters in books written by men. Feminist critics have observed that in general—there are exceptions—male authors deal with female characters in one of two ways: by omitting them or stereotyping them. Some of the established classics of literature have few (if any) female characters; *Moby Dick* is a good example, as is any of Shakespeare's history plays. But amplifying the voices of women, however marginal, in such texts can sometimes provide an important counterpoint to male-oriented traditional criticism. Women, this approach assumes, can be as interesting as men, even when relegated to minor or marginal roles. (We shall consider other forms of feminist criticism in later chapters.)

Of several possible feminist approaches, *Burr* invites consideration of the limited roles allotted female characters in its pages. "Roles" may be an ambiguous term here. In one sense, "women's roles" in the novel mean the kinds of lives women are represented as leading, the options that seem to be available to them. In another sense, "women's roles" can refer to the artistic uses to which a writer typically puts female characters. (Secondary characters in fiction, for example, are often used to provide necessary information, to serve as foils to a main character, or to symbolize a philosophical position.) Of course, these multiple senses of the term "women's roles" can overlap. Too, as is sometimes forgotten, the feminist critic needs to stay alert to the attitude a book projects toward the women's roles it portrays. Although two novels may portray women as subservient to men, one may endorse what the other deplores. All critics should be wary of attributing to a novel or to its author the beliefs of any given character or of a represented society.

Overall it is fair to say that *Burr* presents its female characters almost exclusively in relation to one or more men. The novel's few female characters seem to be included primarily to illuminate the personalities of either Burr or of the novel's narrator, Charles Schuyler. Turning a fem-

inist lens on *Burr*, however, asks us to pay close attention to the few
female characters both as artistic devices and as representations of human beings in a particular society. Such attention can enrich one's reading of the novel and deepen one's sense of social inequity, its conditions
and in what circumstances it can be evaded. In *Burr*, female characters
appear as wives, mistresses, and whores or brothel keepers. Of course,
the temporal setting of *Burr* limits the kinds of roles women can plausibly be assigned. In the period 1775–1836, there simply were few women
earning livelihoods outside domesticity, domestic service, or family busi-
nesses.

Despite the conventionality of women's roles in *Burr*, the novel could
be called feminist in some of its sympathies. It is true, certainly, that the
roles Vidal assigns most women in this novel are those generally defined
by sexual relationship to one or more men: wives, mistresses, whores.
Thinking of such roles in the abstract, it is tempting to define them,
rather cynically, as bargains in which women exchange sexual favors for
financial support. In *Burr*, however, surprisingly few wives and mistresses fit comfortably into this pattern; Burr's certainly do not. Both
Burr's wives were widows when he married them. An old friend describes the first Mrs. Burr to Charles: "A very plain woman. . . . And
sickly from the cancer even then. And not a penny to her name" (83).
Theodosia Prevost may have been poor by some standards, but she
brought to the marriage the Hermitage, "a fine house" (107).

And then there is Madame Jumel. As Charles realizes (12–13), Burr
married his second wife primarily for her money, which he needed to
finance yet another of his schemes to rule in the American West. (In this
case, he bought up land grants in the Texas territory, to be settled by
German immigrants.) Several marriages and liaisons in *Burr* are similar,
including those of Washington and Hamilton. Even Jefferson's mistress
serves to increase his wealth; their numerous offspring, after all, become
his slaves. (To a plantation owner, slaves are capital, as Vidal's *Lincoln*
will remind readers.) Although we can assume that Sally Hemings has
little choice in the matter, most of the women in *Burr* choose or accept
husbands and lovers for other than financial reasons. In aggregate, the
portrayal of wives and mistresses in *Burr* raises interesting questions
about what men and women want from each other.

Burr focuses primarily on its male characters and thus does not offer
much material for speculation on such matters. Still, the novel hints at
modes of self-determination for women even in a society that constrains
their options so narrowly. Perhaps *Burr*'s most interesting deviation from

predictable feminine patterns is the role of spy. Burr's recollections of the American Revolution include two women who were spies for the British. The first is Margaret Moncrieffe, a pretty thirteen-year-old. Despite her father's being a major in the British army, in 1776 she is staying with General Putnam of the Continental Army. Burr records her impertinence to General Washington at dinner; in his presence she defiantly proposes a toast to British Commander General Howe (75). No one but Burr seems to think it odd that this Tory sympathizer spends her time watching the revolutionary troops' encampment from the roof (75). Nor does anyone become suspicious when she undertakes a set of flower paintings to send to her father. Her treachery is exposed by her flustered reaction when Burr asks whether she believes in a language of flowers; the paintings encode information about troop movements. At that point, he persuades the general to send Margaret elsewhere. It may seem incredible that someone could with impunity live in a general's house, openly declare allegiance to the enemy, keep a close eye on troop deployment, and regularly send messages to an enemy officer. Margaret, however, is young, female, sexually attractive, and—Burr suspects—sexually active with General Putnam and perhaps others. The men do not take her seriously enough or do not credit her with enough intelligence or initiative to acknowledge that she is potentially dangerous. It is not, therefore, wholly surprising or simply self-serving when Burr credits himself with recognizing her scheme. Elsewhere in the novel, Burr attributes his success with women to the fact that he treats them like men; he also insists, "Women have souls, Charlie! They really do" (67). Unlike many men of his time, Burr allows women sufficient humanity to be nefarious.

A similar, better-known case is that of Peggy Shippen Arnold, wife of notorious traitor Benedict Arnold and probably the lover of Major André, who recruited Arnold to the Tory cause. In *Burr*, we meet Peggy after Arnold and André have been arrested and she is being taken to Philadelphia. She has insisted to her captors on spending the night at the house of her old friend, Theodosia, and Burr is there as well. (He is at this point engaged to marry Theodosia.) Peggy enters raving, wild-eyed, claiming that her baby has been murdered, and shrieking in terror of a phantasmic hot iron. Left alone with Theodosia and Burr, she drops her pose and boasts of having deceived Washington, Lafayette, and Hamilton by pretending to be insane, thus avoiding being implicated in her husband's treason. Writing retrospectively, Burr attests to how seriously the Revolutionary commanders underestimated Peggy Shippen

Arnold: "She was able in one day to dupe Washington, Hamilton and Lafayette" (133).

Burr hints that extraordinary circumstances, such as war, permit some women to break traditional molds, but the novel also includes the sad story of Helen Jewett. (In his Afterword, Vidal affirms that Helen Jewett indeed existed and met the fate described in *Burr*.) In the novel, Helen functions primarily to illuminate the character of Charles Schuyler. If Burr is characterized in part by his sympathetic understanding of women, Charles is revealed as rather pathetically dense in such matters. (Of course, Burr is much older than Charles, but in the novel's sequel *1876*, Charles remains bemused by women.) His interactions with Helen also suggest that he is painfully lacking in self-knowledge. Charles recognizes that sexual desire drives him to Mrs. Townsend's brothel (and to other brothels). It is not unusual that he should find Helen especially attractive. He learns something of her life and her ambition to be a dressmaker, suggesting that he may resemble his biological father (Burr) in respecting women as individuals, unlike his legal father, who beat Charles's mother and locked her out of the house to die. Charles's decision to rescue Helen from Mrs. Townsend's brothel and set up housekeeping with her is more difficult to understand. He seems to act on impulse, oblivious to his own motives and interests as well as Helen's feelings.

Charles consistently writes of Helen as mysterious, alien, and unfathomable in her temperament and whims. Sometimes she is reclusive, sometimes gregarious. Charles reacts to her changing moods as if they were forces of nature, as unpredictable and as beyond human comprehension or control as an early frost or an earthquake. He seems simply incapable of assessing Helen's actions as sentiently motivated. He is mystified when, after her miscarriage, Helen flees back to work in Mrs. Townsend's establishment. Because readers see Helen only through the narrator's descriptions, her motives may ultimately remain as opaque to us as to Charles. Still, one interpretation seems plausible. It is easy to imagine that Charles's attitude toward Helen could become insupportable. Charles confesses in his journal that he thrills to the risk of being seen in public with a woman when the truth about her could ruin him (425). Helen might well tire of being his naughty secret. It seems plausible that, whatever Charles's fantasies, Helen feels more whore than wife, more burden than helpmeet. Charles finally admits to himself, "I have spent over a year inventing my own Helen Jewett and now she has gone back to being her own Helen Jewett" (514).

It is important to note that fictional characters, male and female alike, are just that—fictions. Their motives, desires, anxieties, their very existences are constructed by readers out of information provided by a novelist. As a general rule, we can say that there is never a single, definitive interpretation of a character. Often, however, we can rule out some interpretations as inconsistent with a text. Thus, there can be no single "right" answers to questions about Helen's motives. Indeed, precisely because we are given only limited and exterior information about her, it is difficult to eliminate any given interpretation of her as implausible or inconsistent, more difficult than it is to rule out potential readings of Burr, Schuyler, Leggett, or Hamilton. Helen is arguably the most important female character in *Burr*; certainly she is the one we see most often. Yet she is presented more as an enigma than as flesh and blood, more as a perception of Charles's than as a represented person in her own right.

In sum, we can say of *Burr* that its female characters are relatively marginal to plot and their depiction is subordinated to a primary interest in male figures. To look closely at these marginal characters, however, is to understand some important things about a period in which women's choices were so narrowly circumscribed. Taking such a perspective on *Burr* suggests the costs to both women and men of devaluing half the human race; it also suggests, however, that even in repressive environments, women can resist (and have resisted) their dehumanization. It is disturbing that in the novel the Revolutionary War offers some women escape from conventional constraints, as other wars have also done. Widespread death and mayhem are high prices to pay for independence. It may be worth noting that perhaps the most attractively presented woman in all of *Burr* is Dolley Madison. (Coincidentally, Burr describes her husband, James Madison, as the truest republican of all the founders). Arguably, the saddest lesson of Gore Vidal's *Burr* is that as a nation we have yet to live up to James Madison's standard: a truly representative republic—one, we now understand, where the voices of every man and every woman can be heard.

Lincoln
(1984)

Written after *Washington, D.C.* (1967), *Burr* (1973), and *1876* (1976), *Lincoln* is the fourth of Vidal's "American Chronicles" in order of composition but second in the chronological order he now recommends for their reading. The final chapter of *Burr* is dated 1840; *Lincoln* begins in February 1861 and ends in April 1865, covering the time from Lincoln's arrival in Washington as president-elect through his assassination. A brief final chapter, set at a diplomatic reception in Paris, suggests some assessments of Lincoln and his presidency. This chapter also introduces Charles Schuyler and his daughter, Emma. Schuyler, it will be remembered, narrates both *Burr* and *1876*, and Emma is the central fictional character in the latter. Their appearance here helps situate *Lincoln* within the familial narrative of Vidal's "American Chronicles," although of the six linked novels it remains the least tied to the Burr-Schuyler-Sanford line of descent.

The Lincoln of Vidal's novel is not the humbly born, rail-splitting, emancipating Honest Abe of schoolroom legend. He is, instead, a complex and sometimes devious politician driven by a vision that will eventually forge the nation anew—and bring down the visionary. Just as *Burr* demythologizes George Washington and Thomas Jefferson, so *Lincoln* does for its own central figure. There is, however, a major distinction. Seen through Burr's eyes, Washington and Jefferson shrink from heroic titans into ordinary mortals, gifted politicians but less than magnificent.

Indeed, in that novel, Washington sometimes seems a buffoon and Jefferson is something of a coward and hypocrite. And both—along with other founding fathers—are dedicated above all to the preservation of property rights. (In *Burr*, the title character exempts James Madison, calling him the "only true republican," and in an Afterword Vidal asserts that he thinks more highly of Jefferson than does his fictionalized Burr.) Vidal's Lincoln, on the other hand, emerges as a grander, subtler, more mysterious personage than the sentimentalized icon of legend. Lincoln is the novel's protagonist in the deepest sense of the word, not only its chief character but also a driving force in the terrible national *agon* (battle, struggle, contest) that was the Civil War.

In *Lincoln*, subtitled "A Novel," Vidal creates a fictionalized portrait of Lincoln consistent with the written record. (Of course, there are contradictions within the historical evidence. Such contradictions offer a rich field for both novelists and historians.) As Vidal notes in one of his essays about writing *Lincoln*, he read many primary and secondary sources, the most important of them being Lincoln's own writing. In his commitment to historical fidelity, he also relied on historian David Herbert Donald ("Lincoln and the Priests of Academe," *United States* 675; a distinguished Harvard professor, Donald has recently added a well-received biography of Lincoln to his many publications on the period). Some academic historians objected to Vidal's unsentimental depiction of Lincoln (for his responses to their objections, see *United States* 664–707). Several of the historians' complaints simply demonstrate a misunderstanding of novelistic narration, an inability to distinguish between a character's views and an author's. (To be fair, this misconception is widespread, not at all limited to historians.) For secondary characters drawn from historical personages, such as John Hay and Salmon P. Chase, Vidal has relied largely on their diaries and letters. For characters whose names but little else are matters of record, such as David Herold, Vidal feels free to invent plausible details. In general, Vidal remains faithful to recorded facts—which, however, sometimes contradict each other.

For all the important incidents in the novel, Vidal can cite recognized sources to support either their accuracy or their plausibility. His novelistic interpretation of Lincoln as tragically driven by ambition is, of course, open to debate. A useful companion piece to Vidal's *Lincoln* is Merrill D. Peterson's *Lincoln in American Memory*, a judicious survey of Lincoln's "afterlife" in American culture and myth. Among its many strengths, Peterson's book reminds readers that to write about Lincoln—

whether as historian, biographer, poet, novelist or screenwriter—is to select which recorded "facts" to accept and which to reject.

PLOT DEVELOPMENT

In *Lincoln*, Vidal retells a story whose outcome is well known. From the beginning of the novel, we know that the Civil War will be joined, that the North will win, and that Lincoln will be assassinated by John Wilkes Booth. Like a Greek tragedy or one of Shakespeare's history plays, *Lincoln* exploits our knowledge of events while tempting us into wondering how things might have turned out otherwise—and why they didn't.

Vidal narrates the events of *Lincoln* in chronological order. His focus remains on the White House years, though at times secondary figures or the president's own reminiscences supply details of Lincoln's earlier life. Vidal emphasizes his portrait of Lincoln as president, a mature man in action, rather than indulging in a speculative portrayal of his protagonist's psychological development. *Lincoln* foregrounds its central figure as embattled: outwitting his political rivals, struggling to keep Virginia and Maryland in the Union, wrestling with issues of slavery and emancipation, frustrated by a series of recalcitrant generals and lost or indecisive battles. Eventually, Lincoln summons Ulysses S. Grant, who has steadily been winning Union battles in the West, despite his notoriously heavy drinking. This is a turning point for Lincoln and *Lincoln*; once Grant takes charge, the Union proceeds to win the war. Still, as late as August 1864, it seemed likely that McClellan, the failed general turned politician, would defeat Lincoln for the presidency. But on September 2, 1864, Sherman and the Union army occupied Atlanta, assuring Lincoln's re-election. Lincoln, of course, was assassinated within months of his second inauguration.

Lincoln has prepared for this assassination from the beginning. The novel opens with the president-elect's furtive arrival in Washington City (D.C.), complete with a newly grown beard and two bodyguards. He has altered his itinerary to avoid Baltimore. Lincoln and a few trusted supporters have taken these precautions because of rumors that the Baltimore "plug-uglies"—local street toughs—intend to shoot him as his train passes through the town. As Vidal stresses, this assassination plot is only one of many. Almost immediately, the novel introduces nineteen-year-old David Herold, a restive young man who believes the "wild boys"—Washington's equivalent of Baltimore's plug-uglies—will kill Lincoln before he can take office. Historically, Herold worked as a delivery boy at Thompson's drugstore near the White House and became involved with John Wilkes Booth in the plot to assassinate Lincoln. Though little is known about the young man otherwise, Vidal's fictional portrait is persuasively buttressed by the circumstantial evidence, and Herold's adventures provide a useful subplot for the novel. Herold serves as a conduit between Confederate conspirators and the White House; more important, he is also the reader's eyes and ears on the ordinary inhabitants of the Southern city that is the Union capital.

The loyalties of David Herold and his cronies remind readers that for Lincoln, Washington was a hostile environment. Across the Potomac River from Virginia and separated by Maryland from securely held Union territory, Washington is a city more Southern than Northern. One historian observes that "with the exception of Baltimore, there was probably no city in any of the loyal states in which there were more citizens disloyal to the United States than in the country's own capital" (Hanchett 9–10). In effect, Lincoln must conduct a war from a Union enclave within Confederate territory. Vidal reminds us that Lincoln is also a minority president, having received less than 40 percent of the vote. To Washington City, he is an outsider, a Westerner, a bumpkin. And his Cabinet includes his two most powerful rivals, William H. Seward and Salmon P. Chase. Thus, even as Lincoln prosecutes the Civil War, he must negotiate conflicts within his administration. Like David Herold, Chase and his daughter, Kate, supply a thematically resonant subplot to Lincoln's story. Chase's political aspirations and Kate's movement toward marriage have considerable narrative interest in themselves, but the Chases also represent the Washington establishment and its objections to Lincoln. Thus, both subplots underscore the hostility surrounding the novel's protagonist.

There are problems within Lincoln's household as well. Many are tied directly to his wife, Mary Todd Lincoln. Mrs. Lincoln is willful, tormented by headaches, and subject to intermittent bouts of insanity. Although not unsympathetic to Mary, Vidal's novel emphasizes the difficulties she caused for her husband. Throughout the novel, Lincoln obviously feels anxious not only about his wife's physical pain but also about what she might do next. Mrs. Lincoln's extravagance in refurbishing the White House and in expanding her own wardrobe lead her into debts neither she nor the president can possibly afford. That indebtedness exposes her to political scandal and the appearance, at least, of impropriety. (Later in this chapter, we shall consider Mary Todd Lincoln from a feminist perspective.)

CHARACTER DEVELOPMENT

Vidal's portrayal of Lincoln depends upon the novel's choice of narrative point of view. In Vidal's thriller *Dark Green, Bright Red*, Peter Nelson, "fascinated and a bit puzzled," watches General Alvarez: "The General was neither tall nor short, neither fat nor thin. Like many public men, he tended to be more general than particular: the reflection of many people's opinion of him" (8). This comment points directly to the strategy Vidal employs to explore the complexity of Abraham Lincoln. The omniscient narrator provides us with the thoughts of other characters about Lincoln but never with Lincoln's own thoughts, only his words and others' impressions of his moods. Indeed, although technically accurate, the term "omniscient" may be misleading here. *Lincoln*'s narrator provides us access to the perspectives and motives of several secondary characters, but those of Lincoln himself remain enigmatic.

We see Lincoln through the eyes of several characters, including Elihu B. Washburne, who has known Lincoln since their days as Illinois lawyers; Mary Todd Lincoln, who loves her husband; and David Herold, a Confederate sympathizer who considers Lincoln the enemy. The figures most important in creating Vidal's prismatic portrait of Lincoln, however, are Salmon P. Chase, William H. Seward, and John Milton Hay. (In the process, each of these also becomes a well-developed character in his own right.) As Lincoln's secretary, Hay is sympathetic to Lincoln throughout, admiring but hardly awestruck. Seward, Lincoln's one-time rival for the Republican presidential nomination and now his secretary of state, begins by drastically—almost disastrously—underestimating Lincoln. Seward initially intends to be the power behind a Lincoln who is merely a figurehead, but he learns how wrong he was. Precisely because Seward is initially antagonistic and condescending toward Lincoln, his growing respect and admiration help keep readers' sympathies with Lincoln, even when their preconceptions are disrupted.

Salmon P. Chase, secretary of the treasury and later chief justice of the Supreme Court, also underestimates Lincoln. Unlike Seward, however, Chase never quite recognizes Lincoln's strength of will and political savvy, and he comes to hate him. This miscalculation eventually leads to Chase's political humiliation, a humbling not wholly compensated for by his appointment to the office of chief justice. The novel thus includes perspectives on Lincoln from differing attitudes as well as from several distances.

Lincoln debunks sentimental components of the Lincoln myth, refuses to accept the "cornball Disneyland waxwork" (*United States* 664) of popular biography—or more accurately hagiography (a technical term for the biography of a saint). Several strategies combine to defuse the image of Lincoln as a plaster saint. First, Vidal insists upon the physical body. Lincoln suffers from constipation (120); his hands sometimes shake as he delivers an important speech (66); he chews methodically—horselike— upon apples (250–51). He may have contracted syphilis as a young man (289); and he catches smallpox while in office. His clothes are ill-fitting, like those of the villain-protagonist of his favorite play, *Macbeth*. Many of these details come from the collected papers of William Herndon, Lincoln's law partner in Illinois. Some agreed upon facts, such as the presidential constipation, Vidal refers to throughout. More scandalous possibilities, such as syphilis, are alluded to by other characters in the novel, but always presented as conjecture. (As Vidal points out, all Lincoln biographers must draw on the gossipy Herndon, but they do so selectively. Peterson notes that as of 1990, Herndon was being rehabilitated as a reliable source, 392.)

Vidal's very human Lincoln knows the art of the political deal. For example, because of political debts incurred in securing the Republican nomination, he is compelled to appoint Simon Cameron as secretary of war, an action Lincoln calls the most disgraceful thing he has ever done (250). Cameron is corrupt, slothful, and unscrupulous. Yet Lincoln and the Union are stuck with him until he is enticed—with an ambassadorship to Russia—into resigning. (Despite Cameron's faults, he controls Pennsylvania politics, so Lincoln cannot risk antagonizing him.) Cameron's replacement, Edwin M. Stanton, is a flawed man, "mercurial and vain and compulsively duplicitous," but he is financially incorruptible and a hard worker (270; cf. 308–09).

Lincoln finds other compromises necessary. Perhaps the darkest of Lincoln's politically motivated actions is retaining General George B. McClellan as general of the Army of the Potomac. At first, McClellan seems an inspired choice. He trains 200,000 ragtag recruits into a real army, no mean accomplishment. He and his soldiers respect each other, and he is highly skilled at directing the logistical and engineering tasks preliminary to military engagement. Yet he exhibits a remarkable reluctance to engage his well-trained troops in battle. After considerable lost time and numerous missed opportunities, Lincoln would dearly love to replace McClellan, yet he cannot—or will not—until after the congressional elections of 1862. As commander-in-chief, he has the legal authority to do so, but he fears the political consequences. Despite McClellan's dilatory approach to fighting the war, he is extremely popular with his army and the public.

Lincoln, we see, is not at all above playing politics, even when doing so runs counter to his convictions. The subordination of principle to expediency appears most forcefully in his actions regarding slavery. (This is one of the matters over which *Lincoln* angered some professional historians, although Vidal can cite specific sources for the sentiments he ascribes to his protagonist.) Lincoln detests slavery as an institution, but he is also thoroughly aware of slavery as a political issue, indeed a political minefield. To be elected and re-elected president, Lincoln has to mollify, or at least avoid wholly alienating, the various wings of his own fledgling party. There are radical abolitionists—some single-minded ones, such as Charles Sumner, some deeply committed but not to the exclusion of other concerns, such as Chase. There are the moderates, among whom Lincoln numbers himself. And there are those, such as Seward, who oppose slavery if asked but for whom the issue is secondary. The Emancipation Proclamation, it will be remembered, freed slaves only in the Confederate states and specifically exempted states that remained in the Union. Repeatedly, Vidal's Lincoln stresses that he has the constitutional authority to free slaves in the rebel states as a matter of "military necessity" but lacks authority to free slaves within the Union. He does insist, however, that once the war is over, he will propose a constitutional amendment outlawing slavery throughout the United States. And he also insists that the abolition of slavery in the South be a condition of peace. Donald's 1995 biography argues that Lincoln backed away from this insistence (559–60), perhaps indicating yet another shift in the prevailing academic view of Lincoln. Donald documents Lincoln's long-standing support for establishing colonies in Africa or Latin America for freed slaves—a particularly sore spot for the historians who attacked Vidal's novel in the 1980s. (Vidal, incidentally, predicted that in the 1990s the black separatist movement would lead to yet another round of revisionism and "Lincoln the colonizer reestablished" (*United States* 695).

Because *Lincoln* presents its protagonist from the viewpoints of several other characters, the novel inevitably provides portraits of these secondary figures themselves. Johnny Hay, for instance, who will appear as an elder statesman in *Empire*, is here a young man making his way in the world. Secretary of State Seward emerges as a shrewd politician, but intensely loyal to Lincoln once he recognizes the intelligence and will that lie behind the president's folksy and often self-deprecatory manner. More interesting than these supporters of Lincoln, however, are two of his antagonists, Salmon P. Chase and David Herold, whose hostility toward Lincoln is nearly pathological. Even as their personalities emerge, Chase and Herold stand for the two arenas in which Lincoln must contend. For most of the novel, Chase serves in Lincoln's Cabinet and persuasively represents the considerable opposition Lincoln faces from members of his own party. David Herold is a generally unremarkable citizen of the nation's capital; Southern in his sympathies, he becomes a part-time Confederate spy and eventually participates in Booth's assassination plot. Herold's story reminds readers that Lincoln is never far from mortal danger.

Lincoln portrays Salmon P. Chase as a complicated, even contradictory man, a skilled politician who combines "cordiality and aloofness" (157). He is, however, no match for Lincoln, who outmaneuvers him time after time. Chase holds strong moral views, including absolute opposition to any perpetuation of slavery; however, he is rankled by the thought of Lincoln receiving any credit for emancipation. Sincerely Christian, he is also ambitious, longing immoderately to be president. As secretary of the treasury, Chase succeeds brilliantly in financing a war more expensive than any preceding it, but as a private man he is comically, almost ludicrously, obsessed with collecting the autographs of famous people. (His treasured collection includes signatures of Henry Wadsworth Longfellow, Julia Ward Howe, and Queen Victoria.)

Despite Chase's chronic shortage of money, he steadfastly refuses to accept "gifts" from banking interests or to sell permits to conduct trade with the rebel states. He does, however, allow his underlings to issue legal trade permits only to his friends. Further, he is well aware of building a national political organization by appointing hundreds of Treasury agents across the country. And in insisting on an income tax, he cannot help thinking of the additional thousand or so Treasury agents he will be able to appoint—and eventually recruit to his own campaign for the presidency. Patronage in the form of awarding government jobs to political supporters was widespread in the 1860s, but Chase is uncomfortable when his acute awareness of potential patronage intrudes on his public policy decisions (179).

Perhaps the strongest demonstration of Chase's conscience appears when he decides that a precious (if only to Chase) letter from Ralph Waldo Emerson is about Treasury business and must therefore be held in that department's archives rather than in his private collection. This scrupulous and personally painful sacrifice is significant; without it, readers might well dismiss Chase as either hypocritical or profoundly self-deluded. Rather, Vidal depicts a genuinely moral man whose ambition for the presidency corrodes his morality and blunts his ethical judgment. Relinquishing the Emerson letter clarifies the terms Chase has hewn for his political ethics and serves as a tangible, almost sacramental, gesture that reassures Chase of his own integrity. Immediately after the novel reports the surrender of the letter, Chase tells the powerful banker Jay Cooke that he can no longer accept dividend checks for stocks he doesn't actually own. (Cooke has been managing Chase's money for him, to the Secretary's enrichment.) Chase will, however, regard any campaign funds Cooke raises as "a public and not a private matter" (435). He seems to have drawn his moral boundary: as long as he refuses out-and-out bribes destined for his own pocket, he can keep his conscience clear, or at least at bay. As long as he keeps his own hands clean, the good he hopes to accomplish as president outweighs his distaste for the financial grubbiness that surrounds him.

It is significant that the conversation with Cooke occurs at a reception following the announcement of Kate Chase's engagement to Governor William Sprague. Chase regards Sprague as an ignorant, loutish drunkard. This "boy-governor," however, is rich and willing to finance Chase's political aspirations. Deeply conscious of his own honor, Chase nevertheless sacrifices his daughter to his political ambitions. To be fair, this marriage is originally Kate's idea, in accord with the assumptions of her time and class. John Hay, however, who often provides commentary on other characters, has a revelation after Kate's engagement party. He thinks to himself that, contrary to popular opinion, Chase dominates his daughter rather than the other way around. Hay perceives that "in [Chase's] lust for the presidency, he had thrust his daughter into a loveless marriage so that he might have Sprague's money" (437). (Later in this chapter, we shall consider Kate from a feminist perspective.) Chase comes to an unhappy end, politically disappointed and bitterly aware of his son-in-law's venality and his daughter's misery. One senses that for all his moral delicacy and financial genius, Chase cannot understand quite where he went wrong. Of Lincoln's antagonists, Chase is in many ways the most admirable, but fate and his own ambition do him no favors.

Less admirable, though perhaps more amiable, is another of Lincoln's

enemies, David Herold. In temperament, Herold resembles several of
Vidal's early protagonists, although he lacks the privileged background
most of them share. He is young, physically attractive, and intelligent
(though minimally educated). He longs for adventure and finds himself
enmeshed in intrigue, but his natural indolence guarantees that he will
be a recruit rather than an initiator. All along, David wants to undertake
dangerous, romantic, dashing missions. His superiors in Confederate espionage, however, insist that he is most useful where he is—at Thompson's drugstore, delivering prescriptions to the White House, picking up
bits of information, and well positioned to poison the president should
the decision to do so be made. (Historically, it is unknown whether Herold was directly involved in the attempt to poison Lincoln's "blue mass"
laxative. Vidal depicts him as perfectly happy to accept credit as a poi-
soner when Lincoln falls ill but passively innocent of any decisive action.)

Numerous details prepare the reader for Herold's attraction to John
Wilkes Booth, a fascination that embroils him fatally in the plot to assassinate Lincoln. Early in the novel, on the day of Lincoln's first inauguration, Vidal tells us that David longs for a brother (54). To Herold,
Booth represents glamour—in the word's old connotations of bewitch-
ment and enchantment. He embodies all that Herold would like to be.
Herold, after all, is perpetually surrounded by women: his widowed
mother, his seven sisters, brothel madams, and other older women who
coddle him, one way and another. For Herold, taking risks for the Confederate cause is entangled with his notions of manliness and ties to
other men. It is no accident that his first excursion carrying a message
into rebel territory coincides with his decision to grow a moustache. And
after the assassination, Herold thinks "[A]ll that mattered was that
Wilkes had thought that he, David Herold, had done as he was told,
and that they were now, the two of them, friends and true brothers,
immortal" (652).

THEMATIC ISSUES

With *Lincoln*, Vidal dismantles the popular legend of Lincoln; the effect, however, is not to diminish Lincoln but to magnify him. The novel
is more concerned with character than with theme. Arguably, Lincoln's
character, in all its contradictions, simply is the theme. Although other
of Vidal's recurring themes appear—venal journalism, empire, founding

moments—*Lincoln* is above all about perhaps the most complex figure in American history.

Harsh as it sounds, to understand Vidal's Lincoln, one must recognize the argument that he placed preservation of the Union ahead of adherence to the Constitution; many of his actions bordered on the tyrannical. Indeed, one could well argue that the so-called "imperial presidency" is ultimately a product of Lincoln's administration. Vidal's novel reminds readers of two Lincoln policies that must be seen as anti-democratic, from nineteenth- as well as twentieth-century perspectives. First, when a shortage of volunteers makes military conscription necessary, Lincoln favors permitting a reluctant draftee to pay someone else to take his place—but not cheaply enough to diminish the availability of the poor (215). Three hundred dollars is the proposed price, an amount roughly equal to the annual wages of a typical worker. This practice was satirized as venal at least as long ago as Shakespeare's *Henry IV* plays, which antedate Lincoln's presidency by nearly three hundred years and Vidal's novel by nearly four hundred. And, as Vidal reminds us, Lincoln knows his Shakespeare. (For one of many examples, see 526.) Although it is unfair and rather silly to fault historical personages for thinking and behaving within widespread assumptions of their own time, Lincoln must have recognized the inequity of his draft legislation and decided to implement it anyway. (The 1863 Conscription Act allowed a draftee to hire a substitute or pay $300 to the government, leading to the bloody New York draft riots in which 119 people died. Historians generally agree that the rioters were enraged less by the draft itself than by the option for the rich to buy their exemption; see 455–60.) Although entirely factual, the Lincoln of conscription laws is not the humble democrat of legend.

Even more alarming is the light in which Vidal places Lincoln's suspension of habeas corpus. Again, the novel depicts Lincoln as apparently willing to undermine democracy in order to save the Union. A writ of habeas corpus requires an official to bring a prisoner into court and account for that prisoner's detention. At stake here is the fundamental right of a detainee to see the evidence that warranted his or her arrest. Arguably, this is the single most important principle distinguishing free from totalitarian governments. That is, the single strongest defense against government by autocratic whim is the principle that people cannot be incarcerated without due process, knowledge of the charges and evidence against them, and the right to a speedy trial. Our physical bodies are subject to the rule of law but not to the caprices of individual magistrates. (That this principle is sometimes circumvented does not reduce its importance.)

The Constitution allows the suspension of habeas corpus in times of public danger: "The Privilege of the Writ of Habeas Corpus shall not be suspended, unless when in cases of Rebellion or Invasion the public Safety may require it" (Article I, Section 9). The Civil War may have been such a time, but over 13,000 people were arbitrarily arrested, and the specific incidents Vidal includes in *Lincoln* demonstrate a patent abuse of presidential authority. Many arrests of newspaper editors were ordered by Secretary of State Seward: "Seward's strategy was to hold the editors for an indefinite period; then, without ever charging them with any crime, he would let them go—to sin no more" (233–34). In effect, criticism of the president was construed as seditious.

Even shadier—and more tyrannical—is the use of arrest and threats of arrest to hush up Mrs. Lincoln's financial peccadilloes. To spare Lincoln embarrassment over his wife's misconduct, Seward uses the threat of arrest and unlimited detention to coerce Mrs. Lincoln's White House accomplices (and tempters) into committing perjury when Congress investigates what we would now call "leaks" of incriminating documents. (Mrs. Lincoln bears at least partial responsibility for these leaks; she was not always discreet.) By having Seward carry out the dirty work, Vidal deflects disapproval from Lincoln to an extent, but Seward acts on presidential authority and in presidential interests. (Donald asserts that the years following 1861 "would see greater infringements on individual liberties than any other period in American history," 304. For the counter view, see Mark E. Neely, *The Fate of Liberty* [1991].)

Given Lincoln's precise references to constitutional authority with respect to slavery, readers may find strange his apparent willingness to stretch the interpretation of Article I, Section 9 as far as—some will say farther than—can be constitutionally defensible. This apparent discrepancy between executive authority and presidential deed is a matter of historical record, as are many of Lincoln's other contradictory words and actions. To the historical facts, insofar as they are known and agreed upon, the novelist can contribute a coordinating motive, a psychologically plausible explanation for such contradictions. For Vidal's Lincoln, "the Union" is a numinous entity, palely shadowed in the Constitution but not defined by it. Lincoln's actions make coherent sense only if one attributes to him a dedication to the Union, or the idea of the Union, that verges on the mystic and the monomaniacal. To the exclusion of all other concerns, Vidal's Lincoln is obsessed with, even possessed by, his commitment to preserving the United States as a single nation. Out of the documentary record, Vidal interprets Lincoln's nature and constructs a narrative able to grapple with the complexities of that nature and its consequences, both private and public. Rejecting romantic and didactic biography, Vidal retells Lincoln's story in the austere genre of classical tragedy. In its purest form, tragedy ends with a restoration of order and a promise of communal healing, but always at a terrible cost. In Vidal's novel, the Civil War is tragic and Lincoln a tragic hero. Our sense of Lincoln's larger-than-life stature, and hence his eligibility for tragic status, is enhanced by the assessments other characters voice. For instance, Elihu Washburne, who knew Lincoln in Illinois, tells Seward that Lincoln "isn't really like other people" (12). Seward, initially contemptuous of the new president, finds himself thinking, "Lincoln seemed to him like some bright, swiftburning substance that, once ignited, could not be extinguished until it had burned itself entirely out" (564).

In part, a tragic sense of inevitable doom is bred by our knowledge that Lincoln will be assassinated at the pinnacle of his achievement. As noted earlier, the tension is amplified by the subplot of David Herold's espionage and his infatuated friendship with John Wilkes Booth. Further, attempts to kill Lincoln appear throughout the novel (e.g., 369, 447, 572). Reinforcing this pattern, Vidal presents Lincoln's own premonitions of his fate. To Governor Curtin of Pennsylvania, for example, Lincoln says, "I was chosen to do a certain work, and I must do it, and then go" (396). Of course, he could be speaking of the electoral process, but the phrasing resonates with foreboding. When Charles Sumner urges Lincoln to withdraw from the 1864 election in favor of General Grant, Lincoln refuses, saying that his desire for power has gone: "There is nothing left of me. But there is still the President. He must be allowed to finish the work that he was chosen to do. . . . I have known for some time now that when this conflict is over, I end" (568–69). Lincoln also dreams prophetically; in one dream:

> Grim-faced people were filing past the body. Some were sobbing, others simply stared, horrified. Lincoln crossed to one of the soldiers who stood at the room's entrance. "Who is dead in the White House?" he asked.
> "The President." . . . "He was killed by an assassin." (640)

Part of the tragic sense, from Aeschylus to Shakespeare, is that in embracing their destinies, tragic heroes and heroines see too much to persevere in the dailiness of ordinary life. Highly relevant is John Hay's elegy at the novel's end: "Lincoln, in some mysterious fashion, had willed his own murder as a form of atonement for the great and terrible thing that he had done by giving so bloody and absolute a rebirth to his nation" (657).

Vidal's Lincoln never doubts that the Union must be preserved, whatever the cost. But he also recognizes and accepts as his personal burden the horrific carnage of the Civil War. Of his ultimate judgment on Lincoln, Vidal has written, "I regard that statesman's blood-and-iron response to the withdrawal of the Southern states as a very great evil; hence his tragedy; ours too" (*United States* 699). In another essay, Vidal describes Lincoln as a "literary genius who was called upon to live, rather than merely to write, a high tragedy" (*United States* 707). It is clear that Vidal considers Lincoln a tragic figure, and that *Lincoln* is intended as a tragedy.

The novel assigns Aristotle's definition of tragic response to John Hay: For Lincoln, he feels "pity and awe" (556). (Aristotle's *phobos* is usually translated as "fear," but awe for a ruler or divine being is also possible.) For anyone steeped in classical tragedy, even more telling may be Lincoln's aside to Seward, in which he denies any conventional religious beliefs but admits that he believes "in fate—and necessity." He explains, "I believe in this Union. That is *my* fate. . . . And my necessity" (46). "Necessity" here suggests the Greek word *anankē*, which it only weakly translates. For the classical Greeks, *anankē* could refer to death, erotic passion, fate, doom, blood ties, and divinely imposed obligation, always implying compulsion and often connoting violence. "Necessity" in this sense is inescapable and irresistible; its consequences are irreversible. And it haunts tragic heroes.

Although the foremost theme of *Lincoln* is the tragedy of Lincoln and the Civil War, several other of Vidal's recurring themes appear in the novel. The press, for instance, is at once unreliable and powerful, wielding enormous influence, unfettered by external constraints or accountability. As in *Julian* and *Creation*, in *Lincoln* Vidal focuses upon a founding moment, a critical juncture in time when history moves decisively in one direction rather than another. (Vidal's second novel, *In a Yellow Wood*, turns on a private or individual version of this theme; his later novels often place whole civilizations or nations at metaphoric forks in the road.) To a provocative extent, *Lincoln* forcefully reminds us how easily the Union and Confederate states could have divided permanently into separate nations.

This reminder does not ignore the North's overwhelming advantage in manpower; in *Lincoln*, General Grant wins military victories through sheer doggedness. He refuses to retreat even when his army is suffering horrendous casualties. Where Northern casualties are great, so will be those of the South, whose smaller population simply cannot afford to lose as many troops. The Union always has the human resources, the steady supply of cannon fodder to win the war. The question in *Lincoln*, as it was historically, is whether Northern political support for this war will persist long enough for numerical superiority to prevail.

The theme of empire is less developed in *Lincoln* than in other of Vidal's "American Chronicles," but it is there. Most specifically, imperial aspirations are identified with Seward, who (to oversimplify a bit) would prefer that the Union let the Southern states secede in order to concentrate on expansion in other directions; he even shares Aaron Burr's old dream of annexing Mexico. (As secretary of state under Lincoln's successor, Andrew Johnson, Seward arranged the purchase of Alaska, an acquisition much mocked in its day, but which no one now would dismiss as "Seward's icebox.")

A FEMINIST READING OF *LINCOLN*

The previous chapter defined feminist criticism and one of its variations. As noted there, some literary works by men present stereotypes of women, often negative ones. Feminist criticism can come to the defense of characters a narrative denigrates, arguing that their apparent flaws arise from an unjust and inequitable social order. Here we look at two female characters whose behavior is, ultimately, unlikable. Traditional, male-oriented criticism has deplored such figures or blamed them for the problems they cause male protagonists. Feminist critics, on the other hand, can look at flawed female characters and ask whether the literary texts suggest social causes for these flaws. Identifying destructive social circumstances cannot license the bad behavior of individuals, but such identification can alert us to the costs and consequences—for women and men—of rigidly enforced gender-specific roles.

As noted in the previous chapter, *Burr* implies a notably limited range of roles for women. But American political life of the late eighteenth and early nineteenth centuries was an almost exclusively masculine realm. Similarly, *Lincoln* presents a society that constrains women, as it charts some of the costs of those limitations. Like *Burr*, *Lincoln* presents women most often as wives, mistresses, prostitutes, madams, servants, and—on two notable occasions—spies. Still, the novel hints that the overall status of women has improved in the years between the Revolution and the Civil War. We learn, for example, that Lincoln once gave a speech advocating women's suffrage. *Lincoln* also includes women who support themselves but not as prostitutes, servants, or wealthy widows. There is, for example, a widow who owns "a grocery shop back of the Navy Yard" (170); she gives young men groceries in exchange for "dally[ing] with her and enlivening the sadness of her widowhood" (170). David Herold lives with her for two months and thinks of her as "the ham lady" (260). Herold's own mother "presides over a furniture shop" (16), and Mrs. Surratt runs her family's truck farming business while her dying husband exhausts himself in Confederate espionage. Elizabeth Keckley, a free black, is an excellent dressmaker. She becomes something akin to a family retainer or paid companion to Mrs. Lincoln, but her specialized skill protects her from dependence. (It is worth remembering that in *Burr*, Helen Jewett aspires to become a dressmaker. Given Vidal's careful research, we can perhaps infer that this trade was one of the first sorts of skilled labor available to respectable women. Notably, Keckley wrote a book, *Behind the Scenes* [1868], about Mary Lincoln.) Too, the novel includes several actresses, though one could hardly call acting a respectable profession for women in the mid-nineteenth century. All this is not to say that the ham lady or Lizzie Keckley would necessarily have led enviable lives. Given the choice, most women would surely have chosen the circumstances of a Kate Chase or a Mary Todd Lincoln over those of a grocer or a dressmaker. Still, from one feminist perspective, *Lincoln* is most interesting for its developed and sympathetic depictions of two upper-class and unfortunate women.

The first of these, Kate Chase, feels compelled to marry money. It is not her personal financial need that motivates her, however, but rather her desire to further her father's political career. In several of the "American Chronicles," Vidal depicts intense father-daughter relationships, and in *Lincoln* we see such a relationship from both sides. Salmon Chase is devoted to his daughter, she to him, and both to his political ambitions. As the novel begins, Chase seems well positioned to run for president in 1864; what he lacks is money. He may also lack something of the requisite ruthlessness and single-minded desire, but Kate has enough of those qualities for both of them. To ensure her father's campaign financing, Kate marries the odious Governor William Sprague of Rhode

Island, whose family has made a fortune in the textile business. Ultimately, the marriage is unhappy, Chase is politically outmaneuvered and humiliated by Lincoln, and Sprague's treachery almost deprives his father-in-law of the office of chief justice of the Supreme Court. To keep his cotton mills running, Sprague has been evading the Union blockade of Confederate harbors, providing the Confederacy with arms and ammunition in exchange for help in smuggling cotton from Texas to Rhode Island. His actions are treasonous, and only Secretary Stanton's efforts prevent Sprague's arrest, which would inevitably have required Chase's resignation as chief justice. Kate has married, to no avail, a man she hates, and she is pregnant. (In *1876*, she has become the mistress of Senator Roscoe Conkling, whom Vidal describes elsewhere as "New York State's great lord of corruption" [*United States* 730].) Despite beauty, intelligence, and charm, Kate Chase is not a very admirable, or even likable, character. *Lincoln*, however, suggests that the world she lives in and its expectations for women must take some blame for her shortcomings. The feminist point here is that Kate is thwarted by the biological accident of being born female. She has the intelligence, will, and connections to succeed in the politics of her day. Because she is a woman, however, she shifts her ambitions onto her father and, in effect, peddles her womanliness to further his career. *Lincoln*'s portrayal of Kate is extended and persuasive, but ultimately one-dimensional. Kate is, above all, ambitious; all her actions proceed from that single fact. Her single-mindedness mirrors that of the Lincolns. Herndon, Lincoln's former law partner, hints that Lincoln married Mary Todd for reasons not unlike those that lead Kate Chase to marry William Sprague. According to Herndon, Lincoln's connection to the Todds enabled him to achieve his ambitions (286). The story of Kate's marriage may encourage readers to consider whether Lincoln has made a similar choice and, perhaps, whether he has paid a similar price. (That Kate's sex precluded her pursuit of her own ambitions does not mean that every ambitious man can rise unimpeded.)

More directly, the novel invites us to compare the fates of Kate Chase and Mary Lincoln. Mary Todd Lincoln is ambitious for her husband; her own success in the world is contingent on Mr. Lincoln. It should be noted that the Lincolns are mutually and steadfastly committed to their marriage, to such an extent that we cannot disentangle either the ambitions or the welfare of one from the other. Unlike Kate Sprague's, Mary's ambitions for the man in her life are fulfilled. This success, however, does not protect her from misery and madness. She is reckless with her own future and her husband's. There is no doubt that her extravagance is ultimately self-destructive. Her debts and the alliances in which they embroil her risk Lincoln's undoing as a leader and as a politician.

Wisely, Vidal does not impose a precise diagnosis on Mary Todd Lincoln's mental distress. (He does have Herndon hint at but refrain from asserting directly a possibility that Vidal has entertained outside the novel, that Mary Lincoln contracted syphilis from her husband. Thus her madness could stem from paresis, the late stage of that disease. See *Lincoln* 290, and *United States* 692.) More relevant here than the causes of her illness are its symptoms. Even madness is not everywhere and always the same. Mary Lincoln's compulsive spending, for example, takes forms particular to her circumstances. Men in the mid-nineteenth century certainly could bankrupt themselves, but (in fiction at least) they tend to do so through gambling, drink, or bad judgment in business. Mary, on the other hand, spends wildly on clothing and interior decoration, two stereotypically feminine interests. The association between women and overspending on clothes has a long history. For example, in sixteenth-century England, sumptuary laws regulated the kinds of clothing people of differing ranks could wear. These laws were often justified as protecting prosperous merchants from being impoverished by their wives' extravagance. Too, it is arguable that the nineteenth-century United States witnessed an increasing identification between women and their houses, particularly those things purchased for their houses. Machine-made furniture and other household goods increased both the available choices and the numbers of people able to afford them; the more choices, the more readily selection among them can be taken to reflect upon the chooser.

Mary Todd Lincoln's circumstances also allowed her to go much deeper in debt than would have been possible for most women. Merchants obviously felt secure in selling her goods on credit, and some—as *Lincoln* emphasizes—counted on political favors in exchange for extended credit. And Mary knew it. It seems plausible that the spendthrift symptoms of her mania were triggered by a desire to exercise power and the perquisites of high office. She no doubt gives herself some credit for Lincoln's election. One need not accept Herndon's claim that Lincoln married Mary Todd in order to further his ambitions; it remains clear, however, that in terms of money and influence, Lincoln made a politically advantageous marriage. Indeed, having brought so much to the marriage, at least in tangible terms, Mary may have resented the subservience automatically expected from a woman.

At any rate, although we can never know for certain the precise causes of Mrs. Lincoln's madness, it remains relevant that her symptoms were so quintessentially feminine for her time and social status. We shall also never know how many Kate Chase Spragues or Mary Todd Lincolns invested all their ambitions in a man, in a sense living vicarious lives. At the least, feminist criticism can remind us that what looks like shrewishness may be a symptom of social inequities rather than a sign of personal or feminine flaws.

1876
(1976)
and *Empire*
(1987)

Because of the thematic and political continuities between *1876* and *Empire*, and because the historical implications suggested by the former appear to have been borne out by the national experience related in the latter, we have chosen to discuss those two novels in one chapter. *1876* tells the story of a presidential election that was apparently subverted by political functionaries of American commercial interests. In brief, the Republican Party made an arrangement, under the aegis of a congressional panel known as the Commission of 1877, with Southern Democrats to abandon Reconstruction in return for the White House and a continuation of unregulated *laissez-faire* capitalism. *Empire*, whose story follows on the heels of the Spanish-American War of 1898, relates the next phase of that triumphant capitalism's dominance of American affairs: the United States' annexation of the old Spanish colonies in the Caribbean and the Pacific in order to expand its markets and establish a military presence in Asia.

Given the focus of the two books, we have chosen a Marxist interpretation for our alternate reading. Although Marxism as a prescriptive tool for social ordering has been a demonstrable failure, Marxist criticism retains considerable diagnostic and explanatory powers, and, in this case, seems particularly apt.

1876

HISTORICAL CONTEXT

In 1876 the German archaeologist Heinrich Schliemann proved that an old Western myth was grounded in reality when he uncovered the ancient Greek city of Mycenae, the reputed home of King Agamemnon. In the same year Alexander Graham Bell stretched the social-historical envelope in the other direction with his invention of the telephone. The United States celebrated its centennial, and the World's Fair was held in the old national capital of Philadelphia.

As the year drew to a close, Samuel J. Tilden was preparing a speech for his inauguration as the nineteenth president of the United States. But Tilden, the reform-minded Democratic governor of New York, never gave that speech; instead, Rutherford B. Hayes, his Republican opponent and the apparent loser of the recent election, delivered one of his own. The immediate results of that historical anomaly are well known and perhaps continue to plague the country today. Briefly, the political machinations that overturned Tilden's election are as follows: A commission was established by the so-called Compromise of 1877 to adjudicate the matter of disputed election returns in several southern states. The Republican majority on that commission, in return for certain concessions, was awarded the electoral votes of the states in question, exactly the number of votes needed in the Electoral College to swing the election to Hayes. What the Republicans effectively conceded to Southern Democrats was the end of Lincoln's program of Reconstruction; by so doing, they may unwittingly have condemned the country to the climate of racial inequality and hostility that permeates American society today.

1876 is the third of Vidal's "American Chronicles," his recreation of that eventful year when the presidency was stolen and the character of the old agrarian republic changed forever. As companion pieces to *1876* we recommend two dissimilar but equally valuable works about the same era: Mark Twain's novel *The Gilded Age*, and Lucius Beebe's highly entertaining volume of biographical sketches, *The Big Spenders*.

PLOT DEVELOPMENT

In winter of 1875 Charles Schermerhorn Schuyler, the American journalist and narrator of Vidal's *Burr*, returns to his native New York after a hiatus of thirty-eight years in Europe. He is accompanied by his thirty-five-year-old daughter, Emma, the Princess d'Agrigente, widow of a philandering French noble who has left her nearly impoverished. Schuyler's aim is to support the pair with his writing until Emma, titled and beautiful, finds a suitably rich husband among the wealthy burghers of New York. If all goes well, Schuyler will attach himself to the presidential campaign of Samuel Tilden, leader of the Democratic Party's reform wing; if Tilden wins, Schuyler will be offered the ambassadorship to France, his daughter's future will be secure, and he will live out his life comfortably in Paris.

Readers of *Burr* will remember that Schuyler left the United States in 1838 when he was appointed to a diplomatic post by then-President Martin Van Buren. (Though Schuyler is fictional, Burr did have illegitimate children. In the novel, but never spoken of between them, Schuyler and Van Buren are half-brothers. Indeed, the old rogue Burr may have had a better claim to the sobriquet "Father of His Country" than did George Washington.) Schuyler might happily have stayed in France, but the disastrous Franco-Prussian War of 1870–71 and the financial panic of 1873 have wiped out his savings and forced him home, where he hopes to recoup his losses. Because of his minor celebrity as a writer and the fascination Emma holds for the American aristocracy, the Schuylers gain entree into the different, never entirely separate, realms of politics and society. What binds those worlds together and fuels the national ethos, Schuyler discovers, is an unabashed and seemingly unslakeable thirst for wealth. Though he may be appalled by the pervasive avarice of his countrymen and the venality of their politicians, he is not entirely indifferent to the charms of money himself, and the money is in the United States. Whatever else he may think of it, America is his last chance.

Immediately after landing in New York, the Schuylers' prospects brighten. Schuyler is commissioned by his old friend and editor William Cullen Bryant to write a series of articles in the style of Washington Irving's *Knickerbocker Tales* for the *Evening Post*. Simultaneously, the young reprobate James Gordon Bennett Jr., publisher of the *New York Herald*, hires him to delve into the workings of the scandal-ridden Grant administration. (Bryant, Bennett, and Irving are accurately portrayed, holding positions and views consistent with the historical record. Of course, Vidal does invent dialogue and specific adventures for them.) While Schuyler insinuates himself into the world of politicians and deal makers, Emma advances in high society. Vidal's artifice here suits his literary purpose admirably. What is essentially one protagonist—Charles/Emma—in two guises allows him to explore two spheres of society with two congruent plot lines. Emma will make her way in the world of the rich while her father chronicles the most bizarre election in American history.

In short order Emma is affianced to the thoroughly respectable and thoroughly boring John Day Apgar, a young lawyer of impeccable background and better prospects. (The fictional Apgars are perhaps modeled on the family of Vidal's stepfather, Hugh Auchincloss). Emma may not reciprocate her doting beau's passion, but she is, after all, getting older. She has two adolescent sons in France, one with a precocious and embarrassing mustache. Marriage to Apgar and inclusion in his extensive and well-connected family would be a most timely and satisfactory, if unexciting, match. More exciting, if ultimately less respectable, is Emma's attachment to William and Denise Sanford. (Like the Apgars, the Sanfords are fictional. Their son Blaise will play a part in *Hollywood* and *Washington, D.C.*) Sanford is a wealthy and rudderless boor who affects the pose of a self-made man. His enormous fortune, however, derives largely from his marriage to the charming and unaffected Denise, who soon becomes Emma's closest friend and confidante. The alliance between the two women is a natural one; both are essentially European in outlook and attitude (Denise's family is of the old New Orleans Creole aristocracy), and both deplore the provincial conventions of the American society they move in. When Denise becomes pregnant—a dangerous proposition, because a previous miscarriage nearly killed her—she turns to Emma for advice and pays for it with her life when she dies in childbirth.

POINT OF VIEW

Schuyler, although an American, is a man of Old World sensibilities and tastes. He has been away from his native country for nearly forty years, most of that time in Italy and France, where he was a diplomat and a working writer. During his years in Europe, Schuyler was connected to the nobility—he was even an unofficial member of the French court—and though he's no snob, the crude democratic energy of America dismays him.

At sixty-two, though hardly ancient, Schuyler is in poor health and considers himself an old man, the antithesis of what the United States is all about. He also considers himself an alien in his own country; his long absence and his work are regarded by many as somehow unpatriotic.

He did, after all, write a book called *Paris under the Commune* (that title is the subject of a joke that runs throughout the course of the novel), an account of an experiment in collectivism imposed following the Franco-Prussian War. But if Schuyler is different from the general run of Americans, he's different in a way that gives him a vantage point particularly well suited to Vidal's purpose. Because he has been an expatriate writer (a tradition that includes Irving, Henry James, Ernest Hemingway, and Vidal himself), his view of the United States is not clouded by the nativist assumptions so dear to the hearts of the American politicians and tycoons he comes to loathe. Schuyler is finally a rueful, if not entirely pessimistic, witness to the American scene. "I have always felt," he tells us, "that somewhere in this corrupt and canting American society there still exists in certain men a sense of what the good society must be" (109).

CHARACTER DEVELOPMENT

When Emma subsequently ends her engagement to Apgar and marries the widower Sanford, her father is distraught. Is Emma, in effect, a murderess? Schuyler will never know, but he will have reason to think back on his earlier wonderment at his own daughter:

> I do not really believe as much in heredity as I do in the ordinary circumstances that shape a life, but there is no doubt that Emma and I have in our veins most curious blood. I am the illegitimate son of Aaron Burr, and though I do not much resemble in appearance or character that elusive, marvellous, amoral man, I do sometimes see, staring at me from beneath Emma's beautiful level brows, the eyes of Aaron Burr, absolutely intense and entirely resolute— the eyes of a world conqueror. (129)

Ultimately, Emma remains as much a mystery to us as she does to her father. Her perception of the world and its possibilities is unsentimental, and her *modus operandi* is calculating, if not homicidal. The product of two worlds, one old and enervated, the other new and rich in possibilities, she is thoroughly cynical and self-possessed, a born survivor and a perfect match for the United States as it nears the end of the nineteenth century.

But Emma is a fictional construction, her character is constrained only by artistic sensibility and a few limitations imposed by factual data. The historical players present another problem. For the most part, through their writings, speeches, and the reminiscences of their contemporaries, these figures are known quantities; their characters as manifested in their actions are too well documented to allow for much authorial invention.

Vidal's favored technique is to reveal them in private conversation with, or overheard by, the Schuylers. For example, Schuyler has a dinner chat with Mrs. Astor, the "Mystic Rose," grande dame of super-rich American society. (It was Mrs. Astor who coined the phrase "the four hundred" to designate the *crème de la crème* of American high society. That was the number of the elite who could comfortably be fitted into her ballroom.) With economy and the telling phrase, Vidal paints the comic miniature portrait of a scatterbrained miser:

> *She* began *in medias res* . . . though I had not a clue as to what she was talking about.
> "People make such trouble."
> "That has been my experience."
> "They *will* gossip."
> "True."
> "They will tell untruths, Mr. Schermerhorn Schuyler."
> "I have heard them tell untruths, Mrs. Astor, and quite gratuitously, too."
> She frowned, not liking, I suspect, the long word which no doubt made her think of overtipping. (291; italics in original)

The political cast is accorded similar treatment. Figures long relegated to history texts are rounded into novelistic form through physical description and imagined speech; those conversations provide depth to the characters and enliven the historical exposition. Typical of the technique is the presentation of Samuel J. Tilden. As Schuyler recounts his first meeting with Tilden we at once register the physical man, a period fashion note, and a brief insight into the religious factionalism of nineteenth-century America:

> The hair is grey and cut . . . short. . . . He wears no mustache, beard or side-whiskers. If only for this continence, I hope that he becomes the President and sets the nation a new style. Since the war no one has actually been able to get a good look

at any American face, so fantastic are the beards and whiskers, in imitation for the most part of General Grant. . . . I found myself staring down at the pale face with the large nose and curiously arched lip (dentures that do not fit?). (133)

Tilden shuts his "hooded . . . dull gray eyes" and speaks: "It is most perplexing. Much of our Democratic support is Catholic. But then there are all those Baptists and Presbyterians in the party, too. Such a noise they make" (134).

Even noisier than the Protestant contingent is Vidal's rendition of the bibulous newspaper publisher, James Gordon Bennett Jr. (known to his scandalized contemporaries as Bennett the Younger, and to posterity as the founder of the *International Herald Tribune*). On the evidence, Bennett was something of a real-life Jekyll and Hyde character whose catalytic elixir of choice was a high-octane cocktail known as the "razzle-dazzle." But as Stevenson wrote a horror story around the theme of human duality, Vidal uses that same theme, in the person of Bennett, to comic effect. In the process, he exposes some of the pretenses of genteel society; the Bennett of *1876* is a sad and self-destructive man who serves as an unflattering mirror to the upper class.

THEMATIC ISSUES

Vidal's American histories have consistently addressed the problem of political corruption, and *1876* continues the theme most forcefully. The emphasis in this novel is on the corrosive effect of concentrated wealth on democratic processes, and on the cynical application of wealth to deflect democratic institutions such as the ballot from their legitimate expressions.

The onset of what we call the Gilded Age, roughly the last quarter of the American nineteenth century, coincides with the centennial of the Declaration of Independence and provides the social milieu of *1876*. The Industrial Revolution, imported from Britain and brought to full, pungent bloom in the United States, was changing the face of the American landscape. A rural agrarian society was becoming an urban manufacturing one, and mercantilist policies in furtherance of those changes—chief among them the imposition of protective tariffs and a reliance on cheap labor—made possible the amassing of enormous individual fortunes. Those policies also made inevitable the rigid stratification of social classes and an enormous economic gap between the rich and the laboring poor.

Inevitable, too, was the use of concentrated wealth as an instrument of political leverage that perpetuated the American version of mercantilism. In 1876, it should be remembered, U.S. senators were elected by the states' legislatures; it sometimes happened that the members of those bodies were not indifferent to the chilly allure of cold cash. In the case of more democratically elected offices, it was not unheard of that a candidate's henchmen might go directly to the public to purchase its votes on a more personal basis. If mercantilism is now but a distant memory in the United States ("free trade" seems to be the current rallying cry of the monied establishment) and today's political panderers (the mass media, Vidal would argue) are more subtle, the fundamental issues would seem to be the same.

EMPIRE

Though further removed in time, the histories of the American War of Independence and the American Civil War are likely to be more familiar to the reader of today than is the Spanish-American War. The War of Independence established a sovereign United States and legitimized the idea of revolution for the European intelligentsia. The Civil War, for good or ill, fixed the primacy of federalism and rendered moot some long-debated constitutional points. That it required an intramural blood-letting of ghastly magnitude to do so attests to the passions of the people who waged it and at least partially explains its continuing fascination for their descendants. 1898's Spanish-American War, the "splendid little war," as John Hay called it, makes no such claims on the popular imagination. "Little" it may have been, but at a remove of nearly a century, "splendid" rings a hollow note.

The war lasted a mere four months and casualties were relatively light, but the geo-political changes effected by the American victory were enormous and immediately apparent. The Spanish Empire, which had its New World roots in the fifteenth century, was dismantled in a matter of weeks and reassembled under new management. Spain's possessions in the Caribbean, including Cuba, fell into the United States' orbit, as did the Philippines in the Pacific; whatever illusions the inhabitants of those islands may have had about independence were soon put to rest by American military occupation.

And whatever illusions the world may have had about the United States as an isolationist agrarian republic were laid to rest, too. As the twentieth century began, the country joined the European powers and Japan in an all-out race to subdivide the rest of the globe—but not without a fair amount of self-righteous posturing. The motives and rationale for that land-grab and the guise of altruistic piety its chief engineers donned for the occasion constitute the political story of *Empire*.

The fictional accompaniment is the continuing saga of Aaron Burr's descendants; in this installment Burr's great-granddaughter, Caroline Sanford, takes the leading role when she buys a failing newspaper and turns it into a political power base to rival the publishing empire of William Randolph Hearst. Caroline is also the fictional link to the great political and intellectual figures of the day, as well as the high society Vidal introduced us to in *1876*.

POINT OF VIEW

The narrative voice Vidal employs in *Empire* is the omniscient one; the sheer number of characters, both fictional and historical, as well as the physical and dramatic terrains they occupy would likely preclude any other narrative vantage point. The engaging and personal voice of Charles Schuyler, whose reminiscences and observations relate *Burr* and *1876*, has no effective counterpart here. Whereas the garrulous, anecdotal voice of Schuyler was well suited to the socially intimate nature of the early republic, a more emotionally removed and impersonal tone is better suited to tell the story of the great power thatublic becomes in *Empire*. The historical saga is seen primarily through the eyes of Secretary of State John Hay (readers of *Lincoln* will remember the elderly secretary as "Johnny" Hay, that president's youthful aide). Hay, like many of Vidal's observers (Eugene Luther of *Messiah*, for instance, or Cyrus Spitama of *Creation*), is old, sick, and tired; he knows that he's dying, and he knows that his own imminent death will coincide with the death of the old republic.

The continuing fictional story of Aaron Burr's illegitimate line focuses on Caroline Sanford, Schuyler's granddaughter. Caroline's perspective in *Empire* resembles her mother Emma's in *1876*. She, like Emma, is European in upbringing and outlook, and like her mother, Caroline will find an unsuspected opportunity in the United States.

PLOT DEVELOPMENT

Caroline's father—a wealthy, if deranged, American expatriate—has been killed in an accident, leaving his daughter and her elder half-brother, Blaise, to contest the terms of his badly written will. Blaise maintains that he has control of the entire estate until his sister turns twenty-seven; Caroline believes that her half of their enormous legacy is forthcoming much sooner, when she turns twenty-one. (The legal contention, incidentally, turns on the similarity between the written French digit one and the American seven). The fictional contretemps between brother and sister parallels the historical crisis of the day. At the same time, Vidal introduces the "Five of Hearts," a group of elderly friends whose distinguished intellectual and political ancestries can be traced to the colonial period. Their presence, although a diminishing one, serves to bind the fictional and historical narratives and provide another textural layer to the novel. They also come to symbolize the changing of the American guard and the metamorphosis of the national character.

The story begins at the English summer home of Senator Don Cameron and his wife, Elizabeth. Among their houseguests are the American ambassador to England, John Hay, and Hay's wife, Clara. The Hays' son Del has invited Caroline, en route to New York from the family estate in France, to join the party. (All, save Caroline, are factual persons.) Del's amorous feelings for Caroline are not necessarily reciprocated. He hints at marriage, but she is preoccupied by the upcoming battle with her brother. The two pre-eminent Henrys of American letters (James the novelist and Adams the historian) enter, and Adams provides a brief gloss on American naval strategy. News arrives that the Spanish have surrendered; the Caribbean now belongs to the United States and the Philippines is up for grabs. Chapter 1, the reader will note, is busy, but a careful reading will be rewarded by a clearer understanding of later developments.

President McKinley summons the ailing John Hay to Washington and appoints him secretary of state, in which position Hay will oversee the consolidation of the new American empire. His task, however, is complicated by more than age and failing health. A Filipino uprising against the American occupation, European intervention in China, Japanese militarism, and the imminent collapse of Czarist Russia are only some of the problems that the old man faces. When McKinley is assassinated, Hay tenders his resignation to McKinley's successor, the bumptious

Theodore Roosevelt. Roosevelt refuses to accept that resignation, and Hay is in for the duration.

Juxtaposed with the historical maelstrom around Hay is the continuing story of Aaron Burr's fictional line. Blaise Sanford, we learn, has left Yale before graduation and joined the staff of William Randolph Hearst's scandal-mongering *New York Journal*. Caroline moves to Washington, D.C., and uses her temporary "allowance" to buy the respectable but moribund *Washington Tribune*. To the amazement of Blaise—and everyone else in the newspaper business—Caroline revitalizes the *Tribune* with the same style of lurid sensationalism popularized by Hearst himself. In the process she becomes a figure of importance in the capital, moving with ease between the social and political realms much as her mother and grandfather did in *1876*. Less conveniently, she also becomes pregnant by married U.S. Senator James Burden Day, but she finesses that potentially catastrophic *faux pas* by marrying her lawyer, who also happens to be her distant and financially strapped cousin. (Emma, the child of that pregnancy, will become a player in *Hollywood*, the next installment of Vidal's American series). Blaise and Caroline are eventually reconciled and become partners in the *Tribune*, a satisfying, if somewhat facile, coda to the fictional shenanigans.

CHARACTER DEVELOPMENT

Of particular interest are Vidal's portraits of two central and historic characters, the newspaper publisher William Randolph Hearst and the career politician Theodore Roosevelt. Both men apparently thought the world of themselves and consequently, as Vidal demonstrates in their private conversations, loathed each other. Both also thought themselves the heroes of the Spanish-American War, Hearst because his chain of sensationalist papers had inflamed public opinion in favor of the war, and Roosevelt because, as under-secretary of the Navy, he had largely orchestrated the successful military operations (to say nothing of his grandstanding charge up San Juan Hill).

Vidal exploits the similarities between the two men to create a kind of sibling rivalry that brings out the worst in both their characters. Those similarities include single-mindedness and self-absorption to a degree that makes them oblivious of anyone else's interests and blind to their own contradictory natures. Hearst, for instance, though he keeps a succession of mistresses and panders to the basest of instincts with his lurid newspapers, is something of a public moralist. Laughably (for those who have been to Hearst's castle at San Simeon), he also considers himself an aesthete, a connoisseur of the fine arts, though his tastes run to kitsch, vaudeville, and chorus girls. For his part, Teddy Roosevelt was a self-styled "conservationist" who slaughtered wildlife in his leisure hours (Vidal gives us Roosevelt rhapsodizing over the glories of the hunt), and a Nobel Peace Prize-winner who loved war. (He was, in fact, awarded the prize for his efforts in negotiating the end of the Russo-Japanese War.)

That Vidal emphasizes the significance of Roosevelt and Hearst in this fiction is no mistake. They were outsize personalities whose private agendas exerted undue influence on American history. Vidal's artistic apprehension of the two—and his own thematic purpose—become clear when we appreciate the restraint of his brush. He takes what he wants from the record, but stops short of caricature. The warts may be in high relief, but the surrounding flesh is accorded credible weight. From a pair of well-documented, if lamentable, historical characters Vidal creates a couple of archetypes to personify his real ogres: the media (Hearst) and twentieth-century colonialism (Roosevelt).

THEMATIC ISSUES

The dominant theme of *Empire* is one of consummate greed in public and private life; the territorial acquisitiveness of the American government in Washington is mirrored by the insatiable avarice of the wealthy social set in New York. That thematic resonance comes to boisterous life in a New York restaurant where Caroline is amazed by a scene of un-apologetic gluttony.

> The latest Victor Herbert musical contained a highly minatory song called "I Want What I Want When I Want It." . . . [T]hey had dined at Rector's, and when the singer from the musical comedy entered the restaurant, he boomed out, "I Want . . . " and the entire restaurant took up the chorus, and on the word "want" everyone banged a fist on the table. It was like a war being conducted by very fat people against—the waiters? or everyone on earth not as fat or as rich as they? (440; second ellipsis in original).

Or at least everyone not as fat, rich, white, and Christian as they. As the newspaperman Hearst inveighs against the "Yellow peril" (the Japanese this time), the Protestant McKinley convinces himself that he has been commissioned by God to Christianize the Filipinos, most of whom are Catholic. Sanctimony and self-delusion were the order of the day, and those who had, wanted more.

A thematic counterpoint is provided by the friends known as the Five of Hearts; they represent a gentler tradition of the American spirit, one that dwindles through attrition during the course of the novel. Henry Adams, John and Clara Hay, and the adventurous polymath Clarence King are the four surviving Hearts when Caroline Sanford learns early on of the group's existence. (The fifth Heart, Adams' wife Marian, had committed suicide years earlier by drinking photographic chemicals; why she made that gruesome exit isn't known.) The Hearts' philosophy, not so much explicitly formulated as lived, promotes the theme of friendship based on refined and mutually held sensibilities as the ideal social norm. (If that notion seems somewhat epicene, even precious, by contemporary standards, it may be that we've come unmoored.) "Remember us," Adams tells Caroline near the end of his life. Yes, Vidal says, remember them and think of what we've lost.

Finally, Vidal would have us think about the continuing debasement of public conversation in America as presented in the popular press. Readers of *1876* will remember that William Cullen Bryant, a genuine literary figure, was Schuyler's editor at the *Evening Post*. Under Bryant, the *Post* presented reasoned and stylish political discourse that attracted a fairly wide readership. But how impossibly, and unprofitably, high Bryant's standards appear only twenty-five years later when compared with those of William Randolph Hearst in *Empire*. The trend, Vidal suggests, is ever downward.

A MARXIST READING OF *1876* AND *EMPIRE*

Marxist literary criticism derives from the work of Karl Marx (1818–1883), a seminal figure in the philosophy of modern economics. Though much of Marx's thinking and analysis seems obsolete today (he could hardly have anticipated twentieth-century technology), and given that the social systems imposed under his name have been horrific failures, certain of his principles remain powerful explanatory tools. Marx postulated the essential importance of economics in human affairs, arguing that a given society's economic system and its modes of production shape that society and the people within it.

Under capitalism, Marx would say, as people become alienated from the work they do and the mode of production, relations among people, and people themselves, become reified. That is, people come to be thought of and treated as commodities, objects for sale and consumption. The novels *1876* and *Empire* can be seen to illustrate the process of reification.

Charles Schuyler of *1876* has written a book called *Paris under the Commune*, a description of the two-month period in 1871 when the beleaguered and exasperated Parisians democratically elected a municipal government that openly declared and implemented its communist principles. As noted earlier, various characters in the novel congratulate Schuyler on his book, but nearly all of them misremember its title. This, in part, is Vidal's running gag about the transience of literature, but it is also something more; Freudians would explain that slips of the tongue and lapses of memory often occur around topics of anxiety. And the characters Schuyler encounters have good reason to be anxious about civil rebellion, communism, and social revolution. As depicted in *1876*, American society is a nightmare of capitalist greed at its most vicious.

Without invoking all the complexities of Marxist theory, we can point out that everybody and everything in *1876* are commodities to be bought and sold. Both the historical and fictional plots turn on the universal commodification of American life. Emma, as a potential bride, is for sale, and so is the presidency of the United States. Each of the novel's sales, however, is morally legitimized by social camouflage, so it will be useful to consider the range of goods represented in the marketplace of *1876*. First, through his journalism, Schuyler offers his mind and memory for sale. Then he makes a tawdry commercial endorsement on the strength of his minor celebrity; having been given a reduced-fare trans-Atlantic passage, he regales a gang of reporters with overly fulsome praise of the ship's amenities. "I sang," he ruefully admits, "for all our suppers" (8). Of course, Schuyler has little choice but to sing for his supper. All of his capital was wiped out in the financial panic of 1873, a debacle brought about by a gang of Wall Street speculators who tried to corner the gold market. Reduced to selling himself, Charles hopes to peddle his political allegiance and his newspaper columns to the cause of Governor Tilden for a cushy ambassadorial appointment. He also hopes to ensure his daughter's future with a favorable (i.e., lucrative) marriage. "I am, frankly," he tells us, "desperate, and would sell Emma to the highest bidder" (66). He later recants, but Emma's subsequent engagement to John Apgar is—on her part, at least—a matter of mercenary convenience.

Sexual prostitution is a recurring motif in *1876*, too, and Charles notes the similarities between politicians and whores. During a visit to a Washington bordello he reminisces about his golden youth: "forty years ago when Leggett and I would prowl . . . getting to know the good brothels . . . as now I am obliged to learn the Cabinet of General [President] Grant" (105).

Or, as Roscoe Conkling says to Charles, "So much is for sale, Mr. Schuyler" (211).

"So much" includes the following on the political menu of *1876*:

- A nomination for a cadetship at West Point: $5,000, payable to your congressman
- A seat in the U.S. Senate: $250,000, payable to the party of your choice
- Florida's Electoral College votes: $200,000; Louisiana's: $1,000,000 (sorry, cash only); South Carolina's: the blue-plate special at a piddling $80,000
- A team of a horses with accompanying receipt for $1,700: $3 (sorry, available only to Ulysses S. Grant, president of the United States)
- The *pièce de resistance*—Charles "I don't care if they print it backwards" Schuyler's article about the slightly less than fascinating Empress Eugenie: $750.

The above is only a sampler of the treats available at the larger banquet. Of those, the most delectable (or unsavory, depending on one's taste) is Emma's gruesome selection. Although she denies having deceived her best friend, the novel leaves little doubt that Emma duped Denise Sanford into carrying a surely fatal pregnancy to term. When Denise dies in childbirth, Emma marries Denise's widower William, a man with nothing to recommend him but a fortune established on his dead wife's inherited wealth.

Empire, as Marxist criticism might have it, portrays the logical extension of the capitalist impulse at domestic play in *1876*. Not content with the commodification of native assets—the land, the resources, and the disturbingly restive laboring class—American capitalism sought to extend itself in the colonial arena occupied by its natural competitors, Japan and the imperially minded nations of Europe. To do so, it became necessary to make abstract, to objectify as tactical commodities, the nations and peoples it targeted for colonialization.

Chief among those targets in the Spanish Empire were the Philippines. Alfred Thayer Mahan, a naval strategist and friend of Theodore Roosevelt, with Senator Henry Cabot Lodge and Henry Adam's brother Brooks, pressured McKinley to supplant the Spanish in those islands, even though the American government had a tacit agreement with the Filipino rebel leader Aguinaldo to respect Philippine independence after the war. Mahan contended that failure to establish an American presence in the Far East would constrict the expanding American industrial capacity and lead to a "socialist" redistribution of excess production at home. Further, Adams argued that the next "great war" would be between the United States and Czarist Russia. The Russians, he said, "must either expand drastically, into Asia, or undergo an internal revolution" (33). At least in that regard, a Marxist would agree that Adams was prescient.

Last, a Marxist critic might make something of religion (that "opiate of the masses") as a rationale for American imperialism in *Empire*. Vidal portrays McKinley as suffering from a mild case of religious dementia—he seems to have had some intimate conversations with God—that his advisers were able to exploit for their own purposes. The majority of Filipinos, as noted earlier, were Catholics, and the majority of Americans, including McKinley, were rather staunch Protestants. It is not surprising then, that whatever McKinley's private feelings about *Realpolitik*, he seems to have been convinced that the Filipinos needed to be Christianized for their own good. That particular conversion never took place in the Philippines, but in the Marxist view another one did: The islands and the people in them became commodities in the capitalist marketplace.

Hollywood
(1990)

At the beginning of the second administration of Woodrow Wilson
(1917) Europe was in the middle of the Great War (not to be called World
War I until the onset of World War II). Wilson had pursued a policy of
neutrality since the war's onset in 1914, but when the revolutionary government of Russia dropped out of the fighting, tilting the balance in favor
of the Central Powers (Germany and the Austro-Hungarian Empire), the
United States was dragged in on the side of the Franco-British allies. A
German victory in Europe would have been inimical to America's own
expansionist designs. Consequently, the task confronting Wilson was to
build public support for an unpopular war. His difficulties in creating
that support were compounded by a significant German-American population that wanted no part in a war against the old country and a general population that wanted no part of Europe at all. To sell the war and
inflame public opinion against Germany, Wilson created a propaganda
agency headed by the journalist George Creel. That agency, euphemis-
tically known as the Committee for Public Information (CPI), saw in
popular entertainment—particularly that new form of popular entertainment, the *photo-play*—a singularly felicitous venue for public suasion.
And so it was that Hollywood went to war. And at this juncture Vidal
fuses the historical and fictional elements of his story, as he sends the
Washington newspaper publisher Caroline Sanford, at Creel's urging, to
Hollywood to spread the patriotic word.

Concurrent with the war, and twice as lethal (10 million war deaths compared with 20 million deaths by illness), was an epidemic of influenza that originated in China but came to be known as the Spanish flu. In 1917 the U.S. Congress, in an effort, perhaps, to console a beleaguered nation, enacted Prohibition. While it may have been a splendid piece of secular prayer, the Volstead Act was not a hit with a sizable part of the American public, though it eventually ignited the entrepreneurial spirit of Al Capone, among others. The following year an armistice was signed between the Allies and Germany, and the deposed Czar Nicholas II, last of the Romanov dynasty, along with his family was murdered by their Bolshevik successors. Not to be outdone, the U.S. Post Office confiscated and burned a shipment of James Joyce's novel *Ulysses*.

NARRATIVE POINT OF VIEW

Vidal tells the fifth of his American histories, *Hollywood*, in an omniscient voice informed by the craft of film making. Hollywood, the California state of mind in the American consciousness, is not only the title but the metaphor that informs his story of the United States in the years from the second Wilson administration through the presidency of the hapless Warren G. Harding. Vidal's fictional creations—the continuation of Aaron Burr's illegitimate line of Schuyler-Sanfords—serve as the cameras that record the historical action. Caroline Sanford and her half-brother Blaise, co-publishers of the *Washington Tribune*, are positioned again (as in the preceding *Empire*) to capture the social backdrop and dish the dirt about notables of the era. The fictional Democratic Senator James Burden Day pans in for the close-ups on the historical figures *sans* makeup and records their private conversations as well as their public oratory. Jesse Smith, a political errand boy for the Ohio Republican boss Harry Daugherty, is the intimate lens that pierces the smoke-filled rooms of the Republican convention that nominates Harding in 1919. (Smith prefers the nickname Jess, 6.) Through Jess's eye we are also made privy to Harding's philandering and the vaulting ambition of Harding's wife, whom Smith titles "the Duchess." The set designer and general interlocutor is Vidal himself. When a physical description is needed, Paris in 1917 or dusty Santa Monica in the 1920s, he provides it. When an explanatory historical aside is necessary to the reader's understanding of the action, Vidal delivers it succinctly and returns to his director's chair.

PLOT DEVELOPMENT

Corruption—of popular entertainment by the government, and of the government by political hacks—drives the two storylines at the heart of *Hollywood*. Caroline Sanford goes to Los Angeles to convince the studios to produce films sympathetic to the Wilson administration's pro-British position, that is, films designed to inflame public opinion and stifle dissent. Improbably, Caroline soon finds herself in front of the camera, which, as they say, loves her. Under the *nom de cine* Emma Traxler, she plays a mother searching the French battlefields for her lost son in an epic called *Huns from Hell*. (Vidal isn't just clowning around here. When George Creel went to Hollywood for the CPI he himself produced a movie with the overwrought title *The Kaiser: Beast of Berlin*.) An overnight, if middle-aged, sensation, Caroline is now privy to the inner workings of Hollywood and the publicity machine that serves it. She has an affair with the director Timothy X. Farrell, a young Boston Irishman whose egalitarian tendencies are construed by some as communist sympathies. Their romance fades, but the two become partners in a production company, and they begin to formulate a newer, more sophisticated, approach to film-making. This new approach, Caroline believes, will supersede the crude opinion-making of the sensationalist ''yellow'' press and bring her the power enjoyed by her old friend Hearst. To that end, she sells her half of the *Washington Tribune* to her brother Blaise and moves permanently to California.

Back in Washington, Blaise has insinuated himself into the maneuverings of the administration and its Republican adversaries. After the armistice is declared on November 11, 1918, Wilson, with Blaise in tow, leads the American delegation to the peace conference in Paris. Blaise catches up with his French connections—and makes some new ones—and the Treaty of Versailles is negotiated, including provisions for establishing a League of Nations. Wilson returns to the capital, but before the treaty can be ratified by the U.S. Senate, he suffers a debilitating stroke. Ill and probably incompetent at this point, Wilson is unwilling to compromise on relatively minor points. The treaty's opponents (notably the self-interested Lodge and the isolationist Senator Borah of Idaho, with some backstage help from Alice Roosevelt Longworth) manage its rejection on the Senate floor and Wilson fades into history, setting the stage for the seeming debacle that was the Harding administration.

Warren G. Harding was a newspaper publisher from Marion, Ohio, and the protege of political operator Harry Daugherty, who master-minded Harding's election to the U.S. Senate in 1914. Intelligent, gregarious, and attractive, Harding became the Republicans' candidate for president when the 1920 convention was deadlocked among other contenders. During his campaign against the Democratic nominee James M. Cox, his call for a "return to normalcy" resonated pleasingly within the electorate, and he was elected by a large majority. When he took office, unfortunately, the new president brought with him some old friends. Out of loyalty—or cronyism—he nominated Daugherty as attorney general, Charles Forbes as chief of the Veterans' Bureau, and Albert B. Fall as secretary of the interior; Vidal gives us Daugherty's gofer, the Marion haberdasher Jesse Smith, to record the larcenous hijinks that ensue.

Smith's days take him from mornings at the White House, where he functions as the duchess's fabric consultant and arranges the president's extramarital recreations, to afternoons at his unofficial office in the Capitol Building, where he sells contraband liquor from government warehouses. His main focus of action, however, takes place in the evenings at a bungalow on K Street, where Harding's coterie plays honest poker and deals from the bottom of the deck with supplicants for government contracts. Smith learns of Fall's complicity in the Teapot Dome scandal—a scheme in which the secretary illegally leased the naval oil reserves in Elk Hills, California, to the Mammoth Oil Co. and the Teapot Dome, Wyoming, reserves to Pan-American Oil—and Forbes's fraudulent dealings at the Veterans' Bureau. A Senate investigation is launched, and Smith, who knows too much, is shot to death while under the protection of the FBI. Daugherty's Justice Department subsequently brings a finding of suicide, and the matter is soon forgotten.

Crosscutting to Hollywood, Vidal develops a parallel milieu to mirror the one in Washington and lend a bi-coastal balance to his story. Through no fault of her own, Caroline is implicated in another mysterious death 3,000 miles from the K Street house; this one, however, involves drugs, a famous director, and a pair of misguided, if highly photogenic, actresses. Structural symmetry is consummated when the cover-up machine of the Los Angeles Police Department goes the Justice Department one better and tries to pin the historically factual murder on the butler. Art imitates life, or life imitates art imitating life.

CHARACTER DEVELOPMENT

Presidents Wilson and Harding are the two players of primary historical interest in *Hollywood*, and Vidal, as head of wardrobe, fits them out
with distinctive personalities and a full range of idiosyncratic accessories.
He also casts them, in their private moments, against type; in so doing
he creates a pair of credible fictional characters to play out their historical
destinies.

Woodrow Wilson's public persona was certainly shaped by his academic background; he was a professor of history and, before his election
to the governorship of New Jersey, the president of Princeton University.
Regarded by the public as rigid, didactic, and authoritarian, there was
nothing about his conduct of the war or his petulance when the Senate
rejected his presentation of the Treaty of Versailles to contradict that
perception. Such, however, is not the stuff of which leading men are
made; Vidal gives us instead a privately passionate man with an amorous past (something only whispered at in his own time) who is at once
a mordant wit and a frustrated vaudevillian. After the treaty fails he
speaks to Blaise Sanford of his hatred for Theodore Roosevelt: "[O]ut of
Roosevelt's private rage and malice, and, yes, malignant evil, he could
not bear that anyone else might ever get credit for benefitting the world.
. . . I regard his death as a true blessing and I pray that no such monster
ever again appears upon the scene, preaching mindless war." But moments later, his rage dissipated, Vidal's Wilson does a comic turn. "The
face, totally slack, was cretinous and comical. The body drooped, com-
plementing the face. 'I'm Dopey Dan,' he sang, 'and I'm married to Mid-
night Mary' " (207–08). On that note, the president of the United States
does a grotesque little dance and takes a bow. Vidal's Wilson is clearly
not the icy pedant of popular imagination.

Nor is the Harding of *Hollywood* the amiable nonentity so many of his
constituents thought him to be. Rather, he is portrayed as a canny but
well-intentioned political operator with some all-too-human frailties (bad
taste in friends, and an eye for a pretty girl and the nearest closet, for
instance). Harding was generally thought to have been maneuvered into
his party's nomination by Daugherty, but Vidal takes us backstage at
the convention, where we eavesdrop on Harding's own calculated assessment of his chances:

"I know there's a temptation to go along with what you
think might be the winner, General Wood, and I know there
are a couple of fellows pledged to me who're trying to per-
suade you to switch tomorrow on the first ballot and throw
the nomination to [Wood]. . . . he's not going to be nominated, ever. . . . We're still very much in business, and we're
still the state that the Republicans have to win to win the
election." (291)

Astute and humane, admittedly fond of cigars and the occasional whiskey, Harding emerges as the victim of his own good nature. Tellingly,
he compares himself with his predecessor. Wilson, Harding acknowledges, was a great man, and he is not. He will do what he can to earn
the public's love, if not its awe. Unfortunately, he never became the ben-
eficiary of either emotion, but Harding is well cast as minor tragic figure
rather than pilfering buffoon.

On the purely fictional side, Caroline Sanford is the same formidable
and single-minded operator she was when last we saw her in *Empire*.
But this time she's ten years older and an experienced hand in the publishing and political worlds of Washington, D.C. She retains, if not much
in the way of innocence or naivety, the same supreme self-confidence
that made her a success in the newspaper business and the same determination to know how things work. This time she focuses her considerable talents and determination on the business of making movies.

Caroline is fictional, but two very real women played a part in her
creation. The first was Mlle. Marie Souvestre, a free-thinking French-
woman who founded girls' schools at Fountainebleu and, later, at Allenwood, in England. Apparently Souvestre was an unapologetic agnostic
who instilled in her students (among them the outspoken Alice Roosevelt) a bracingly realistic view of the world and an utter disregard for
failure. It is from Allenwood, we learn in *Empire*, that Caroline graduated. The second of the women Vidal draws upon was an old friend.
Responding in an essay to an incredulous reviewer in the *Washington
Times*, Vidal says, "[He] also tells us, basking in his ignorance, that no
young woman—like my invented Caroline—could have taken over a
Washington newspaper and made a success of it. But less than twenty
years later one Eleanor Patterson, whom I knew very well, did just
that and published the earlier *Washington Times-Herald*" ("How I do
what I do if not why," *At Home* 276). Given the Souvestre-Roosevelt-

Patterson pedigree, then, we can understand that Hollywood is over-matched when Caroline hits town.

THEMATIC ISSUES

Hollywood, the factory of illusion, is Vidal's metaphor for the political dream machine that manufactures its own truth for mass consumption. The gap between the governed and their elected rulers is wide, he tells us, and the buffer between them is a blurred rendition of reality more palatable to the electorate than the reality itself. The thesis is self-evident and requires little explication; a particular passage in the novel states it succinctly and might even be an appropriate disclaimer preceding the nightly network news of our own day. Caroline Sanford, the editor, is watching herself on screen as Emma Traxler, the actress. But she is also watching the others in the room as they watch the fabrication on the screen, and she sees that they are transfixed, as if in a dream. The moving picture, she understands, an artifice made of light passing through strips of celluloid, creates its own world, one that includes its audience. Caroline envisions possibilities beyond mere entertainment: "Reality could now be entirely invented and history revised. Suddenly, she knew what God must have felt when he gazed upon chaos, with nothing but himself upon his mind" (186).

A PSYCHOANALYTIC READING OF *HOLLYWOOD*

The term "psychoanalysis" does double duty, referring to the psychological theories of Sigmund Freud (1856–1939) and to the psychiatric practices they imply. Both theory and practice have been modified by Freud's followers, but his central insights remain the ground of psychoanalysis. From its early days, Freudian psychology has inspired literary criticism. This fact should not be surprising; Freud himself often ventured into literary commentary, and he regularly acknowledged that great writers had anticipated his own discoveries.

Freud's writings, not to mention those of his followers and explicators, run to thousands of pages. There will be room here for only a quick outline of some important points. First, and perhaps most shocking to his contemporaries, Freud insisted that sexual impulses are present from infancy on. In order to live in a community, children learn to repress socially unacceptable desires rather than act upon them. Repression is a process of forgetting, of excluding repressed feelings from the conscious mind. Such feelings are not wholly erased, however. Rather, they reside in our unconscious minds and continue to exert pressure on our thoughts and behavior. Sometimes, repressed material impels people to persist in counterproductive—neurotic—actions. The goal of psychoanalytic therapy is to uncover the unconscious impulses behind neurotic behavior—hence, the importance of dreams.

When we sleep, the mechanisms of repression relax a bit and "unacceptable" thoughts begin to surface in dreams. Some degree of censorship remains active, however, so repressed memories and desires enter dreams in disguise. Freud called dreams "the royal road to the unconscious," but they require interpretation to penetrate their disguises, to decode their symbolic elements. Here, we shall take a Freudian approach to *Hollywood*, analyzing one pattern in the novel as if it were a dream.

A brief justification of this procedure may be in order. Freudian critics have most often "psychoanalyzed" either characters or authors. Such studies can be enlightening, as long as one remembers that fictional characters lack unconscious minds and an author's psyche is only one factor in creating the ultimate shape of a work of art. Too, some of Freud's specific points now seem dubious. For example, his account of a boy's psychosexual development (through the Oedipus complex) may fit the patriarchal family of late nineteenth-century Vienna better than other family constellations. And most people agree that Freud's developmental hypotheses need considerable adjusting if applied to females. Finally, it seems likely that Freud's thoroughgoing stress on sexual symbolism owes something to his own historical circumstances. With all these reservations, Freud's account of mental processes, of the psychic economy, remains persuasive. The concepts of repression, the unconscious, and dreams as symbolically laden seem as valid as ever. Literary critics can take a cue from psychoanalysts in locating a starting point for interpretation: Look for a minor element that recurs more often and seems more heavily emphasized than strictly necessary.

Although a minor character in the novel's action, Jess Smith is important as a narrative consciousness through which we witness many scenes in the novel. And, both early and late in the novel, Smith's appearances are marked by references to the closet that holds his terrors (see, for example, 53, 62, 107, 152, 402, 404, 406, 408). Sheer reiteration argues for according this closet symbolic significance. Freud insists that dream-symbols are repeated in such sources as proverbs, fairy tales, and so on

(Freud, *General Introduction* 166). Thus, we can begin by considering current metaphoric uses for the word "closet." In everyday parlance we speak of skeletons in one's closet, of homosexuals coming out of the closet, of people being "closet ———s," with the blank being filled by anything from "queen" to "liberal" to "wrestling fan." Closets carry connotations of secrecy, a secrecy maintained because its possessor feels ashamed, embarrassed, or endangered by the secret. (Some readers will also think of "water closet," British for toilet.)

The first description of Smith's fears suggests that his closet, the closet in the hallway of his house, represents homosexuality. In this closet, behind "an old winter coat and a stack of galoshes, horror reigned. Only his driver George dared enter that closet; and return unscathed and sane" (8). The contents of the closet are consistent with a sexual reading: "galoshes" are also called rubbers, as are condoms, and an overcoat is a standard symbolic equivalent for condoms (see Freud, *Dreams* 166). In Freudian analysis, the interpretation of a symbol often hinges on puns or analogous functions. Homosexuality could be implied in the fact that only George can safely enter Smith's closet, and Smith's short-lived marriage was not a success, though he and his wife remain close friends. If Smith is or fears that he may be a closet homosexual, some of his political duties make good sense. He would pose no sexual threat when he escorts Mrs. Harding to social functions or serves as go-between for Harding and his mistresses. As we might expect in a Vidal novel, however, the hypothesis that Smith is homosexual is neither particularly interesting nor explanatory. The plot neither requires nor precludes any specific sexual preferences on Smith's part. The novel stresses his fear of the closet more than would be warranted by a homosexuality that never becomes relevant to the action.

Let us consider, then, whether the novel includes other literal or metaphoric closets. As it happens, *Hollywood* is haunted by closets, by small dark places and large dark secrets. Besides the closet of Smith's psychic horrors, there are the closets in which Warren G. Harding commits adultery, the "closet" out of which director William Desmond Taylor never comes and which his associates contrive to keep closed at all costs after Taylor is murdered. This latter "closet" can be considered that of the entire movie-making industry at the time. Threatened by censorship, the film business simply couldn't afford additional scandal.

Some closets are communal secrets a community withholds from outsiders. Roughly equivalent spaces include the Senate cloakroom, a scene of political decision-making shielded from public scrutiny, and the smoke-filled hotel room where the Republican Party bosses settle on Harding as their presidential candidate. The backrooms of American politics resemble the individual unconscious in that negotiations, competing interests, and sometimes shady motives work behind the scenes to shape public life. So too, in Freudian theory, one's conscious life is continually at the mercy of unconscious desires and negotiations.

One of the odd details in the novel offers yet another small, confined space. Near Blaise Sanford's newly purchased house in Virginia stands an old cabin, still occupied by its original tenant, an emancipated slave. This former slave lived through the Civil War, refused to move out of his cabin, and continues in his old age to despise all Yankees except Lincoln. As might happen with a dream, this small, extraneous image signifies beyond its apparent irrelevance. Following the novel's pattern of small, enclosed spaces, this slave cabin and its inhabitant—who links the novel's present to the Civil War—are emblems of slavery, the skeleton in America's closet, the dark past which shadows the present.

Finally, there are the surprisingly small sound stages where myths are made, as well as the darkened theaters through which these myths are disseminated. Hollywood has often been called a "dream factory," and Vidal takes this metaphor seriously. Caroline and her partner/lover Timothy X. Farrell decide quite deliberately to make movies that will subliminally civilize Americans. Tim argues that Hollywood has been "supplying the world with all sorts of dreams," so why not use movies to shape the collective dreams of a population?

Caroline shudders as she restates Tim's program: "I was going to say we can invent the people. Can we?"

Tim replies, "Why not? They're waiting to be invented, to be told who and what they are" (346).

Taken together, these assorted confined spaces—closets, cabins, studios—seem to represent a national unconscious, the backrooms and dark memories of a people. And gradually, Smith comes to represent that people. For a political insider and a participant in government corruption, Smith remains oddly childlike. He is, for example, the perfectly responsive audience for Caroline's propaganda movie, *Huns from Hell*, responding to each new image precisely as the moviemakers hope. In a process of reversal typical of dreams, through the course of *Hollywood* Smith moves from being the man terrified of a closet to being a representation of that which others need to relegate to a metaphorical closet, to ignore. That is, Smith takes on a double role as a national unconscious in human form and as an emblem of the body politic. Literally, he is murdered because he has become a repository of secrets, like a closet. In this sense, he must be "repressed" by the powerful crooks he has helped to bilk the American public. In the logic of dreams, people and things often change into their opposites and often "condense" into one symbol multiple associations. Something along these lines happens with Jess. He is power's dirty secret, yes, but he also provides a visceral and visual image of what is happening to the United States in the 1920s. From the novel's beginning, Jess suffers from asthma, diabetes, and high blood pressure. Without pushing the analogy too far, we would note that each of these ailments can be seen as a malfunction in the body's economy, in its orderly maintenance of the organism. Asthma interferes with breathing, with access to fuel (oxygen). Diabetes—insulin deficiency—disturbs the conversion of fuel (food) into new cells and energy. High blood pressure, perhaps, demands more of the body's "transportation system" than it can bear. In the larger body politic, and especially in Harding's corrupt Cabinet, the accumulation of wealth has replaced the normal executive functions of government; the system is running on money. For a while, as Harding's cronies grow rich, Smith has a respite from all his ailments and from his fearsome anxieties. But as the conspiracies of corruption begin to unravel, his health worsens. By the novel's end, though injected insulin has become available, Smith's illness does not respond to treatment. In his last few appearances, he has had an appendectomy and the surgical incision will not heal. This detail is logical enough; diabetes indeed can retard healing. The image of the suppurating wound, however, even as Smith sings his favorite refrain, "My God, how the money rolls in," becomes an image for a damaged body politic corrupted by greed.

Washington, D.C.
(1967)

Vidal has said that the idea of a long-running American family saga came to him after he had written *Washington, D.C.*; that fact will explain an apparent gap in the fictional continuity between this novel and its immediate predecessor in the series chronology, *Hollywood*. Readers of the other five books in the group will note that the direct, though illegitimate, line of Aaron Burr is no longer in evidence, though a painted portrait of Burr plays a small supporting role. That seeming anomaly, however, will prove no impediment to the reader's pleasure or edification. As with *Empire* and *Hollywood*, the narrator is omniscient. The story revolves around the interconnected lives of Burden Day, a U.S. senator with lively, if slightly antique presidential aspirations; Day's ambitious assistant, Clay Overbury; and Peter Sanford (in whom Vidal has incorporated some autobiographical clues), the son and antagonist of the wealthy and unscrupulous newspaper publisher, Blaise Sanford.

The story takes place in the years from Franklin Delano Roosevelt's second administration through Dwight Eisenhower's first—the late 1930s to the middle 1950s. At the outset the United States is nearing the end of the Depression and the beginning of its involvement in World War II (1941). Four years later the dropping of two atomic bombs on Japan ends the hostilities, leaving the United States and the Soviet Union the two pre-eminent world powers. The former allies—actually co-belligerents—immediately face off in the so-called Cold War (which was to heat up

considerably in Korea, and later in Vietnam), and anti-communism becomes a tenet of faith and the standard political currency for the American Right. The House Committee on Un-American Activities
investigates and brings charges against several Communist Party members (and their sympathizers or "fellow-travelers"), and two alleged
spies, the Rosenbergs, are executed for passing atomic secrets to the Soviet Union. By the novel's end television has evolved from technological
novelty to the prevalent medium of popular entertainment, and a new
threat to social stability, a thing called "rock and roll," is about to make
its noisy debut.

PLOT DEVELOPMENT

The two complementary storylines of the novel, one political-historical,
the other fictive, are initiated simultaneously, in 1937, at Laurel House,
Blaise Sanford's estate in suburban Washington. A party celebrating the
defeat of FDR's scheme to pack the Supreme Court with liberal justices
is underway. The guest of honor is Burden Day, who led the fight against
the plan in the Senate. Jubilation is the dominant mood, especially for
the host, who sees himself as the architect of Roosevelt's humiliation.
While self-congratulatory speeches and toasts are delivered in the ballroom, the adolescent Peter Sanford roams the grounds outside and discovers his sister Enid and Day's assistant Clay Overbury *in flagrante* in
the pool house. His jealous reaction mirrors the politically incestuous
gathering indoors, but when Peter confronts Enid with what he's seen,
she lies, implicating another man. That lie sets the moral tone for what
follows, a cautionary tale of lives built on and eventually destroyed by
deceit and self-delusion.

To Blaise's initial rage, Enid and Overbury elope, but he is eventually
reconciled to his son-in-law when he discovers in the younger man a
surrogate champion for his own thwarted ambitions. Through his newspaper, the *Washington Tribune,* he makes a popular war hero of Overbury
and orchestrates his election to Congress following the truce. Enid, by
now a schizoid alcoholic and an embarrassing political liability, is conveniently shunted into an asylum; divorce wouldn't play, after all, in
Overbury's home district. Blaise then begins the destruction of his old
friend Burden Day, whose Senate seat will be the next rung in Overbury's climb to power. Disgusted by his father's machinations, Peter rejects the assumptions and prerogatives of the elder Sanford and begins

publishing a leftist magazine even as Congress and the judicial system are telling American "radicals" to 'fess up and shut up. Blaise's wife, Frederika, meanwhile, has decamped the domestic wars and busies herself with the social management of Laurel House. At the novel's end—which coincides, appropriately enough, with the ascendancy of Eisenhower—Mrs. Sanford is exhibiting symptoms of premature senility, as is the constitutional republic itself.

The disintegration of the Sanford family parallels events on the national scene; the body politic comes to resemble a family as splendidly dysfunctional as its fictional analogue. While Blaise the patriarch flouts conventional paternal limits and alienates his children in pursuit of his own ends, so does the American presidency under Roosevelt and Truman arrogate to itself the authority and trappings of a dictatorship. (For example, the "relocation" of Japanese-Americans into camps during the war prefigures Enid's incarceration in a mental institution.) And Congress, impelled in part by popular hysteria, legislates its own subordination to the executive when it delivers Roosevelt's wartime powers as commander-in-chief to Truman by acquiescing in the extension of the draft and approving U.S. military intervention in Korea.

CHARACTER DEVELOPMENT

The factual characters in *Washington, D.C.* play a less active role than do those in the other novels of the "American Chronicles," and Vidal recreates them in a style more photographic than literary. Of course, the writer's artistic license was somewhat limited in this case; the historic types are of quite recent vintage, and Vidal knew many of them in his childhood and adolescence. His pictures of those types—the major political players of the era—are skillfully rendered, but tend to be rather more decorous than the depictions of some of their counterparts in the earlier histories. The Roosevelts, Trumans, and Eisenhowers, for instance, walk through the book relatively unscathed; even the egregious demagogue Joseph McCarthy is spared the characteristically harsh light of Vidal's authorial camera.

Fortunately for the reader, such is not the case with three of the four members of the fictional Sanford family: the manipulative patriarch Blaise, his dotsy wife, Frederika, and their malicious daughter, Enid. They are Vidal's inventions and subject to his singularly unsentimental and sardonic eye, but their value lies in the family dynamic; as individuals they hold no particular interest for us. Some critics have suggested the characters represent members of Vidal's own several families; if so, they have been artistically transmuted into grotesque archetypes. Blaise Sanford, it should be noted, will merit much more attention in *Empire* and *Hollywood*.

More interesting by far are Peter Sanford and Burden Day. The younger Sanford, when first we meet him, is a frustrated teenage voluptuary who submerges his perpetual horniness in calisthenics and hors d'oeuvres. He views the adult world around him with adolescent condescension and affects a cynical detachment that disguises, if thinly, a nearly unbearable need to connect with life. A short stint at the University of Virginia is followed by a brief and unsatisfactory job at his father's newspaper. The war, however, initiates a sea change in Peter's life; he joins the Navy and encounters a group of Bohemian Marxists, most notably Aeneas Duncan. Engaged by his new friends' fervor, if not their persuasions, he becomes an avid reader of history and makes an educated man of himself. At war's end he establishes a magazine antithetical to Blaise's newspaper and falls in love with Diana Day, Burden's daughter. Ultimately, his acquired self-knowledge will liberate him from the incestuous family web.

Not to be liberated is the aptly named senator, Burden Day, would-be president and eventual victim of Blaise Sanford's machinations. He carries on his back not only the baggage of republican (note the small ''r'') sensibilities, but the lingering hatred of his long-dead father, that ''sardonic and violent man'' (27), who took a Union bullet in his shoulder at the battle of Chicamauga in opposition to the tyrant Lincoln and later disowned his son for betraying ''the people.'' In addition to carrying that considerable load, Day serves as the transitional figure—the bridge— between the united states of America and that corporate entity, the United States of America. In his office Day keeps a bust of the Roman republican Cicero (most of his colleagues think it a bad likeness of William Jennings Bryan), and in his pocket the misshapen bullet that struck his father, a nagging memento of ancient valor.

In the late 1930s the senator is middle-aged and at the height of his political power. He is, barring American entry into the war, the logical successor to Roosevelt. Unfortunately for Day, America does enter the war and the president runs for a third term. In 1944 the dying and vindictive Roosevelt runs again and names Truman his running mate, effectively thwarting Day's presidential chances forever. By 1948, Day is a spent force, politically and physically. At Blaise's behest he had years earlier accepted a bribe in exchange for a legislative favor; that single indiscretion has forced him from the Senate, and the world he knew is at an end. Stoically (shades of Cicero), he resigns himself to the passing of the old order, and in suicide is reconciled with his father.

THEMATIC ISSUES

The acquisition and manipulation of power drive the storyline of *Washington, D.C.*, and the nature of power itself is the theme of this novel, perhaps Vidal's most pessimistic. Those political and familial dynasties that dominate the narrative require power to regenerate themselves and to service the cadres of retainers that accrete to them. Power has other uses as well. For Blaise Sanford the exercise of power fills an unnameable void. He is insecure in himself: his inheritance bought his position; he is emotionally disconnected and sexually ambivalent. Thus, he wields his power to create a contained universe, himself his own sun. For Enid Sanford, a reservoir of indiscriminate hostility, the power that springs from her leverage as Clay's wife and Blaise's daughter is a bludgeon she swings to inflict pain and incite fear. Her brother Peter, who imagines himself indifferent to power's allure, is in fact fascinated by it; he eventually makes a career for himself talking about it. None of these characters, however, or any of the career politicians who populate the capital (including Franklin Roosevelt), has illusions about the nature of power or their relation to it. They simply adore it for its own sake and are its willing handmaidens.

But Burden Day is different; he would make power his servant, the means by which he will accomplish a great thing—the destruction of Roosevelt for his usurping the prerogatives of "the people." Therein lies Day's *hubris*, his overreaching pride, a crucial element in any good tragedy and the seed of his own ruin. (It would seem that Nemesis, the Greek goddess of retribution and sometime bestower of power, is at work here and classically diligent in her labors.) As befits a tragic hero, the senator is first raised to power and then annihilated according to strict Olympian protocol. Fate smiles on him and he is placed above other men. His ambition (the presidency and his intended deflection of the nation's preordained course) overreaches his station and affronts the heavens. Subsequently, he begins conversing with his long-dead father (whom the gods would destroy, after all, they first make mad). And finally, his one great misdeed resurfaces to dash his hopes and consign him to oblivion.

AN INTERTEXTUAL READING

Intertextuality can be defined as the interrelationships among various texts. ("Text," by the way, is the currently preferred term for books, song lyrics, advertisements, and anything that can be analyzed as a symbol system.) The study of intertextuality includes the long-established search for sources of major literary works. Typical questions in source study would be: What reading influenced Chaucer's writing of *The Canterbury Tales*? How did Shakespeare adapt Holinshed's history in *King Lear*? A very general form of such questions is: How are new books made from old books?" Recent critics have been especially interested in asking how new books change old books. Initially, this question seems nonsensical; how can a book change after it's been written and its writer has died? The notion of intertextuality implies that no text is ever "finished" once and forever. Instead, the text is "completed" time and again by each of its readers, and the way a reader completes a text will be influenced by other texts he or she has read (or seen, or heard). That is, for example, you may well read *Romeo and Juliet* differently after watching *West Side Story* or *Hamlet* differently after seeing a production of *Rosencrantz and Guildenstern Are Dead*.

Consider Vidal's *Washington, D.C.* When the novel was published in 1967, readers surely understood it as the story of one young man's coming of age in a psychologically destructive family. Multiple betrayals provide the backdrop for Peter Sanford's debilitating unease, and his dark secret (incest) is paralleled by James Burden Day's own secret (he took a bribe). The link between Peter and Senator Day is Clay Overbury, their common rival and Peter's brother-in-law. Although politics are of some significance in the text, it is, in its own context, less a political novel than a family drama set against a political background. In the first full-length critical study of Vidal, Ray Lewis White (1968) described the book as the story of a young man searching for personal integrity in a corrupt world. At that time, White's assessment was undoubtedly correct. However, by 1976 Vidal had published both *1876* and *Empire* and the critics were looking at a trilogy. In 1982 the critic Robert F. Kiernan, reading *Washington D.C.* in a new context, described Peter Sanford not as an exemplar of personal integrity, but as the emblem for a republic in decline. More important than the two critics' different (though not incompatible) analyses of Peter, however, are the markedly different assessments of the scope of the novel. What seemed in 1968 a fairly straightforward story of one individual, by 1982—in its new context—had become a commentary on national decline.

Alert readers of Kiernan's criticism of the trilogy may notice the absence of women in the essay. Understandable for *Burr* (see our chapter on that novel), pardonable (if a bit unfair to Enid) for *Washington, D.C.,* the omission wildly distorts *1876.* Emma is easily the most interesting character in that novel, and her fate rather than Schuyler's is the apt fictional counterpart to the historical events. To be fair to Kiernan, however, it is now easier to recognize Emma's centrality with the additions of *Lincoln, Empire,* and *Hollywood.* First, Vidal's technique in depicting Emma resembles that used for Lincoln. Both characters are described entirely from the outside; we are never told their thoughts. Both, ultimately, are enigmatic. Second, the spirit of Emma haunts *Empire* and *Hollywood* in the person of her daughter Caroline, who is the protagonist of those novels and, like her mother before her, the fictional equivalent of a nation in transition. Once the "American Chronicles" are completed, the liaison between Caroline Sanford and James Burden Day anticipates that between Peter Sanford and Diana Day—who look pretty good when compared with Caroline and Day's offspring Emma, a dim bulb and a red-baiting McCarthyite. At any rate, when *Washington, D.C.* is read as last in the series, Enid must be seen in the light of Emma and Caroline, more as a character in her own right and less as a pawn in the rivalries of men.

Finally, as the sixth of the "American Chronicles," *Washington, D.C.* is likely to seem neither simply the story of one man's coming of age nor an allegory for the debilitated republic. Instead, it becomes the coda to a much larger story about imperial America. Some elements of the novel that struck early reviewers as melodramatic (Day's vision of his father in Civil War uniform, for instance) now seem entirely appropriate, historically resonant gestures in the larger context of the American past.

VIDAL'S INVENTIONS

Vidal's Inventions: An Introduction

While Vidal was working on and experimenting with historical novels, he was also writing what he has called his "inventions": *Myra Breckinridge* (1968), *Two Sisters* (1970), *Myron* (1974), *Kalki* (1978), *Duluth* (1983), and *Live from Golgotha* (1992). Several of these inventions can be located within identifiable genres. *Two Sisters*, for example, is Vidal's foray into the "non-fiction novel," a form in which writers as their own main characters blend reportage with self-revelation. *Kalki*, for another example, participates in the tradition of apocalypse, a long-standing variety of literature that foretells the end of the world. *Myra Breckinridge*, *Myron*, *Duluth*, and *Live from Golgotha* are surrealistic fictions that resemble what the critic Robert Scholes calls "fabulations." That is, they reject traditional realism, take pleasure in form and formal experiments, cheerfully display their authors' artfulness, and repeatedly call attention to their status as fictions (see Scholes 1–4).

Unlike many fabulations, however, Vidal's inventions are deeply informed by the traditions of classical satire. Like historical fiction, satire is as old as Western literature itself, and includes such masterpieces as the Homeric mock-epic *Battle of the Frogs and the Mice* and the plays of Aristophanes. The satirists who have most influenced Vidal's inventions, however, are the classical Romans and their eighteenth-century English followers. Wide reading in the classical canon is not required to appreciate Vidal's inventions, but it helps.

Whatever other genres they combine, Vidal's inventions take satire as their mode. They are outrageous rather than inviting and fantastical rather than realistic in any literal-minded way; they are prepared to violate equally aesthetic expectations and moral sensibilities. Traditionally, the behavior represented in satire is intended to scandalize; shock and ridicule are used to educate or improve the audience. That is, satire presupposes a standard against which its characters are measured and found wanting. Although highly comic, Vidal's inventions are morally serious; satire always is.

Like any humorous fiction, Vidal's inventions will not be to everyone's taste. Something either strikes you funny or it doesn't, and no amount of explication or argument is likely to change that response. Further, Vidal often refuses—in the inventions—to make concessions to his audience. In the historical novels, Vidal is careful to provide readers with the background information necessary to follow the storyline and its significance. Indeed, he writes these books partly in reaction against a widespread ignorance of history. In the inventions, however, readers are on their own. To miss an allusion—whether to *auteur* theory or to the Book of Ruth, to Georgette Heyer or to Ronald Reagan—is to miss any chance to get the joke at hand. And to miss Vidal's links to Petronius, Lucian, Apuleius, Rabelais, Swift, and so on is to risk missing the satiric point altogether. This statement may seem—should seem—obvious, but looking at magazine and newspaper reviews of the inventions could lead one to wonder whether some reviewers think *Satyricon* is a brand of deodorant, *The Golden Ass* a night club, and *Gulliver's Travels* a jolly adventure tale for tots.

The problem of an audience that has not read widely is exacerbated by a favorite technique of Vidal's for conveying his satire. In the inventions, Vidal often couches social satire as literary and linguistic parody. (Parody mocks a cultural form or format by exaggerating its characteristic features.) That is, specific problems and flaws in society are represented through parodies of literary (or subliterary) genres and other linguistic activities, such as advertising and journalism. Through parodies of public language, Vidal pillories American public life in the late twentieth century. Thus Vidal expects readers to know both popular and so-called elite cultures. Again, such parodic satire may not appeal to everyone, which is fair enough, as is arguing that the satire fails. But beware of reviews that fault these books for unrealistic characters, implausible plots, or moral "degeneracy." One might as well read restaurant reviews that fault a pizzeria for not serving tacos.

A second and related technique in the inventions is Vidal's combination of elements from a host of genres within a single novel. This hybridizing of familiar forms can be disorienting; such artistic dislocation helps transport readers from everyday reality into the wild landscapes that are Vidal's specialty. In the following chapters we shall try to provide a compass for exploring the surreal, hybrid worlds of Vidal's inventions.

13

Two Sisters
(1970),
Myra Breckinridge
(1968),
and Myron
(1974)

From 1964, when he published *Julian*, Vidal's novels can be divided into two categories: the historical novels (including the "American Chronicles" discussed in Chapters 7 through 11) and the experimental, darkly comic tales, which Vidal sometimes refers to as "inventions" ("Interview," Parini 280). The first three inventions are *Myra Breckinridge* (1968), *Two Sisters* (1970), and *Myron* (1974). Although different in many ways, these three novels share several themes and techniques. All three juxtapose the 1940s with the 1960s and assess the role of movies in American life. Each in its own way blurs boundaries between art and life, particularly those at the intersections of everyday life and Hollywood films. Of the three, *Two Sisters* is the least successful, probably because its confessional mode is uncongenial to Vidal, who has often insisted that he is not the subject of his writing. Further, the techniques Vidal enlists to wedge some ironic distance between author and character coexist uneasily with a recurrent melancholy tone. Still, *Two Sisters* is an important book in Vidal's canon. As it probes intersections of art and life, this novel can be seen as bridging the partially autobiographical *Washington, D.C.* and the other, less immediately personal, American historical novels to follow. At times, *Two Sisters* also moves close to the surreal, rehearsing characters and motifs to appear in the later comic inventions. It can be argued that *Two Sisters* enables the move from *Myra Breckinridge* to *Myron*, in which parody, broad humor, social commentary, and acute portrayals of anxiety and desperation are delicately balanced. It will be useful, therefore, to look briefly at *Two Sisters*, preparatory to a fuller discussion of the Breckinridge novels.

TWO SISTERS

Two Sisters has two subtitles: *A Memoir in the Form of a Novel* (on the title page) and *A Novel in the Form of a Memoir* (on the dust jacket). As this initial ambiguity suggests, *Two Sisters* is Vidal's experiment with the "non-fiction novel," a genre that blurs the lines between novel, autobiography, reportage, and social commentary. (Other examples of non-fiction novels include Norman Mailer's *Armies of the Night* and Truman Capote's *In Cold Blood*.) Like many of Vidal's novels, *Two Sisters* experiments with the narrative juxtaposition of voices and times. The novel opens in its own present, 1969: The riots at the 1968 Democratic Presidential Convention in Chicago have occurred, *Myra Breckinridge* has been published, and astronauts are circling the moon. The first-person narrator is represented as Vidal himself, commenting on the state of American public culture even as he confronts private events of his past. This confrontation is forced upon V. when an old friend and lover, Marietta Donegal, insists he read a notebook and screenplay by Eric Van Damm, a man they had both known in Paris more than two decades earlier. (For clarity, this discussion will use "V." for the narrator/character and reserve "Vidal" for the book's author.) Marietta wants V. to exploit his Hollywood connections to sell Eric's script to the movies.

Two Sisters consists of V.'s narrative, which incorporates Eric's notebook, addressed to his twin sister, Erika. In turn, this notebook embeds a movie script, *The Two Sisters of Ephesus*, within Eric's account of writing the script in Paris in 1948. The screenplay itself is set in 356 B.C. and tells of two rival sisters, Helena and Artemisa, and their half-brother, Herostratus. Among the people Eric writes about is V., that is, the narrator of *Two Sisters* and stand-in for its author, Gore Vidal. As we might expect, Eric's version of events does not always match V.'s memory, so Eric's narrative is frequently interrupted by V.'s comments. In effect, *Two Sisters* intertwines at least three narratives: first, the screenplay of *The Two Sisters of Ephesus*; second, Eric's first-person account of events in Paris, 1948, particularly as it reveals a romantic triangle among Eric, Erika, and V.; third, V.'s 1969 rethinking of his entanglement with the twins and theirs with each other. At the novel's structural center is the story of Eric, Erika, and V. Complications of this triangle are gradually revealed as well as paralleled across all three storylines.

In general, *Two Sisters* explores how a writer's experiences can be transmuted into fiction. Crucial to this exploration is Eric's movie script, which explicitly draws upon the tradition of *roman à clef* ("novel with a key," one that includes characters who are thinly disguised versions of well-known people). Such novels, and their filmed equivalents, present readers with an enjoyable guessing game, one that in our time might well be called "Spot the Celebrity." More important, *roman à clef* can be understood as an emblem or quintessential instance of how novels are written. Writers, after all, draw upon people they've known in order to represent people in fiction. (Obliquely at least, *Myra Breckinridge* and *Myron* make the equally important point that novelists also derive their characters from other narratives.)

Through the voice of V., Vidal works some interesting twists on the tradition of *roman à clef*. After the first section of *The Two Sisters of Ephesus*, V. comments: "As much as I dislike those who try to identify fictional characters, I find myself wondering who—and what—Eric has in mind" (48). (Vidal employs a narrative trick: He denies the general validity of a way of reading in order to insist on its specific applicability to the text at hand.) Later, V. confirms the relevant identification and simultaneously asserts his own authority on the topic (as well as Vidal's, of course): "For some years the press has enjoyed relating me to the *ci-devant* [has-been] tragic empress of the West (yes, Eric's screenplay provides analogies) because my onetime stepfather is currently Jackie's stepfather" (169). That is, both Vidal's mother and the mother of Jacqueline Bouvier Kennedy and her sister Lee were married to Hugh D. Auchincloss. If readers interpret *The Two Sisters of Ephesus* as a *roman à clef*, they may take comfort in the fact that V. does so as well, observing that Eric writes thinly disguised autobiography. V. recognizes quickly that Eric's script will never sell, and he settles cozily into both script and notebook as gossip fest. That is, V. reads the script for clues to the natures of the twins who once fascinated him. Of course, the putative script antedates some events it alludes to, further complicating its status as *roman à clef*. We might describe Eric's script as having not one but two keys, one to "real life" celebrities, the other to characters in *Two Sisters*. In fact, it would be worthwhile to examine at length the variations Vidal works here on the principle of "novel with a key." For the purposes of this chapter, however, we can simply note that *Two Sisters* demonstrates Vidal's self-conscious fascination with the interanimations of life and narrative. As we shall see, versions of this interest pervade *Myra Breck-inridge* and *Myron* as well.

MYRA BRECKINRIDGE AND MYRON

For practical purposes we have discussed *Two Sisters* before the Breck-inridge novels, which indeed invite direct comparison. It is worth re-membering, however, that *Myra Breckinridge* was published in 1968, an iconoclastic year, just after *Washington, D.C.* (1967) and not long after *Julian* (1964). *Myra Breckinridge* shocked many readers—some with delight, others with outrage—and seemed a radical departure from all of Vidal's earlier novels. From a more distanced perspective, however, *Myra Breckinridge* can easily be seen as an imaginative fusion of material from the two historical fictions that preceded it. In order to write *Julian*, Vidal immersed himself in Roman history, and as James Tatum has re-cently pointed out, Vidal's ingrained sense of Rome and Roman eroti-cism informs *Myra Breckinridge*, along with all of Vidal's novels ("The *Romanitas* of Gore Vidal," Parini 199–220). Vidal has noted that the ori-gins of *Myra Breckinridge* are in Petronius and Apuleius (*Views From a Window* 173). (Petronius and Apuleius antedate *Julian* by a couple of centuries, but their echoes in *Julian* are obvious.) *Washington, D.C.*, itself perhaps inspired by Vidal's immersion in the late Roman empire, cru-cially involves what we would now call "media hype" in the selling of a political candidate. Further, the novel sketches a dysfunctional family in which the mother is vague and self-absorbed, the daughter retreats into alcoholism and neurosis (perhaps psychosis), the father helps de-stroy his daughter and in some sense at least is in love with his son-in-law, while the son rejects the father who has ignored him and killed the sister he incestuously loved.

It may be argued that Vidal recasts dissolute Rome as contemporary Hollywood and rewrites a dysfunctional family as a parodic familial configuration in which Myra, within her own fragmented psyche, em-bodies the gamut of familial roles. In other words, *Myra Breckinridge* draws from many of the same sources as *Julian* and *Washington, D.C. Myron*, the sequel to *Myra Breckinridge*, reworks much the same materials, but with a tragic edge to its satiric thrust. Finally, we should note that *Washington, D.C.* anticipates one device vital to the Breckinridge novels. Just as Myra often tells us that she is being one or another movie actress at given moments, so characters in *Washington, D.C.* think of themselves and others in similar terms.

PLOT DEVELOPMENT IN *MYRA BRECKINRIDGE* AND *MYRON*

Myra Breckinridge is a comic tour de force, recounting the Hollywood adventures of the title character in her own voice. Once Myra has introduced herself, she recounts her meeting with Buck Loner, formerly a singing cowboy of radio and movie fame and the uncle of Myra's ostensibly late husband, Myron. The property on which Buck's lucrative Academy of Modeling and Drama is located was willed jointly to Buck and his sister, Gertrude, Myron's mother. Myra, who claims to have been left penniless after Myron's death, has come to collect her share of the inheritance, now a multimillion-dollar parcel of real estate. Lawyers will have to work out the details of Myra's settlement, but in the meantime Buck offers her a job teaching "Posture and Empathy" at the Academy.

Myra doesn't seek her lawful inheritance simply out of greed. She has plans and ambitions, and she intends to finance them with Myron's half of the estate. Her secret mission is *"the destruction of the last vestigial traces of traditional manhood in the race in order to realign the sexes, thus reducing population while increasing human happiness and preparing humanity for the next stage"* (36, italics in original). Toward this goal, Myra rapes a dim-witted acting student, Rusty Godowski. The once gentle Rusty reacts to this violation by becoming the sadistic lover of Letitia Van Allen, a tough-talking, hard-drinking, and promiscuous Hollywood agent. In a parallel development, Myra is surprised to find herself feeling increasingly tender toward Mary-Ann Pringle, another acting student and Rusty's former girlfriend.

Meanwhile, Buck's lawyers do their best to undermine Myra's claim on Buck's property, and Myra enlists her friend, the analyst and dentist Dr. Randolph Spenser Montag, to swear that he witnessed her Mexican wedding to Myron. Buck and his lawyers believe they have triumphed when they prove that Myron is not dead. Myra, however, overcomes; she and Dr. Montag announce that Myra and Myron are one and the same, distinguished by a sex-change operation. Shortly thereafter, Myra wakes up in a hospital; she has been unconscious for ten days following a hit-and-run automobile accident. To her horror, she is resuming a masculine form even as Myron reasserts control of their shared psyche. The novel ends with a postscript by Myron, written after he's read Myra's diary. At the novel's conclusion, Myron is happily married to Mary-Ann, raising dogs and writing a television series.

Myron, the sequel to *Myra Breckinridge*, opens in April 1973. The bewildered Myron finds himself on the set of a 1948 movie, *Siren of Babylon*, which moments before he had been watching on late-night television. He is understandably upset and worried about returning to Mary-Ann, their Chinese catering business, and the pedigreed dogs they breed. Myron's peculiar circumstances are explained in the next chapter, which begins ominously: "Myra Breckinridge lives!" (220). Indeed, it was she who emerged from Myron's splintered psyche and transported him back to 1948 and *Siren of Babylon*. For the rest of the novel, Myron and Myra battle for control of the body they share. Myron struggles to find a way back—or forward—to Mary-Ann and 1973, but Myra has another agenda. She continues her mission to eradicate the worship of masculinity and thus halt overpopulation. To her worthy if immodest goal of saving the human race, she has now added a plan to save the Metro-Goldwyn-Mayer movie studio, primarily by preventing the producer Dore Schary from destroying the studio with dull, uplifting movies. Myra's plan will be advanced by a movie she intends to make, one in which the actor Steve Dude is transformed into Stephanie Dude, "a joyous, fun-loving sterile amazon, living a perfect life *without* children, and so an example to the youth of the world, a model for every young male, and our salvation, humanity's as well as Metro's" (373).

Myra is sidetracked, however, when she mysteriously comes to inhabit the body of Maria Montez, the star of *Siren of Babylon*. (Montez was a real movie star, but *Siren of Babylon* is Vidal's invention, though distinctly reminiscent of the era described.) Myra relishes her life as a star until the crucial moment when she presides over the opening of a Penney's department store. There she crosses paths, as well as lives, with ten-year-old Myron and his mother. Myron explains: "So that was it. The crunch. The next thing I know I am sitting here in the TV and rumpus room in front of the TV, watching the last credits of *Siren of Babylon*" (411). At last Myron understands a childhood bout of insanity: Maria Montez was inhabiting his body and speaking Spanish, while he (as Myra) was occupying that of the movie star.

POINT OF VIEW IN *MYRA BRECKINRIDGE* AND *MYRON*

Early in *Myra Breckinridge,* the heroine asserts that "the only useful form left to literature in the post-Gutenberg age is the memoir: the absolute truth, copied precisely from life, preferably at the moment it is happening" (17). And such indeed is the effect imitated in Vidal's novel. Most of the story is told in the form of Myra's diary, kept partly as therapy, partly to give readers "an exact, literal sense of what it is like, from moment to moment, to be [Myra]" (4). The impression of contemporaneous recording is conveyed in several ways. Sometimes, Myra indicates that she is writing even as she is doing so; for example, "People want to sit with me, but I graciously indicate that I would rather make these notes. They respect my writing at odd times in public places" (33). Often she begins a new chapter by stating her location, as in "I am sitting in a booth at Schwab's drugstore" (67) or "I am home now" (73). A few chapters stop abruptly, apparently in mid-composition: for example, chapters end with "while" (27), "excited" (113), "and" (128, 162), "now" (156), "then" (200); none of these is followed by any punctuation. Generally, no attempt is made to account for such breaks in the narrative, disjunctions that suggest Myra's instability. Finally, like several other of Vidal's diarist narrators, Myra puzzles over her choice of words. Surely, Vidal is poking fun at two literary vogues: insistently self-reflexive prose and the flat, declarative listing of uncontextualized detail characteristic of *le nouveau roman,* the French "new novel," as written and theorized by Nathalie Sarraute and Alain Robbe-Grillet, among others. (Vidal's essay "French Letters: Theories of the New Novel," is well worth reading as a preface to *Myra Breckinridge, United States* 89–110.) Fortunately, Vidal did not indulge his urge to spoof so far as to replicate the tedious protagonists of many such fictions. Instead, Myra's exuberant energy sweeps us into her fantastical escapades. We may disapprove of Myra's behavior at times, but she never bores us.

Interspersed among Myra's notebook entries are excerpts from Buck Loner's dictaphone discs. The excerpts are presented as if transcribed verbatim, with no punctuation beyond capital letters and an occasional voicing of "period paragraph" or "exclamation point paragraph." Buck's recordings resemble stream-of-consciousness narration, in the manner of James Joyce, as the dictaphone machine records spontaneous, disorganized, and uncensored speech. (Vidal had experimented with stream-of-consciousness in his earlier novel, *The Season of Comfort*.) The ending of one disc suggests that this resemblance is deliberate. There, Buck is recording recent events while receiving an erotic massage: "Myra asked permission to use the infirmary tonight God knows why I suppose she is mixing up some poison which it is my prayer she takes Jesus Milly dont stop Milly Jesus Milly" (126). Some readers will be reminded of the end of Joyce's *Ulysses*: "then he asked me would I yes to say yes my mountain flower and first I put my arms around him yes and drew him down to me so he could feel my breasts all perfume yes and his heart was going like mad and yes I said yes I will Yes" (783). These readers may then ponder the name "Buck"—a highly appropriate monosyllable for a greedy singing cowboy, but also a name shared with Buck Mulligan, an important figure in *Ulysses*. (And Molly Bloom, whose reverie is quoted above, has a daughter named Milly.)

Indeed, *Myra Breckinridge* begins as a parodic pastiche of several recognizable literary styles, although Vidal seems to lose interest in most of them as the novel proceeds. We've already mentioned *le nouveau roman* and modernist stream-of-consciousness. Also skewered is pretentious criticism of literature and film, especially archetypal film criticism that seeks cinematic equivalents for ancient gods and goddesses. (Myron, it should be remembered, was also a film critic.) Lampooned as well is the unpretentious but no less hackneyed puffery of fan magazines: "[T]he light Max Factor base favored by Merle Oberon among other screen lovelies makes luminous my face even in the harsh light of a sound stage" (25–26). Pornography's reliance on simile and metaphor is echoed in Myra's descriptions of her assault on Rusty (129–51). And throughout, characters repeat clichés of off-the-rack morality and conventional wisdom.

Much of the humor in *Myra Breckinridge* derives from the juxtaposition of various speech and literary styles. Catherine Stimpson has called *Myra Breckinridge* and *Myron* "a carnival" of levels of language ("My O My O Myra," in Parini 195). In part, Myra enchants readers because she has mastered so many ways of speaking. Within the novel, she dominates people far more often through verbal agility than through her maniacal physical strength (more stressed in *Myron*). We could call *Myra Breckinridge* a contest over which verbal idiom will prevail. No doubt to the regret of most readers, it is the stilted, platitudinous banality of Myron and Mary-Ann that persists at the novel's end. For the time being, Myra has been silenced. She will, however, return.

In *Myron*, the voices of Myron and Myra alternate, as now one and then the other takes control of the body and notebook they are compelled to share. This alternation in point of view helps make *Myron* quite different from *Myra Breckinridge.* In the earlier novel, the only counter to Myra's vision of the world is that of the contemptible Buck Loner. Otherwise, we are offered only Myra's megalomaniacal perception of her own actions. In *Myron,* however, we also see events from Myron's perspective, and we witness his efforts to tidy up the assorted messes Myra makes in his absence. Too, as various characters shun Myron after a spell of Myra's dominance, readers may decide that Myra is less charming and irresistible than she believes.

Like *Myra Breckinridge, Myron* is high comedy and high camp, but it is also shadowed by the genuine pain of madness. In *Myra Breckinridge,* readers may well join Myra in celebrating her release from Myron and masculinity; most will mourn her dwindling into the suburban clichés Myron embraces at the novel's end. In *Myron,* however, we witness consequences of Myra's behavior as well as Myron's fear and despair at losing control of his body and his mind. *Myra Breckinridge* encourages us to believe that Myra is somehow authentic, Myron a social imposition of rigid, destructive gender norms; *Myron,* however, depicts multiple personality. Myra admits as much when she says, "Certainly my work is superior to that of Joanne Woodward whose performance in *The Three Faces of Eve* is but the palest carbon of my own story" (319). (The Eve of this movie suffers from multiple personality. Woodward and Vidal are longtime friends. See *Palimpsest,* especially 277–80 and 296–99.) Myron is risible in his allegiance, however garbled, to sanctimonious platitudes. But his labored conventionality, apparent in his prose style, can plausibly be read as a poignant attempt to shore up a precarious sanity. None of this means that *Myron* is not often hilarious, or indeed that *Myra Breckinridge* is without tinges of darkness. What is worth noting is how much difference point of view makes in the tone of the two novels.

In this respect, *Myra Breckinridge* and *Myron* have significant precursors in the short stories of Edgar Allan Poe. Poe is the master of mad and monomaniacal (obsessed) narrators, whether the opium addict of "Ligeia" or the guilt-ridden murderer of "The Tell-Tale Heart." The real terror of such stories lies less in their macabre events than in the fact that, as readers, we are led to accept the logic of madmen; it is all we have. *Myra Breckinridge* similarly seduces us, though (fortunately) without Poe's gloom. *Myron* then forces us to recognize our own seduction. Again, it would be unwise to dwell too long on the horror behind the humor of the Breckinridge novels. Myra and Myron, after all, live in a world gone mad; they simply choose different strategies for psychic survival.

CHARACTER DEVELOPMENT IN *MYRA BRECKINRIDGE* AND *MYRON*

In the Breckinridge novels, characters are defined by their speech patterns. As observed earlier, *Myra Breckinridge* is a collage of verbal styles. Linguists use the term "idiolect" to refer to an individual's unique combination of standard language, dialect, vocabulary, and speech patterns. It is reasonable to say that in Vidal's novel, the characters are their idiolects, or perhaps the idiolects are the characters. Mary-Ann, for example, mouths the feminine pieties of her generation (or her mother's). Rusty speaks from a masculine version of the same ethos, in his case a mix of Sunday School virtues and locker-room boasting. The conventionality of their language signals the conventionality of their minds. As noted earlier, Myra is distinguished by her mastery of several speech styles. She tells us repeatedly that she is self-created, a creature of her own will. But of course, she is nothing of the sort. In a literal sense, she was created by Myron and, lest we forget, Dr. Montag. More important, Myra is the offspring of the movies. Repeatedly, she tells us which actress she is performing at a given moment, on which actress in which movie she is modeling her current behavior (see, for example, *Myra* 38, 83; *Myron* 258, 273).

Influenced by the individualistic assumptions of our time, some readers likely believe that there is meant to be a "real" Myra behind all those stars and starlets she imitates. The novel denies us this comfortable illusion. After all, if there is a "real" Myra in the novel, s/he must surely be Myron. It is significant, however, that from the hospital bed, our narrator tells us: "I am assembling an entirely new personality with which to take the world by storm" (205). And the assemblage that results is the Myron of the novel's last chapter, who is obviously distinct from both Myra and the pre-operation Myron. *Myra Breckinridge* suggests that personality is shaped by the ensemble of one's models; assembling a self is a process of emulation.

In terms of characterization, *Myron* is much like *Myra Breckinridge*. Here too, characters are identified by linguistic idiolects. In *Myron* this technique also incorporates the parodic impulse that marks *Myra Breck-*

inridge. Critics agree that several characters in *Myron*—the time travelers or "out-of-towners"—are explicit caricatures of Vidal's literary contemporaries and their prose styles. (Maude is Truman Capote; Whittaker Kaiser is Norman Mailer; Mel and Gene are Jack Kerouac and Neal Cassady. See Stimpson, in Parini 197.) Most important is Mr. Williams, that is to say, Henry James. As all the out-of-towners acknowledge, Mr. Williams arrived there first. He subsidizes all those who follow; he made the rules. And so most American novelists must feel about Henry James, as if they write in his shadow, never quite able to live up to his literary dictates, perhaps disagreeing with them, but never quite able to forget his example.

THEMATIC ISSUES IN *MYRA BRECKINRIDGE* AND *MYRON*

Each of these two novels has themes specific to it. *Myra Breckinridge*, for example, caricatures the superficial wholesomeness of Rusty and Mary-Ann, as well as the deliberate infantilizing Buck inflicts on his students. It is reasonable to equate Buck's Academy with the Hollywood dream-machine more generally, serving pablum, as it does, to an entire society. Until Myra's intervention, no one ever graduates from the Academy. Instead, the students conduct their own awards ceremonies and review their own performances; they prefer guaranteed praise, however fraudulent, to the risks of public scrutiny. A preference for dreams over reality could hardly be demonstrated more explicitly. (There may also be a Vidalian jibe here at professor-novelists, those who seem to write their books for other professors to teach.) We might even question whether Myra's abuse of Rusty is, finally, much worse than Buck's. Myra cruelly destroys Rusty's image of himself, but Buck is a thoroughgoing charlatan who profits from fostering his students' futile delusions.

Censorship, a minor theme in *Myra Breckinridge* and *Two Sisters*, is central to *Myron*, especially in the novel's original version. Written shortly after a Supreme Court decision giving each community the right to set its own standards for identifying and outlawing pornography, the unrevised *Myron* substitutes the names of Supreme Court justices for words often considered obscene. This tactic is hilarious, but the humor makes the point that words are not "dirty" in themselves, only in the context of their social opprobrium. As one reads the unrevised *Myron*, the justices' names indeed become synonyms for the vulgarisms they replace. One can understand Vidal's decision when revising *Myron* to eliminate this time-specific joke, but he does retain a similar effect. That is, Myra frequently imitates actress Kay Francis in the 1944 movie *Four Jills in a Jeep*, especially when she wants something from a man. From the movie's title, Myra coins two verbs: "to jill" and "to jeep." It doesn't take long for a reader to accept these verbs, even to sense the tone of someone jilling or jeeping.

Perhaps the most important theme in the Breckinridge books, as well as in *Two Sisters*, is the one they all share: the fuzziness of lines between fact and fiction, art and life. *Two Sisters* contemplates how writers use materials from their own lives and those they witness. *Myra Breckinridge* reverses this pattern to ask how people model themselves after art, in this case the movies. ("Life imitates art" is a time-honored theme; classic examples include *Don Quixote*, *Northanger Abbey*, and the last section of *Huckleberry Finn*.) *Myron* takes this theme a step further. Through the device of time travel, Myra intervenes in the making of *Siren of Babylon* and other MGM movies; further, in changing the movies, she changes the future. The most remarkable moment in *Myra Breckinridge* and *Myron* has been largely overlooked. The final pages of *Myron* return us from the 1940s of Babylonian sirens to the 1970s coziness of Myron and Mary-Ann's Southern California suburbs. Myron expresses relief that Myra, after all, has been thwarted. Everything is back to normal, Myron feels happily, just as it was before his visit to 1948. But not quite. In the 1973 Myron inhabits, Bobby Kennedy is married to Marilyn Monroe, his brother John F. Kennedy is about to run for president, and Kennedy's opponent will be the governor of California, actress and Republican Stephanie Dude, the "fun-loving Amazon" (416). In other words, by tampering with movies, Myra has changed the course of history. In the preceding chapter, we observed that Vidal anticipated some themes of the recent "new historicist" movement in literary criticism. From *Messiah* on, Vidal reiterates the power of various media to shape our collective national psyche. (His most explicit account of such power can be found in the recent *Screening History*, a series of lectures he delivered at Harvard in 1991.) In *Myron*, and later in *Live from Golgotha*, the science fiction device of time travel enables Vidal to encode as fable or parable his view of a media-saturated society.

A FEMINIST READING OF THE BRECKINRIDGE NOVELS

In the chapters on *Burr* and *Lincoln* we defined and demonstrated two varieties of feminist criticism. Yet a third feminist approach to literature stresses the artificiality of linking biological facts to social fictions. That is, femininity and masculinity are social or cultural inventions that attempt, more or less successfully, to coerce females and males into being certain kinds of people, according to their sex. In this approach, the critic can enlist literature to demonstrate how a society imposes cultural norms of femininity and masculinity. Further, such criticism can expose the artificiality, or "constructedness," of such norms. In this approach, the critic asks what a particular literary text tells us about how our society shapes feminine and masculine types.

This variety of feminist criticism proves extremely productive when applied to *Myra Breckinridge* and *Myron*. Most obviously, both *Myra Breckinridge* and *Myron* insist upon the fluidity of gender and desire. We witness gender as an unstable category: Myra begins as a transsexual, but is surgically reconstructed into Myron once again. Desire is equally unstable. Pre-Myra, Myron was a passive homosexual; as Myra, he rapes Rusty—either an act of "unfeminine" heterosexuality or a reversal of Myron's (previous) homosexual predilections. And then s/he falls in love with the hyperfeminine Mary-Ann, first as Myra, then as Myron—insistently heterosexual. (Repeatedly, Vidal has argued that the customary categories "homosexual" and "heterosexual" are intrinsically false and destructive when applied to people rather than to actions.)

The extraordinary transformations of Myra/Myron through the novel serve, apparently, to "normalize" Myron. By the end of *Myra Breckinridge*, he and Mary-Ann fit a cliché pattern of wedded bliss, necessarily substituting dogs for children but otherwise cheerfully stereotypic. In *Myron*, however, we see that Myra has been repressed but not destroyed. At a certain level of abstraction, we could say *Myron* argues that sexual identity is not achieved once and for all; rather, it requires regular maintenance, must be invented and defended again and again.

The characters in the Breckinridge novels suggest various permutations of sex, gender, and desire. As a cowboy star, Buck Loner enacts one of American culture's macho archetypes, and Buck seems dedicated to maintaining two other stereotypes for masculine success: the sexual athlete and the moneymaker. The masculinity of his financial success is

undermined a bit by its theatrical sources; he remains, however, the masculine custodian of inherited land, and in his Academy he functions as
a father who intentionally perpetuates his children's infantility. Rusty
also begins as a macho archetype: the gentle hunk. After being raped by
Myra, however, he becomes a brutal lover, one whose masculinity is
reaffirmed in the act of beating up women. (This requires the inclusion
of another gender stereotype, the masochistic woman.) Rusty then becomes a "complete homosexual," in the persona of a movie star named
Ace Mann (212). Dr. Montag assures Myron that the rape merely brought
Rusty's "true nature to the surface" (212). Nothing else in the novel
supports this happy reassurance, however, and Dr. Montag is everywhere else an idiot. Thus, questions are raised about Rusty. Is there a
"real" Rusty? He is genetically male, but where would we locate his
masculinity? If the cultural stereotypes for masculinity are natural to
males, which Rusty is *un*natural?

And then there is Mary-Ann. Her women's magazine femininity is
sustained, though twice it seems endangered: first, when she decides to
be a professional singer, and second, when she falls in love with Myra.
(Lesbianism is unacceptable to Mary-Ann, despite what she feels toward
Myra.) The novel thus suggests that the cultural messages promoting
femininity are hard to resist. Most important, for the characters in *Myra
Breckinridge* gender stereotypes become reality because of the tendency
to believe that movies indeed imitate life. What we see repeatedly en-
dorsed comes to seem natural. Worse, behavior and attitudes not reinforced on screen come to be condemned as unnatural. It is this cultural
fact that inspires Myra's strategies for changing society by changing cinematic representations of masculinity.

In *Myron*, several characters (like those of *Two Sisters*) fit the pattern
of *roman à clef*. Here, however, they are doubly identified by their sex-
uality and by their writing style. It is significant for a feminist critic that
the three types most viciously lampooned in *Myron* are exaggerations:
the self-conscious "queer" parody of femininity (there is no behavior
more feminine than that of a drag queen); hypermacho behavior as a
cover, in which brutality toward women is paraded as proof of masculinity; and self-delusion by men who deny their homosexual experiences
or desires, often (like the hypermacho types) behaving brutally toward
women and being aggressively anti-homosexual. (In *Myron*, the three
types are represented by caricatures of Truman Capote, Norman Mailer,
and Jack Kerouac.) In terms of gender (as with other factors), *Myron*
brings to the surface some of *Myra Breckinridge*'s dark undercurrents.

It is important to recognize the ways Vidal's objections to destructive stereotypes overlap with his concerns about various media as pernicious. The Breckinridge novels remind us that movies, television, and books not only reflect but also shape who we are. As they influence our understanding of what women and men should "naturally" be, they project ideals for femininity and masculinity, ideals that Vidal finds unacceptable and that many feminists reject as well.

Kalki
(1978)

When *Kalki* was published in 1978, it looked to be something of an artistic retrenchment for Vidal, an improbable entertainment in the sci-fi genre that afforded him the opportunity to exercise his spleen on some old friends—grasping politicians, the popular media, and credulous religionists. In retrospect, however, the novel seems a remarkably insightful cautionary tale and, further, represents an important developmental phase in the Vidal canon. For instance, the themes that Vidal addressed straightforwardly in *Messiah* (1954)—religious hysteria and manipulation of the popular will by the commercial media—are expanded surrealistically in *Kalki*. Those concerns will later be addressed comically, and more effectively yet, in *Live from Golgotha* (1992). The more serious his purpose, it seems, the more extravagant are Vidal's conceits.

Briefly, *Kalki* is a futuristic affair about a messianic prophet of doom who would save the planet by annihilating the human race. The tale participates in the science fiction mode of extrapolation. (Novels of extrapolation project, or extrapolate, a present situation into the future, usually an ominous one; Aldous Huxley's *Brave New World* is an excellent example in the genre.) Interestingly, the narrative voice is a credibly feminine one, the only such in any of Vidal's novels—excepting, of course, the dubious Myra Breckinridge. Given that the subtext of *Kalki* is man's violence against the natural world, the woman's perspective is entirely appropriate both as sexual metaphor for the ill-used environment, and in tone, which is long-suffering.

PLOT DEVELOPMENT

James J. Kelly is an American veteran of the Vietnam War who has surfaced in Katmandu as the leader of a small religious cult. Appropriately enough, he has assumed the identity of Kalki, a gruesomely baleful deity of the Hindu pantheon; in that guise he preaches a message of cyclical destruction and rebirth. However unappealing his message, Kalki has devised a singular method of attracting new followers: He gives money away via randomly distributed paper lotus blossoms that can be redeemed for cash. Intrigued by this evangelical innovation, and sensing the weird guru's commercial possibilities, the American media flock to Katmandu and fall all over themselves in pursuit of the story.

Kalki, however, is coy; for reasons of his own, he will be interviewed only by Teddy Ottinger, bisexual girl reporter for the lurid tabloid, *The National Sun*. Teddy, being all girl, falls hard for the charismatic Kalki; being all of another kind of girl, too, she also falls hard for Kalki's wife, Lakshmi. Smitten and confused, Teddy abandons her journalistic principles—whatever those are—and agrees to act as a kind of double agent for the cult. She will remain on the story even as she reports back to Kalki about the machinations of his enemies in the outside world. Through Teddy's eyes, we watch the action unfold.

And action there is aplenty. Teddy must contend with CIA double— or triple—agents, and the inconvenience of a kidnapping. Worse yet, she's thrown together with cynical politicians. Kalki dies on national television, is resurrected on the same venue, and sends Teddy on a round-the-world flight to deliver toxic lotus blossoms to all humankind. In Kalki's final television appearance, he proclaims himself Siva the Destroyer (another aspect of the Hindu god Vishnu) and performs the dance of eternity. In Hindu myth, Siva's dance marks the end of the current cycle of existence. And this dance is appropriate indeed; the lotuses Teddy has scattered worldwide carry bacteria fatal to human beings but harmless to other species. They are harmless as well to Kalki and the members of his inner circle, who have been inoculated against them. Thus the only survivors are Kalki himself, Teddy, Lakshmi (a physicist), Geraldine O'Connor (a geneticist), and Giles Lowell (a physician). As Kalki has promised, one cycle has ended and another begun.

Kalki has carefully planned that he and Lakshmi will be parents to a new human race. His followers will be the transmitters of civilization; hence their particular fields of expertise. Unfortunately, the two leaders' blood types prove incompatible and the lucky monkeys inherit the earth. Whether a god or just another nutter, Kelly/Kalki has fulfilled the pattern of Hindu myth.

POINT OF VIEW

All but the last few paragraphs of *Kalki* are narrated by Theodora Hecht Ottinger, a thirty-four-year-old would-be writer and underemployed test pilot. Though Ms. Ottinger goes by the nickname Teddy, it should be noted that "Theodora" translates literally as "gift of the gods." In view of the lethal gift that she unwittingly bestows on humanity, her name carries a load of ironic mischief. Teddy's middle name, Hecht, is a reminder that her parents were Jewish, though enthusiastic converts to Christian Science. That conceit allows Vidal to take satiric aim at some favorite targets, feminist novels of the 1970s and the Christian Science church founded by Mary Baker Eddy. The writers of those novels, Teddy tells us, wanted to shed "the stereotypes of Jewish princessdom, which they confused with all womanhood" (84). As for the creed of Christ, Scientist, Teddy observes, "My father died, confident that death did not exist. It's my theory that Mary Baker Eddy did not exist because death does. That is for sure" (13).

As the celebrated subject of her purported autobiography, *Beyond Motherhood*, Teddy has a vantage point on the business of contemporary letters, as well. That "candid look at my life and hard times as flier, woman, mother, and would-be know-it-all" (3) was actually ghost-written by the dim-witted Herman V. Weiss, hack writer and teacher of literary criticism. (That Vidal joins those occupations is no accident.) Whenever Teddy's journal lapses into clichés, excessive adjectives, or precious substitutes for "he said," "she said," she acknowledges a debt to the style of H.V.W., as she calls Weiss. Thus Vidal, through Teddy, lampoons much of contemporary writing, in which hackneyed phrases and faltering stabs at variety in diction are intended to mask pedestrian thinking. Doubtless, Teddy is speaking for the author when she says, "As entropy increases, energy hemorrhages. Language is affected. Words become mere incantation. When that happens, the end is near, and the cold" (130).

As Teddy is the last—and most skeptical—recruit to Kalki's inner circle, and because she is ignorant of the group's intentions, she is also the ideal narrator of their story. She recounts events as they unfold, avoiding, as she tells us early on, "the historian's best and closest friend, hindsight" (1). Her innocence engages our sympathy while her skepticism anticipates our own, defusing our incredulity in the midst of extraordinary events. The final entry in Teddy's inside history of those events is a brief addendum by Kalki himself. And that voice, intoning the last words of God or the ravings of a lunatic, engages something other than our sympathy.

CHARACTER DEVELOPMENT

Teddy Ottinger, the narrator of *Kalki*, owes her existence in no small part to Amelia Earhart, the feminist social worker and celebrity aviator whom Vidal knew, through his father, when he was a child. In 1932 Earhart became the first woman to pilot an airplane across the Atlantic, and in 1935 the first woman to solo from Hawaii to California. Her attempted round-the-world flight in July 1937 culminated in that most famous of American disappearing acts, Houdini notwithstanding, somewhere in the middle of the Pacific Ocean.

The narrator of *Kalki* is a celebrity in her own right. She is, in fact, the best test pilot in the world and the presumed author of a best-selling autobiography, *Beyond Motherhood*. A divorced mother of two and voluntary payer of alimony and child support, Teddy O. is the sort of woman Earhart might have been had she been born forty years later. The title of Teddy's book refers to the elective sterilization she has undergone: "I had deliberately removed myself from the bioreproductive track or trap that nature had created for me" (3), and establishes her credentials as feminist and advocate for population control. Those credentials are reinforced when she appears on a television talk show and makes a spontaneous remark in favor of Prime Minister Indira Gandhi's sterilization program for the men of India. That opinion immediately enhances her reputation for candor and precipitates an avalanche of hate mail from right-wing Christians.

Teddy's outspokenness and freedom from reproduction do not, however, free her from the inconveniences and sometimes oppressive constraints imposed on her sex, as she is well aware. When she chases down a lead in New Orleans, she finds herself alone on the ominous streets of the French Quarter at night; her reflections on the experience, her frank admission of fear, make her—in that respect, at least—a universal woman, and one justly resentful of the potential danger men represent. Still, a superior woman in what she acknowledges to be a man's world, Teddy is no hater of men. Far from it, as becomes apparent when she meets and is seduced by the mysterious Kalki. "I've never," she teases him in the afterglow of a good time, "had sex with god before" (87). She is an enthusiastically sexual being of eclectic tastes, although a discriminating one, certainly too fastidious to accept the oafish advances of at least one United States senator.

And, like all Vidal's storytellers, Teddy is an astute and acerbic social observer. Her narrative throughout is embellished with erudite and prickly references to religion, history, politics, and literature. As various asides indicate ("I ought to give up meat. I hate how we treat animals. How we betray them" [83]), she has a soft spot for other species, but a willingness to skewer the odd sacred cow when it ranges into view. She is at her core a civilized and humane skeptic, too worldly and wise to cherish any illusions about the human condition, but too engaged with life to be dismissed as a mere cynic.

Kelly is another story altogether, and not a pretty one. Any casual observer of religious cultism in the latter half of the twentieth century will recognize the type immediately: Sanctimonious, apparently devoid of self-doubt, and obsessed with death, he is the antithesis of the loving messiah he proclaims himself to be. Granted that Vidal had the homicidal model of Charles Manson in recent memory when he began writing *Kalki*, it's worth noting that the character more nearly resembles the later and more spectacular cases of the Rev. Jim Jones in Guyana, and David Koresh, late of Waco, Texas.

This is not to say that Kelly, or Kalki, as he would have it, is not a compelling figure. The failed medical student *cum* god has undeniable star quality (or charisma, to use an overworked word) and knows how to use it to his own ends. The fascination that Kalki holds for others, however, stems from a hollowness at his own core; he seems one of those rare creatures whose absolute indifference to his fellows acts as a vortex into which others are swept. That, combined with a highly developed sense of theater—his public appearances, particularly the televised ones, are invariably dramatic and startling—accounts for his literally fatal appeal. Vidal does not so much develop the Kalki character as display him as an aberrant force of nature, a being so profoundly amoral that the adjective "evil" hardly seems applicable.

Comic relief, apart from Teddy's acid commentary, is provided by several secondary characters, notably Johnson White and Giles Lowell. White is a Republican senator and presidential aspirant who seeks to further his ambitions by launching a televised investigation into Kalki's alleged involvement with drug smuggling. Unable to keep his hands off the ladies and given to long-winded inanities in public speech and private conversation, he is a lecherous, self-important buffoon who fools no one but himself and the voters.

Lowell, on the other hand, is a product of Vidal's imagination. A born intriguer and a master of bad disguise, the one-time physician and university lecturer is Kalki's right-hand man. Where a god cannot go unnoticed, Giles Lowell can, usually in an ill-fitting wig and unplaceable accent. His several roles in Kalki's service—exotic animals broker, media strategist, or curry-reeking Indian academic—reflect his taste for deception and suggest, in their multiplicity, a badly splintered personality. Whereas duality is the mode for other characters, be they mortal/immortal, heterosexual/bisexual, or public servant/bagman, Dr. Lowell is as various and unpredictable as he is treacherous.

THEMATIC ISSUES

Kalki is at heart a pessimistic, eschatological novel (eschatology is the theological study of last things), thinly disguised as apocalyptic knockabout, and in that regard it resembles Terry Southern's screenplay for *Dr. Strangelove*. But as Southern was concerned with the particular menace of nuclear weapons, Vidal raises the more pervasive danger of environmental degradation and the political complicity that facilitates it. Senator Johnson White, representing the U.S. government, typically addresses such issues as overpopulation, pollution, and holes in the ozone layer:

> "Teddy, all of this is just plain old-fashioned commie horseshit. . . . They want us to stop expanding the greatest industrial plant the world has ever seen in order to save these toads and moths. . . . The choice is a simple one. Between these toads and moths and useless varieties of birds and fish and a society that offers you everything in the electrical appliance line as well as more hours of free TV than any other nation on earth, on top of which we have a superb military machine second to none." (128)

Ironically, the ecological problems posed in *Kalki* are eventually resolved through the technical skills of that same military machine. James J. Kelly had been assigned to do medical research during the Vietnam War, and in the course of his duties had isolated an exceptionally virulent strain of *Yersinia entercolitica*. (*Yersinia* is the genus of bubonic, septicemic, and pneumonic plagues.) With this bacillus Kalki wipes out the world's human population, except those five who have been inoculated. Within months of humanity's virtual extinction, the air and water cleanse themselves (223, 245). There is something edenic about the novel's close. The last human being, Kalki, is about to make his exit, and the new Adam and Eve (actually Jack and Jill, Teddy's pet monkeys) prepare to inherit the earth.

In a strong sense, *Kalki* works as an allegory of environmental disaster, as pertinent today as it was in 1978. Kalki proclaims that the end of the world, of life as we know it, is at hand. He attracts disciples, but only among the powerless. Those in power (signified by Senator White), as well as the majority of ordinary people, either do not believe or do not care: As Teddy tells us, "World's end was too much to cope with. Far easier to think of Kalki as just another superstar who was about to score an incredibly high Nielsen rating" (199). Kalki and his message are big hits on television and in the tabloids, and he makes the government just nervous enough to arrest him, but no one changes corporate or large-scale behavior in any significant way. Today, we can buy sweatshirts and coffee mugs emblazoned with environmentalist slogans, companies advertise their good citizenship with claims to using only recycled packaging, and municipalities monitor the watering of residential lawns, all in the name of the planet. Meanwhile, there is a powerful and politically seductive movement in Congress to rescind legislation designed to protect air, water, endangered species, and similar non-essentials. (Regulatory acts are routinely condemned as expensive and as intrusions of big government into private enterprise.) It is true that kooks and crackpots have always been around to proclaim the end of the world. *Kalki* asks us to ponder the possibility that one day, given enough unwitting cooperation, they'll be right.

A NEW HISTORICIST READING OF *KALKI*

As noted in the chapter on *Julian*, a favorite theme of new historicist criticism is theatricality as a strategy of power. Julian and Constantius rule through acting the role of emperor. In *Kalki*, the title character goes

them one better: He acts the role of a god. In addition to *Kalki*'s overt
pro-environmentalist and anti-cult themes, the novel also chillingly depicts how easily one man could exploit our amoral media in order to
destroy the human race.

Unlike Julian, Kelly lacks an army. Indeed, he lacks all the coercive
apparatus of the modern state: military forces, secret and not-so-secret
police, judicial authority, prisons, and so on. (It should be noted that, as
observed earlier, Kelly's ultimate weapon—plague—has military origins;
he developed its prototype during his military service. But once the military has served Kelly/Kalki's purpose, he can leave it behind.) Kalki/
Kelly knows that publicity offers another route to power, and he takes
shrewd advantage of the remarkable facility with which television and
other media are willing and accustomed to convert anything into entertainment.

On its surface, *Kalki* takes up a theme introduced in *Messiah* and brilliantly elaborated in *Live from Golgotha*: the merging of religion and entertainment. Time after time, the novel equates the two. Teddy is first
drawn into Kalki's circle when she interviews him for a cynical tabloid,
precisely the sort of newspaper that unabashedly aims to entertain. Kalki
has his own reasons for insisting that he will speak only to Teddy, but
the *Sun* simply wants to scoop *Sixty Minutes*. Teddy admits she has seen
the letters KALKI on top of a building (an ashram, actually), but she just
assumed these were the call letters of a new radio station. When Lakshmi
tells Teddy, "We will admit you to Vaikuntha," Teddy can't help but
think that Lakshmi sounds "like Arlene promising to come up with a
pair of tickets for *The Hollywood Squares*" (39). Teddy scrupulously reports the ratings for Kalki's television appearances: 36.3 for his segment
on *Sixty Minutes*, 46.7 for his appearance after his televised murder (200),
an estimated 49.0 for his final performance (224). He can appear for this
last dance because his double, a bit-part actor, was murdered on screen,
not Kalki himself—yet another instance of religion and show business
overlapping. In the world of televised "religiomercials," a minor actor
can stand in for a god. (For some additional instances of this theme, see
127, 131, 135, 141, 143, 148, 159, 166, 168, 199.) In part, this aspect of *Kalki*
satirizes (or depicts—the reality has gone beyond satire) the ability of
television to transmute anything into entertainment.

In addition to tracking intersections between power and art or entertainment, new historicism seeks to situate literary and non-literary texts
within their historical moment. In a new historicist sense, *Kalki* is a Vietnam novel, though it is set and written after that military fiasco ended.

Kalki was published in 1978, and it seems reasonable to assume that Vidal had Vietnam on his mind. First, the Vietnam War provides the enabling conditions for Kalki's destruction of humanity. As James Kelly, Kalki served in the U.S. military and developed his particularly virulent strain of *Yersinia* under the auspices of the medical corps. Second, but at least as important, it was Kelly's stint in Vietnam that opened his eyes, as well as a chain of contacts, to the lucrative drug trade that finances his crusade. Finally, the Vietnam debacle created numerous fissures and dislocations in American life. Some of these fractures were immediately apparent, such as the interest in various Eastern cults and religions. (As Teddy puts it, "The seventies were a perfect time to start a religion" [77].) Others, like Kelly, went underground, only to resurface in New Age mysticisms or in the militia movements that make today's headlines. Kalki's success depends on a widespread urge to join some organized group that seems an alternative to the government that gave us Vietnam. (Giles Lowell is at least half-mad, but he may be on to something when he rails about the "American Government's dislike of any organization that appears to be more attractive to the citizens of the country than the Federal Government" [151].) A new historicist argument might well be made that just about all contemporary fiction is at some level about how to live in the aftermath of Vietnam, the war itself and the social rifts it exposed and exacerbated.

Returning to the question of media, Vietnam also brought war into homefront living rooms. Although modestly produced and promoted compared with that mother of all television spectaculars, Desert Storm, the nightly news films of carnage in Southeast Asia surely fueled opposition to the war (although possibly less so than did the end of student deferments). But, equally surely, the same films further eroded boundaries between journalism and entertainment. Although *Kalki* is not a Vietnam novel *per se*, it is a novel about the aftermath of that war, about living in its shadow.

When studying particular kinds of literary criticism, it is incumbent upon us to acknowledge their potential blind spots. (All critical methodologies are selective, partial in both senses of the term.) New historicists and related schools of criticism have been faulted for seeming at times to forget that there are pertinent differences between symbolic violence and material violence. For example, the Gulf war was symbolic violence—media spectacle—for most of us; for many people (mostly Iraqis), however, it was deadly. At a certain level of abstraction, *Kalki* personifies the gap between representation and death in the figure of

Teddy. Teddy is a media-created product. She is a celebrity, and distinctions are blurred among her multiple claims to celebrity status. That is, in being simultaneously but indifferently celebrated as author, aviator, and feminist, she becomes a kind of generic or all-purpose celebrity. Kalki, however, sees the three aspects of Teddy-the-celebrity as distinct, each uniquely useful to his plans. (That the reader, as trained by television, is likely to think of Teddy's fame as undifferentiated helps Vidal create narrative surprises toward the novel's end.) It is to one of Teddy's accomplishments, her success as an author, that Kalki attributes his decision to grant her an exclusive interview. This is a cover story, however. Teddy qualifies for Kalki's select group of disciples precisely because of the "feminist" gesture of her elective sterilization: She can bear no children to compete with Kalki's (projected) offspring. Neither she nor the reader suspects this crucial fact. Above all, however, Kalki needs Teddy as a pilot. The full significance of his media spectacles, including Siva's dance of destruction, requires a shift from transmitted images to transported weapons. Without Teddy's airborne dispersion of poisoned lotus blossoms, Kelly would not become Kalki. Kalki—and Vidal—remember what literary critics sometimes forget: however powerful the media are in shaping our lives, and they are powerful indeed, they are only collaborators in potential mass destruction, not the agents of destruction itself. Vidal knows that what he calls the National Security State prevails in large part through the media-induced consent of the governed. But he also knows that the state's military might underwrites media persuasion even as media persuasion works to legitimize coercive power.

Duluth
(1983)

Vidal says that he was walking in Rome, with nothing particular in mind, when the seemingly meaningless phrase *"Duluth! Love it or loath it, you can never leave it or lose it"* ("Interview," Parini 285) occurred to him. From that unbeckoned and singular epiphany of civic boosterism, he concocted the comic novel *Duluth*, a slapstick foray into the surreal in which he explores the central anxieties of the late twentieth-century American psyche and demonstrates the niceties of his own critical invention, "*après* poststructuralism." The setting of *Duluth* is the mythical mega-city Duluth, which occupies a sizable chunk of the North American land mass; a city ten miles from the Mexican border and just across the causeway from New Orleans. It's a city whose evening sky is lighted by the aurora borealis and the occasional conflagration in the *barrio*. The climate in Vidal's Duluth ranges from the subarctic to the subtropical. An alien spacecraft is parked on the outskirts of Duluth, sometimes in the desert, sometimes in Lake Erie; the occupants are either giant centipedes or—worse luck!—communists.

The citizens of Duluth, *Duluth*, and even "Duluth" (a television soap opera set in Duluth but made in Hollywood) occupy a terrain of psychological dementia as wide and deep as the city itself. From the merely balmy to the seriously deranged, they careen through the narrative and several time warps with neither self-consciousness nor self-restraint. Their various passions and pastimes include tax evasion, red-baiting, racial warfare, sexual battery, political corruption, and, most reprehensible of all, social climbing. The denizens of Duluth are, in short, just plain folks.

PLOT DEVELOPMENT

As the action is joined, a sales pitch is served up and two new acquaintances become lasting, if not exactly long-lasting, friends. Edna Herridge, of the real estate agency that bears her name, is driving a potential buyer, the fabulously wealthy Beryl Hoover, newly arrived from the neighboring burg of Tulsa, through the ice-slick streets of exclusive Garfield Heights. While pointing out some of the city's highlights—including the festive lynching of a black man—Edna loses control of the company station wagon and entombs the car in a massive snowdrift. As the ladies wait for the spring thaw and rescue, Beryl tells Edna of her plan to dethrone reigning social arbiter Mrs. Bellamy (Chloris) Craig II and install her own son, Clive, atop the heap of Duluth's *crème de la crème*. Edna tells Beryl all about Duluth and the movers and shakers who move it and shake it, including Edna's brother, the unscrupulous and tremendously vile Mayor Mayor Herridge (alert readers will note here a nod to Major Major Major, of Joseph Heller's *Catch-22*). Edna hints, too, at the secret identity of The Dude, most cunning and powerful of all the Duluth powerbrokers, but before the name escapes her lips the little remaining oxygen escapes the car, and the women die.

But not for long. Thanks to the fictive law of absolute uniqueness, and its corollary, the simultaneity effect, no one ever dies in *Duluth* without resurfacing—and soon—somewhere else. Meanwhile, a political race is heating up and the *barrio* is about to heat up even more. The young Hispanic males of Duluth are suffering a systematic and humiliating campaign of strip-searches by one of Duluth's finest, the beautiful and sensationally uninhibited Lieutenant Darlene Ecks, and they don't like it very much. So little do the *macho muchachos* like it, in fact, that they swear revenge and form the Aztec Terrorists Society, a self-help organization dedicated to burning down their own neighborhood and dismembering Lieutenant Ecks, in no particular order.

Sensing an opportunity to make political hay and a financial coup at the same time, Mayor Mayor Herridge calls in the FBI and the CIA to exacerbate the crisis. After all, His Honor owns the *barrio* and is insured to the hilt. Besides, his opponent in the upcoming election is Lieutenant

Ecks' superior, the chief of police, Captain Eddie Thurow. If the Spanish-speaking electorate casts its votes against Captain Eddie, Mayor Herridge might even tell his mother, the election commissioner, to count their ballots this time. But before his grand strategy is put into motion, the mayor is taken captive by whoever, or whatever, is in the spaceship. While Mayor Herridge cools his heels in the gummy pink spacebuggy, the celebrated author Rosemary Klein Kantor rolls into town, intent on capturing the alluring Clive Hoover for her own rarified social set in the rival metropolis of New Orleans. The best-selling Klein Kantor can't write, but then again, her audience can't read very well. What she can do, thanks to her data banks and the fictive law of absolute uniqueness, is employ any character or narrative line from any fiction ever written. This is not plagiarism, but creation by other means, and the reason that Edna Herridge, though dead in Duluth, is now dead drunk in Beverly Hills, when not starring in the television series "Duluth." Similarly, Beryl Hoover, though presumably pushing up the daisies in her native Tulsa, is alive and well in another Klein Kantor creation, *Rogue Duke*, a serialized potboiler currently enthralling subscribers to *Redbook*.

As Vidal spins his tale from Duluth to L.A. to "Regency Hyatt England" and back again, cohesion of a sort ultimately emerges from seeming chaos. Each of the three storylines is linked with the other two and their common denouement will be seen to have a common origin. Ever adept at literary and sub-literary mimicry, Vidal intertwines several different popular genres (e.g., romance, family melodrama, and TV soap opera) to engineer a kind of narrative triple helix that lives suspended in a culture of science fiction. Mutant strands that break off from the creature and propel *Duluth* to its apocalyptic finale include an extra-terrestrial centipede disguised as Hubert H. Humphrey, and a *deus ex machina* never dreamed of in any philosophy but the author's.[1]

CHARACTER DEVELOPMENT

In *Duluth*, Vidal borrows—or hijacks—conventions from such genres as science fiction, tough-guy detective stories, historical romances, and the Hollywood novel. Further, many of the characters wander in and out of several different fictional worlds contained within *Duluth* proper. Since the first-time reader may find helpful a scorecard of the major players, we offer the following *dramatis personae*:

Mayor Mayor Herridge . . . Mayor Mayor is, oddly enough, the mayor of Duluth and a force to be reckoned with, always. He becomes the unwilling guest of the aliens in the gummy pink spaceship while waging a political campaign of singular viciousness against reform candidate . . .

Chief of Police Eddie Thurow, who longs for higher office—the better to serve his fellow citizens and participate in more graft. There's very little justice in Duluth, but plenty of law and order, and when Captain Eddie needs someone to dish it out he calls on . . .

The beauteous Lieutenant Darlene Ecks, whose sublime disregard for the niceties of *Miranda* is the perfect foil for the masochistic romanticism of her faithful sidekick . . .

Lieutenant "Chico" Jones, a person of color who wants to be known as a "colored person."

Big John is another person of color, who wants to be known as Big John. Big John is at once the major drug dealer in Duluth and the owner of most of the city's dry cleaning outlets, as well as the guy who wins Lt. Darlene's heart, which . . .

Pablo Gonzales wants to cut out and roast over a slow fire. Pablo is the brains behind the Aztec Terrorists Society. Pablo's comrades in the pursuit of civic betterment include a lot of other people named Gonzales, none of whom are related. They are, however, all sub-literate, which is something they have in common with the best-selling authors and social lionesses . . .

Rosemary Klein Kantor and Mrs. Bellamy (Chloris) Craig II. Klein Kantor borrows freely from her data bank containing 10,000 popular novels to create her art, some of which contains medium-length words. Chloris Craig, on the other hand, never learned to write (or steal) more than a few three-letter words. Her own best-sellers are actually produced by her lover . . .

Wayne Alexander, ace reporter for the *Duluth Blade,* and the boy who knows who killed Betty Grable. (Betty, you'll remember, was once married to the novelist Henry James [19].) Finally, we present Chloris's husband, the fabulously rich and terminally blasé . . .

Bellamy Craig II, who doesn't mind in the least his wife's affair with Wayne. Craig, in fact, may not have a mind at all, but he does have oceans of money, and in *Duluth* that's what counts.

It may be misleading to talk about character development in *Duluth*. As the above list no doubt suggests, it is peopled by caricatures of stock characters. Stock characters represent types rather than individuals, and are often associated with particular narrative formulas. Stock figures familiar from recent movies and television include the hero or heroine's wisecracking pal, the airhead, the nerd, the supercilious villain with an English accent, the manipulative blonde, the ruthless lawyer, and so on.

The term "stock character" should be understood as descriptive rather than pejorative. From Plautus to Shakespeare, Molière, Fielding, Austen, Dickens, and P. G. Wodehouse, gifted writers often employed stock or conventional figures. The plausible development of realistic and individualized characters supplies only one of many possible narrative pleasures. Stock characters can be handled skillfully or ineptly, can suit the fiction at hand or annoy readers with their hackneyed predictability. Sometimes, stock characters overlap with stereotypes, a fact Vidal exploits to make both funny and serious points in *Duluth*.

In *Duluth*, Vidal uses at least two techniques to parody clumsy management of the stock figures of pop culture. For one, he takes the ready-made clichés that pass for characterization and skews them, sometimes wildly and sometimes slightly, but always to humorous and pointed effect. For example, *Duluth*'s requisite "spectacularly beautiful blue-eyed goddess" is Lieutenant Darlene Ecks of Homicide (6). Her hobby is strip-searching male Mexicans while "thundering out . . . 'Gimme a piece of okra and a pair of prunes' "; her dream is to "open a boutique" (6)—until, that is, she forces Big John at gunpoint to rape her. She then becomes "at last, a woman. Warm and mature. Loving and giving" (68). How-to books on writing often advise aspiring novelists to "humanize" or "deepen" their characters by giving them a surprising trait or two. As *Duluth*'s Darlene demonstrates, this gimmick is as likely to produce a mishmash as it is to provide the illusion of depth.

Another example of Vidal's parodic fun is the representation of Pablo, an illegal immigrant from Mexico. A would-be rapist, he makes the mistake of accosting Darlene. She overpowers, strip-searches, and humiliates him. Pablo then becomes leader of the Aztec Terrorists Society. This may not sound the stuff of humor, but observe how Vidal pretends to create a Hispanic atmosphere for Pablo: "Pablo is like a god in the barrios, his every wish fulfilled by black-eyed señoritas. Whenever he appears for a *cerveza* in a *cantina*, young and old surround him, giving him *abrazos*" (109). All this is even sillier after we've just been told of Pablo and friends that they are "protected by one million illegal aliens with their age-old Aztec eyes and unbreakable code of *omertà*" (109). In fiction at least, *omertà* is the Sicilian Mafia's word for the code of silence. Again, facile techniques and sloppy writing are exposed as absurd. *Duluth*, it should be noted, also scatters inappropriate French about, sometimes blatantly obvious, sometimes ridiculously inapposite.

THEMATIC ISSUES

Through satire, *Duluth* addresses genuine ills in contemporary society, but it does so obliquely. If one had to assign a single, simple moral to this complex novel, it would run along the lines of: Only a culture gone terribly wrong could produce so much terrible art. The picture we get of Duluth only slightly exaggerates how an outsider, a naive European say, might well imagine the United States from our cultural exports. As will be discussed later in this chapter, this picture is distorted, but the cultural ills it distorts are all too real. Certainly, Vidal's familiar themes turn up in the novel: political corruption, public gullibility, failures of American education, the American lack of historical consciousness, and so on. The direct target here, however, is bad art and, to a lesser extent, pompous literary criticism. But as the novel reminds us early on, "every society gets the Duluth that it deserves" (1).

Rogue Duke is a truly dreadful novel, dishonest in every way. Rosemary Klein Kantor, it will be remembered, doesn't actually write her novels; she patches them together from bits and pieces lifted from other novels. Vidal probably alludes here to a branch of recent literary criticism that focuses on "intertextuality." In its extreme form, such criticism asserts that "people don't write books, books write books." In this view, all novels (or plays, poems, or short stories) derive from earlier literary works rather than from an individual writer's perceptions; hence Klein Kantor's claim to "creation by other means!" As Vidal well knows, there's considerable truth in the premise that art imitates art, and the Breckinridge novels, for example, frequently represent life imitating art, rather than the other way around. Still, *Rogue Duke* in all its badness suggests what can happen when intertextuality is unleashed in the absence of any controlling intelligence. Rosemary Klein Kantor's opus only slightly exaggerates the foolishness of too many books.

Of course, a knowledge of literary theory is not at all necessary to enjoy *Rogue Duke* as a parody of popular historical romances, particularly those of the subgenre "regency romance." (A regency romance is set in approximately the years 1811 to 1820, when the Prince of Wales was regent in England; that is, he ruled in the stead of his mad father, King George III. From 1820 to 1830 he ruled in his own right as George IV. Perhaps the best definition of the "regency" in terms of popular fiction would be the years of Jane Austen.) Although specifically a regency—or rather, "Regency-Hyatt"—romance, *Rogue Duke* compiles the gaffes and gaucheries of bad historical fiction in general. The plot is random, repetitive, and preposterous, but most acutely awkward (and hilarious) are the anachronisms (i.e., details impossible for their putative time) and other bloopers. Rosemary Klein Kantor, or her data bank, seems to think, for example, that the husband of a marchioness is a march (rather than a marquess or marquis [61]) and that "Regent" is the prince's given name, he is "known to his intimates as Reggie" (56). Another slip has Beryl wielding her trusty matchlock in 1914—a bit late for the Napoleonic wars (61). And in a touch reminiscent of *Monty Python's Flying Circus* or *Get Smart*, the document Beryl must steal is tidily labeled, "Secret Plan for the Invasion of France" (113). In a society where many people gain their knowledge of history from popular art forms, it is surely incumbent on writers to be as accurate as possible. (In this context, Vidal's *Screening History* is relevant. There he stresses how much historical information and misinformation people glean from movies.)

Regency romances are only one variety of popular novels that Vidal parodies in *Duluth*. Rosemary Klein Kantor's novels are always referred to as set in the "Regency-Hyatt" period, reversing the name of a hotel chain. This reference satirizes a pervasive device of trashy fiction, repeated references to specific brand names. *Duluth* provides brand names most often in the storyline involving Mr. and Mrs. Bellamy Craig II: sheets (on the sofa) by Porthault, briefcase by Gucci, what-not by Knole, clothes by Valentino, tape recorder by Sony (18–19). It may be that writers who turn their novels into unpaid advertisements for luxury goods sincerely believe they're creating atmosphere or delineating character in the process. Or they may be some combination of cynical and lazy, substituting ready-made status symbols for precisely calibrated observation of human behavior. One suspects Vidal suspects the latter, because he associates brand names most often with the ostentatiously fraudulent

Craigs. Either way, Vidal's satire is double-edged. His immediate target is bad writing, but the specific type of bad writing points to a sad truth about contemporary America. That is, in our consumption-driven society, people's identities seem to be tied up in their possessions. We have a tendency to read each other as our labels, brand each other and ourselves with the names of products. *Duluth* is a funny book, but there is nothing funny about the cultural malaise it chronicles.

Vidal's parody in *Duluth* extends beyond the banalities of popular fiction. His invented term *"après* poststructuralism" pokes fun at an intellectual establishment determined to name its own era and, further, much given to defining itself as after something else: poststructuralist, postmodern, even postcontemporary, for example. Too, *après* provides a giggle at the expense of English-speaking literary theorists who have eagerly adopted French theories, often (as Vidal has pointed out) in ignorance of the specifically French milieu—intellectual, academic, linguistic, sociopolitical—that spawned these theories. It is useful to remember that *Duluth* satirizes Americans as, typically, monolingual (through parodying trashy fiction's superficial sprinklings of isolated Spanish or French words). Further, we might even consider literary critics to be as obsessed with brand names as are the writers and readers of current bestsellers, the only distinction being that literary critics brand themselves with adjectival forms of the names of European thinkers (Marxian, Freudian, Lacanian, Derridean, Bakhtinian, and so on).

The particular branch of literary theory most ridiculed in *Duluth* is one we could call structuralist narratology, which seeks to discover immutable laws that govern all narratives. Too, in writing a novel that announces its narrative laws, Vidal both parodies and participates in the tendency of contemporary novels to be "self-reflexive," to be "metafictions," i.e., to comment within themselves on the writing of novels. There is nothing new about this practice; Henry Fielding, for example, theorizes about fiction throughout *Tom Jones* (1749). And many of Vidal's novels call attention to their status as narratives. (See, for example, our discussions of *Julian, Myra Breckinridge, Burr,* and *Live from Golgotha*.) Still, it seems plausible to conclude that Vidal sees an excess of self-conscious metafiction as a defect that typifies the sort of novel he has often disparaged as written by teachers for other teachers to teach.

In *Duluth* Vidal aims his satire at many targets, so many, in fact, that on a quick reading his technique may seem scattershot. Upon close reading, however, parallels among various trajectories of satire can be seen.

A DECONSTRUCTIVE READING OF *DULUTH*

Chapter 5 described deconstruction briefly and demonstrated ways in which *Creation* unsettles the conventional understanding of speech as fully present and prior to writing, of writing as an imitation of speech. Here, we shall argue that *Duluth* deconstructs the conventional understanding of another pair of terms: "author" and "text." (Poststructuralist critics prefer the word "text" to "work" as a general term.) Ordinarily, and reasonably enough, we think of authors as preexisting the texts they create. Thus, "author" would be the primary term in the author/text pair, "text" the secondary or derivative term. That is, an author is the independent origin of a text, while a text requires an author to provide its existence. In this common-sense view, the author creates, or causes, the text. *Duluth*, however, can be read as dismantling our everyday understanding of author/text.

First, *Duluth* severs the connection between author and text. Like Teddy, the narrator of *Kalki*, Chloris Craig is the "author" of texts she doesn't write. (For that matter, Chloris is the author of books she can't read.) Chloris does not cause a text; instead, her authorship is an effect of the books (texts) published under her name. Because she does not write her books, she becomes an author only after a text is written, published, and publicized. In this case, it is fair to say that texts precede and are the origin of Chloris-as-author. Readers may well object at this point that Chloris only pretends to be an author; the real author is Wayne Alexander, Chloris's lover and ghostwriter. In our ordinary sense of the word, which equates the terms "author" and "writer," *Duluth* affirms Wayne's authorship. But what then do we make of Chloris's claim to authorship?

The Chloris/Wayne pair calls for some redefinition, so that author and writer are no longer understood as synonyms. In this rethinking, the writer creates or originates a text, while the author receives the credit for and the royalties from sales of a text. But, drawing this distinction resolves nothing. First, a ghostwriter, Wayne, for example, comes into being as such only when hired by the author, in this case Chloris. Here, the "writer" is an effect of the author's action. With respect to any given text, author and writer require each other; neither exists independently. (*Duluth* signals this interdependence by making Chloris and Wayne lovers.) At this point, it may seem reasonable to argue that the author originates the writer who originates the text. However, this solution just raises another problem: As defined here, "author" implies a role, "writer" an activity. (Copyright law makes distinctions between authors and creators; in fact, "authors" are often corporations.) And, again with respect to any given text, the role of author cannot be played until a text has been written. Further, once publicly established as author, an author can replace his or her ghostwriter. In the figures of Chloris and Wayne, Vidal satirizes the phenomenon of celebrity authorship, much as he does in *Kalki*. Still, *Duluth* insists that the functions of author and writer can be severed and divided between two or more people; neither can be understood as self-sufficient or as the independent origin of the other. Chloris and Wayne need each other, and Chloris-as-author is an effect of the books Wayne writes.

The other "best-selling authoress" in *Duluth* is Rosemary Klein Kantor, author of numerous historical romances and of *Rogue Duke* in particular. Is Klein Kantor the cause or the effect of *Rogue Duke*? Perhaps she is irrelevant. Klein Kantor "writes" her novels, it will be remembered, by combining bits and pieces from her databank containing 10,000 other novels. If Klein Kantor is the author of *Rogue Duke*, the novel's writer is a word processor. To complicate matters further, neither Klein Kantor nor her computer has full control over the characters in *Rogue Duke*. For example, Darlene wanders into the novel (42), only to be spotted by Beryl just before Darlene seduces (if that's the word) a handsome servant, known outside *Rogue Duke* as Big John. Further, Beryl landed in Klein Kantor's novel independently of any author's, writer's, or word processor's choice.

Duluth presents characters hurtled from life into fiction and operating with considerable independence from an author. *Rogue Duke* is created (originated) by a "central processing unit" from shreds and patches of other fictions and unruly characters. *Duluth* depicts the "central processing unit" as a computer with an immense databank. It is easy enough, however, to see that computer as a symbol for an author. Authors, then, are shown to be preceded by—and useless without—innumerable narratives. The portraits of Chloris Craig and Rosemary Klein Kantor argue that we can as easily see authors as the products or effects of texts as the other way around.

There is an additional complication in that we tend to use "author" to refer to writers of only certain kinds of texts. Many texts are indeed written, but seem to have no authors: the instructions for assembling a bookcase, for example, or the telephone book, traffic signs, nutritional content labels, and so on. We are also unlikely to refer to the "author" of a toothpaste commercial, a routine newspaper story, or a promotional letter from a bank. The word "author" carries connotations of creating something more substantial, somehow, than the preceding examples. Neither Darlene's "Gimme a piece of okra and a pair of prunes"—however vivid—nor Pablo's confessional diary qualifies them to be called authors. Within the fictional worlds of *Duluth*—and Duluth—these "compositions" have serious repercussions. Public importance is apparently not the criterion for an "authored" text. There is something about kinds of texts that determines whether they have "authors." (For further discussion of this matter, see Foucault, "What Is an Author?")

Along these lines, we would argue that Gore Vidal is an author precisely because he has written novels, as well as plays and collections of essays. The precise lines here are not well defined, but it is unlikely that, taken alone, even the large number of periodical essays would call for the term "author." We say, for example, that "X writes for *Time* or *Newsweek*; Y is the author of several short stories and books." Similarly, Rosemary Klein Kantor is called "author" because of *Rogue Duke*, not because of "Duluth," the soap opera. The texts one writes determine whether one is an author. In yet another sense, texts create authors rather than the reverse.

Of course, the final joke in *Duluth* is about authorship. In the last two paragraphs, the reader meets an author who is not human at all, but rather Tricia, the six-foot centipede. Recently arrived in a pink spaceship and leader of a buggy *coup d'etat*, Tricia is rewriting *Duluth*, erased by Klein Kantor. But characters in *Duluth* have moved this spaceship across the landscape simply by moving a thumbtack on a map. Authorship remains a riddle in the world of *Duluth* and *après* poststructuralism.

NOTES

1. Deus ex machina, literally "god from the machine," refers to the staging apparatus in a classical Greek amphitheater by which a god was lowered onto the stage, usually at a play's end and in order to resolve a tangled problem. Thus the expression has come to mean any contrived resolution to a narrative problem.

16

Live from Golgotha
(1992)

One hopes, of course, that Vidal will continue to amuse and edify, delight and instruct us with many as yet unwritten novels. From a critic's selfish perspective, however, *Live from Golgotha* would make a fitting capstone for a remarkable life's work. Subtitled *The Gospel According to Gore Vidal*, this novel recapitulates the themes, genres, motifs, and hobby horses that have woven through Vidal's writing over the past fifty years. Like *Julian* and *Creation, Live from Golgotha* is set in the ancient world; like *Myron* it plays with notions of time travel; like *Messiah* and *Kalki* it ponders religious cults and apocalypse; like *Dark Green, Bright Red* and the Edgar Box mysteries, and for that matter *Burr* and *Duluth*, its surprise ending is carefully prepared for, the clues available to the attentive reader just as in a classic detective story; like *Myra Breckinridge, Myron,* and *Duluth*, it juxtaposes multiple literary parodies. Similarly, *Live from Golgotha* pursues many of the themes one expects from Vidal. The present rewrites the past; politics, religion, and show business are indistinguishable; sexual preference is fluid, unstable, anything but categorical; as exposed in language, late twentieth-century America is dazzling for its amalgam of the pretentious and the banal; Americans are ignorant of the past and unable to recognize the future almost at hand as their economic and imperial power dwindles.

POINT OF VIEW

Live from Golgotha is narrated by Saint Timothy, writing in the first person. At the closest we can get to a realistic level in this surreal novel, Timothy is writing in 96 A.D. of events he has witnessed or been told about over the previous fifty years. Like the narrators of *Julian* and *Messiah*, Timothy writes from memory about the past while under considerable pressure from a threatening present. He intends to write an account of events from the Nativity to the Resurrection of Jesus in order to preserve the story of Christianity as told in the Gospels. To his horror and bemusement, Timothy is frequently interrupted by visitors from the future or, more precisely, from multiple points in future time. Some of the visitors he calls kibitzers—those who watch and comment on the action. Some are merely tourists; a small number, however, want to change the past. Among those who want to interfere with history are General Electric executives Chet Claypoole, Marvin Wasserstein, and Dr. Cutler. (Cutler returns from two distinct future times; his younger self is called "Cutler One," the older, "Cutler Two.") In this novel, figures from the future have the power to erase, rewrite, and scramble the past—and thus the future as well. And, as Saint Paul tells Timothy, without the Gospels, we would have "no Christian story worth telling, no Crusades, Lourdes, Oral Roberts, Wojtyla" (9).

As one might expect, however, *Live from Golgotha* is neither so straightforward nor so solemn as this précis suggests. In fact it is hilarious. *Live from Golgotha* casts a skeptical eye on any certitude, including its own. Roughly, one could say that this novel derives its plot from the New Testament, its technological conventions from science fiction, its mode of suspense from espionage thrillers, its enigmatic format from the classic detective story, and its language from just about everywhere.

PLOT DEVELOPMENT

It is barely possible to list the chronology relevant to *Live from Golgotha*:

1. Jesus is crucified.
2. Paul spreads the gospel (literally, "good tidings") to gentiles.

3. Paul has conflicts with James (Jesus's brother), who tolerates, but doesn't like, sharing a messiah with gentiles.

4. Timothy becomes a follower of Paul's, is circumcised, and eventually becomes a bishop.

5. In 96 A.D., as Timothy dreams his recurring nightmare about the circumcision, Paul appears and warns him that someone is erasing the Gospels.

6. Everything that happened between 96 A.D. and the 1990s happens.

7. In the 1990s, a mysterious figure called the Hacker begins erasing tapes and thus changing history. (The fictional premise here is that all the events of history are preserved only on videotapes.)

8. Armed with a technology for time-travel, NBC arranges to broadcast the Crucifixion live for viewers in the 1990s.

With these last two events, all the preceding ones are altered or threatened with alteration. The general direction of the plot is backward, toward the Crucifixion, which becomes a focal point for confusion. Timothy discovers that Judas, not Jesus, was crucified at Golgotha. The early disciples were perfectly aware of this substitution, but found the myth of resurrection useful in building support for their cause—the overthrow of the Romans. Suddenly, this most significant occasion of Western history is exposed as a fraud. But—and here things get complicated—only for a time. Having discovered the original deception, Timothy cleverly manipulates events for the "Live from Golgotha" broadcast. Through Timothy's maneuvers, on camera Jesus is crucified—in the person of Marvin Wasserstein, who is also the Hacker. Thus present (or future) intervention changes the past, in this case adjusting actual events to match the long lie of history.

Technically, plot development in *Live from Golgotha* resembles that in Laurence Sterne's *The Life and Opinions of Tristam Shandy, Gentleman* (1760). There, Tristam promises readers the story of his life, but he digresses so frequently that we learn almost nothing about his biography. So too, Timothy is charged with recording the life of Christ as given in the Gospels, but he is repeatedly distracted by events as they happen and by his efforts to place his own gospel in context. Like Tristam Shandy, Timothy never manages to write the narrative he's attempting.

Obviously, such a plot could easily come across as chaotic. Vidal anchors the action, however, in conventions drawn from four popular genres: science fiction, fantasy, the espionage thriller, and the classic detective story.

Live from Golgotha depends upon the notion of time travel, or the ability to travel across time as we are accustomed to travel across space. Although scholars who study science fiction debate the topic, for our purposes we can call tales of time travel science fiction insofar as they attribute such travel to a technologically plausible although as yet nonexistent method. In contrast, time travel in the genre of fantasy relies upon magic or the inexplicable. In both cases, convention requires consistency. That is, once the terms and contingencies for traveling from one time to another are established, readers expect that the plot will adhere to its posited conditions. Thus the fact that Vidal mingles modes of time travel is less important, at least in terms of the convention, than that each mode remain internally consistent.

Vidal is scrupulous about maintaining an illusion of consistency. *Live from Golgotha* presents three methods for traversing time:

1. As a hologram recorded on futuristic videotape: "What with rewind and fast forward, *nothing* is ever gone. All you have to do is know how to work the machine" (14).

2. Through a molecular scrambler and transmitter that reassembles objects and—eventually—persons at an earlier date. Thus Timothy's Sony television arrives in 96 A.D.

3. Channeling through a medium: "All of time is just a flat round plate," at least according to the New Age tourists and kibitzers (16).

Each method has its distinctive rules, and Vidal skillfully uses these distinctions both as clues to the novel's mystery and as thematic vehicles.

Live from Golgotha also borrows from the espionage thriller, and does so in ways especially appropriate to a post-Cold War world. Like a good spy thriller, *Live from Golgotha* sets high stakes. In Vidal's novel Timothy's task is to save Christianity and thus preserve Western history as we have known it since the death of Jesus. And, crucial to suspense, our hero has a time limit. Unless Timothy can complete his gospel and successfully hide it before he too is erased by the Hacker, all knowledge of Christ and Christianity will be lost or garbled. Further, the primary action in

Live from Golgotha is a quest for the identity of the Hacker, who is described (à la John LeCarré) as a mole. Questions of the Hacker's identity and motives are managed much as they might be in a classic detective story. Throughout *Live from Golgotha* clues are planted, clues that in retrospect foreshadow events and revelations at the novel's end: Why can Marvin Wasserstein shake hands when the other time-travelers cannot? And just what kind of plastic surgery has the second Dr. Cutler had?

CHARACTER DEVELOPMENT

Live from Golgotha is peopled with figures from the ancient and modern worlds. Most have familiar names, from Nero and Pontius Pilate to Mary Baker Eddy and Shirley MacLaine, and all are familiar types. Unlike the historical figures in the "American Chronicles," most of those in *Live from Golgotha* have been dead for nearly 2,000 years. This temporal distance allows for considerable license in their depiction, as does the novel's satiric and surreal tone. That is, no one could think Vidal is painting a literalistic portrait of Saint Paul or Saint Peter. Indeed, in this novel characterization generally tends toward caricature, with some touches of *roman à clef* (see the discussion of *roman à clef* in Chapter 13.) Priscilla is a good example. Ostensibly a representation of Saint Priscilla, who was an influential early Christian, Vidal's Priscilla is yet another of his thinly disguised portraits of the writer Anaïs Nin. (Maria Verlaine in *The City and the Pillar* and Marietta Donegal in *Two Sisters* also caricature Nin.) Priscilla's many affairs, her complaisant husband, and her extravagant language all suggest Nin. Most important are her diaries. Nin published several volumes of her diaries, often to the discomfiture or outrage of people mentioned in them. So too, Priscilla gives public readings of her wildly inaccurate diaries. (Vidal's response to the diary in which he figures can be found in "The Fourth Diary of Anaïs Nin," *United States* 1149–54.)

Some of the characters in *Live from Golgotha* are simply types, which need no specific antecedents. Chester Claypoole, for example, is the model of an earnest functionary; he shares his surname with at least seven other characters in Vidal's writing (*Visit to a Small Planet*, *Death Likes It Hot*, *Myron*, *Duluth*, and—very briefly—*Burr*, *1876*, and *Hollywood*). A further complication in *Live from Golgotha*'s characterizations is that the novel presents people as inherently unstable. Not that they are necessarily unhinged, although some certainly are, but rather, they change without explanation. Cutlers One and Two offer the best example here. Comic as they are, they raise questions about continuity in human personalities. Are Cutler One and Cutler Two the same person, as the novel asserts, or are they two different people, as the novel also asserts? In a novel whose characters are defined significantly by their loyalties, can the two Cutlers, with their opposing allegiances, be a single person? The novel also rejects memory as a secure source of continuity. *Live from Golgotha*'s only fully rounded character is Timothy himself. And he is utterly confused about when and whether events happened in his "original" past or the past as rewritten under pressure from Saint (as Timothy calls Saint Paul), Claypoole, the Hacker, and so on. According to Saint, what Timothy thinks are his "recollections of Rome" cannot be trusted "since memory is easily tampered with not only by the Prince of this World and other demons but by a constant exposure to CNN on television" (174). At any rate, all the important characters meet on Golgotha in 33 A.D. Some are kibitzers and tourists; some are media hacks; some, however, are determined to claim the Crucifixion for their own causes, their own loyalties, their own corporations.

THEMATIC ISSUES

As suggested earlier, *Live from Golgotha* recapitulates many of Vidal's recurring themes: founding moments, politicized religion, media power, relations between past and present, problems of historiography, the pernicious banality of American public discourse. It is thematically significant that as a narrator Timothy resembles *Messiah*'s Eugene Luther in several ways. Both write about the founding moments of a religion; moreover, they write with the ominous knowledge that their narratives may well be the last opportunity to record these founding events with any accuracy. The situation of *Creation*'s narrator is similar in that he was present at the murder of Zoroaster, and one theme of that novel is the steady erosion and distortion of Zoroaster's teachings by a venal and self-serving priesthood. Along the same lines, one theme of *Messiah* is the calculated peddling of Cavesway by public relations and advertising experts. *Live from Golgotha*, however, refuses such nostalgic comfort, refuses the illusion that there was formerly a pure truth, now corrupted by human greed and hunger for power. In Vidal's novel, Christianity has been from its beginnings a product hustled by a self-promoting priesthood, itself indistinguishable from any other group that combines marketing tactics and show business to move its product. Like any good entertainer, Saint wants to keep his audience's attention, a tough challenge when he must go into dull theological detail. He manages this feat ingeniously: "He invented, all by himself, *with no professional guidance of any kind*, tap dancing" (35). There would be no point to this performance, however, should it fail to produce converts and contributions. Timothy describes the typical founding of a church: "First a hellfire sermon from Saint. Then the collection. Then names and addresses for our master Holy Rolodex while Saint would take appointments for baptisms and so on. Finally, before skipping town, he'd appoint some deacons and deaconesses and lo! and behold the First Pauline Church of Philippi would open its doors for business" (36).

The theology presupposed in *Live from Golgotha* can be summarized as follows. The historical Jesus was one of many claimants to the role and title of Messiah, the king of the Jews who, according to prophecies in the Hebrew Bible, would rescue the Jews from Roman domination. Further, his original disciples were dedicated to overthrowing the Romans in Jerusalem rather than to promulgating belief in any sort of afterlife or salvation. (Vidal uses the term "Zionist" to describe James and his followers; biblical historians have used the term "Zealot" to describe similar groups, but this term is debated.) Saint Paul, then, invented Christianity, primarily by grafting an ethics onto a militant political movement. As Timothy tells us, instead of the "hard-line message" originally preached by Jesus, Paul has created a "nicer, more mature religion" including the "usual vague end-of-the-world predictions but, meanwhile, all God's children would be living by the golden rule" (194). Indeed, for all his hucksterism, Saint Paul comes off pretty well, especially in comparison with his competitors for defining Christianity. This perspective marks a change from *Messiah*, where a cynical public relations expert, also named Paul, organizes and elaborates what began as a small, simple message. In Vidal's view, Christianity is ultimately as death-dealing as Cavesway in *Messiah* or the Hinduism of *Kalki*. (See his essay, "Monotheism and its Discontents," *The Decline and Fall* 73–88.) In *Live from Golgotha*, however, what is valuable about the Christian religion—a system of ethics—was supplied by Saint Paul, a figure Vidal elsewhere condemns. (See *Views From a Window* 100, 300.)

Many writers rehearse the theme of how the past weighs upon the present. In contrast, Vidal keeps reminding his readers that the present also weighs upon the past. That is, every era constructs the history it wants or needs. Vidal's essays responding to attacks on his novel *Lincoln* explicitly make this point. In Vidal's historical novels, he addresses this theme by drawing attention to contradictions between currently accepted interpretations and documentary evidence. In *Live from Golgotha*, he uses the conventional device of time travel to signify almost allegorically ways in which present desires change the reality of the past. If the Hacker—in the present—succeeds in erasing all the tapes of the early Christian past, he changes history. Further, through the efforts of Timothy and others, the facts of the past are literally altered—to match the lie that has been history. Restated symbolically, recorded history may lie, but that lie becomes the truth.

All this is enough to start one's head spinning, but Vidal turns the screw one more time. The novel's final page reveals that everything the novel has encouraged us to worry about or puzzle over is beside the point. The novel ends with the first page of Timothy's gospel, in which Jesus is born of "the goddess Amaterasu" and we learn that Timothy was born in "Lystra, in Asia Minor, a province of the empire of Japan" (227). The rest is in Japanese. To the victor belong the spoils, including religion. In a conclusion as carefully and deceptively prepared for as Agatha Christie produced at her best, Vidal reiterates a point he has made elsewhere: "If the foreseeable future is not nuclear, it will be Asiatic, some combination of Japan's advanced technology with China's resourceful landmass" (*The Decline and Fall* 10).

Like *Creation* and *Julian*, *Live from Golgotha* argues that religions serve political purposes. Vidal's novel presents a contest for the Crucifixion; the mystery of death and resurrection at the heart of Christian theology becomes a counter in geopolitical power games.

STYLE

Stylistically, *Live from Golgotha* is a parodic masterpiece, laying bare the hucksterism that saturates our society, converting everything from floods to famines to dysfunctional families into television fodder. The novel displays the linguistic mannerisms and recognizable idioms of many categories of speech and writing, most of them dreadful, all available for parodic deflation. This stylistic virtuosity can be seen as the verbal equivalent of the novel's thematic concerns. While amusing in themselves, the stylistic parodies are also vehicles for satiric social commentary. (*Duluth* employs similar techniques.)

The novel's biblical characters often speak the language of the New

Testament as translated in the King James Version. So, in response to James, Paul mutters, "Whom the Lord loveth He chasteneth" (109, Hebrews 12:6), and Peter tells Paul and Timothy, "The grass withereth, and the flower thereof falleth away" (170, I Peter 1:24).

Paul is at least as likely, however, to sound like the leader of a seminar on salesmanship: "Saint always said that after our logo, the cross, the Holy Rolodex was the ball game" (55). He also can sound like an old hand in the world of show business clichés: "A gripping yarn, well told. With a laugh riot in the second act" (145).

This shifting of styles is a running joke in the novel as well as a satiric comment on the banal language of today's commercial culture. Paul's stylistic range, however, may also jolt readers into recognizing the absurdity of making biblical characters speak as if they were Shakespeare's contemporaries. Early seventeenth-century English is no closer to New Testament Greek (*koinē*) than is today's. In fact, the *koinē* of the New Testament was not a literary dialect, let alone an archaic one, so the retention of the King James Version actually runs counter to the original's level of formality. Vidal's novel exposes the practice of assigning seventeenth-century speech patterns to biblical characters as a convention, and a rather silly one at that. A similar point is made when as Timothy flees naked from Nero, Petronius asks him, "Quo Vadis?" This is the Vulgate (405 A.D.) translation's rendering of Jesus's "Where are you going?" at the Last Supper (John 16:5). Equally to the point, it is the title of a 1896 novel by Henryk Sienkiewicz and a popular film of 1951. And literal translation can be amusing as well; Timothy always refers to Saint Peter as "Rock," which is of course an accurate translation of Petrus, but which suggests a thick skull and sounds to modern ears like the stage name of a movie star.

Characters in *Live from Golgotha* also speak the languages of journalism, including television news, celebrity gossip columns, and the self-help and self-discovery twaddle that passes for insight across all of today's print, broadcast, and electronic media. Here are just a few samples: anchorperson, ratings-wise, flacks, learning experience, high fiber, truly supportive, funny money schemes, faux gallique, tastefully appointed, and so on. There are so many targets here that it seems pointless to insist that one or another is primary. Still, the argument could well be made that Vidal aims his sharpest satire at what we could call the pseudo-historical. Much of what passes for historical fiction is no more than costume drama, the representation of thoroughly contemporary characters given a superficial gloss of another time and place through their clothing, possessions, and the odd vocabulary item. (Vidal parodies such novels in *Duluth*; see Chapter 15.)

Such nonsense must irritate Vidal, who works so strenuously to re-capture specificity of language and attitudes in his historical novels. In-deed, even in *Live from Golgotha*—where the collapsing of present and past is calculated—Vidal takes pains to account for Timothy's anachro-nistic language. For example, Timothy tells us that he's decided to in-clude "descriptions lifted from the notebooks of certain *future* writers that, thanks to Chet, it has been my pleasure to peruse" (53). Chet has also supplied Timothy with a computerized phrase selector, "a useful aid to the mastering of an easy selling style during your average es-chatological era" (55; eschatology is the study of last things, the end of the world when the day of judgment is at hand). And at one point, Timothy worries that "the boob tube is beginning to affect [his] prose" (81).

Vidal's linguistic parodies are great fun and perhaps serve as tonic reminders to avoid frozen phrases and automatic cant in one's own writ-ing. But these are pointed parodies, and the verbal jokes speak seriously about serious issues. As we've seen, the religious leaders in the novel speak the languages of salesmanship and show biz. Among Paul's last instructions to Timothy is a reminder to keep "the Follow-up Letters" in mind (173). When Saint Paul competes with the priestesses of Diana at Ephesus, the stakes are couched not as souls but as box-office revenue. There is surely a direct jibe here at television evangelists; *Live from Gol-gotha* was written around the time Jim Bakker, Jimmy Swaggert, and Oral Roberts were making scandalous headlines. It is easy to imagine an in-terpretation of the novel as primarily a satiric attack in the tradition of Sinclair Lewis's novel *Elmer Gantry*, which exposes evangelical avarice and cynicism. To the long-standing theme of exploitation of faith by those greedy for personal gain and aggrandizement, Vidal can add a technological cheapening of religion with a corresponding increase in the number of potential dupes. Given the context of Vidal's other novels as well as his non-fiction, however, the stronger argument is that Christi-anity and other religions, both Western and Middle Eastern, have always been about fund raising and box office appeal. For example, when "Live from Golgotha" is scheduled, Cutler Two explains that the network will give "equal time to Mohammed, while AIPAC has insisted on a twelve-part series based on how Moses and God established the Jews in Pales-tine forever" (199). Similarly, when the director praises Timothy's performance as anchorman at Golgotha, our hero replies modestly, "Well, I am a bishop" (221).

A DECONSTRUCTIVE READING OF *LIVE FROM GOLGOTHA*

Live from Golgotha can be read as a thoroughly and knowingly deconstructive novel. Indeed, there would be little point in a routine deconstruction of *Live from Golgotha* precisely because the novel overtly shares the specific skepticism of deconstruction as practiced by Jacques Derrida. (Readers may want to review the discussion of deconstruction in Chapter 5.) As a philosophical stance, deconstruction is suspicious of every effort to locate centers, origins, and other sorts of organizing principles. Deconstructive techniques demonstrate that the supposed center or origin can easily be seen to depend on or derive from some other center or origin. Literary deconstruction looks for ways in which a given literary text seems to assert some sort of center while simultaneously undermining that center.

Live from Golgotha can be read as deconstructing the founding moment, the center, of Christianity. At the same time, the novel also deconstructs a faith more widespread even than Christianity. Vidal's novel attacks our late twentieth-century faith in live television coverage as a reliable source (or origin) for getting at the truth of events. The novel's title combines the sources/origins/centers to be deconstructed in the novel. *Live from Golgotha*—the very words appeal to a desire to witness for oneself the moment of Christ's Crucifixion and Resurrection. "If only," one can imagine people thinking, "there had been TV cameras to record the Crucifixion and Resurrection, we could know for sure, could be certain of the truth." Such desires are by no means limited to Christians. Any longing for certain, pure, and stable knowledge of the past is likely, in the late twentieth century, to evoke similar wishes. In *Live from Golgotha*, Vidal seems to be arguing that even if we could, by some technological or angelic miracle, view live television coverage of the Crucifixion, say, or the battle of Marathon, or the invention of the wheel, we could be no more certain about ultimate truths than we already are.

Let us consider how *Live from Golgotha* depicts the Crucifixion as the origin/source/center of Christianity. Here the term "logo" is relevant. As Timothy observes, the cross is Christianity's logo. In another instance of Vidal's serious punning, we are reminded that "logo" is both contemporary advertising jargon for a corporate symbol and classical Greek for "word" (*logō*, dative). In the New Testament, the Gospel of John opens, "In the beginning was the Word, and the Word was with God, and the Word was God" (John 1.1). And "Word" translates *logos*, which provides our advertising term "logo." Paul tells Timothy, "It's tough trying to hang on to a trademark" (41). Vidal's novel, of course, recounts efforts of various people and groups to enlist the Crucifixion for their own purposes, to stake a claim to the cross and to define its meaning. We could say, then, that the novel presents a contest for the logo, a contest for the logos.

In *Live from Golgotha*, the logos radiates a divine past, a contested history in the process of being rewritten. In deconstructive fashion, we can state the relevant binary oppositions in *Live from Golgotha* as religion/power and history/power. In many societies religion explicitly authorizes the government. And just about everywhere, the past is invoked to authorize, justify, and legitimize the present distribution of power. *Live from Golgotha* reverses these conventionally assumed hierarchal relationships. Most often, people think of the "ruling class" (under whatever name it is given) as deriving its authority from religion or history or some combination thereof. That is, we ordinarily think that history and religion precede current governmental officials and practices and give them their meaning; hence, for example, a concern for what the founding fathers "really" meant in the U.S. Constitution. As *Live from Golgotha* insists, however, we might more accurately say that the "ruling class" uses its authority to construct a past to serve its own interests. (Of course, such construction need not be deliberate or conscious. Indeed, it is probably all the more effective when the powerful believe their own myths.) The final serious joke in *Live from Golgotha* insists that when power changes hands, the past will change as well. The logo/logos central to our culture will itself be appropriated by the next superpower. In this sense, *Live from Golgotha* can perhaps be seen as a futuristic coda to Vidal's "American Chronicles."

Bibliography

Robert J. Stanton has published an annotated bibliography of writing by and about Gore Vidal through March 1978 (listed below). We have thus included very few entries from that period and, for ease of reference, have retained Stanton's short titles for reviews. Even beginning in 1978, a comprehensive bibliography would swell this book beyond a reasonable size. We have therefore been selective, emphasizing commentary relevant to the novels. We have listed in brackets the editions we cite.

WORKS BY GORE VIDAL

Novels by Gore Vidal

Burr: A Novel. New York: Random House, 1973 [Ballantine, 1982].

The City and the Pillar. New York: E. P. Dutton, 1948. Rev. edn., New York: E. P. Dutton, 1965 [Ballantine, 1979].

Creation: A Novel. New York: Random House, 1981.

Dark Green, Bright Red. New York: E. P. Dutton, 1950. Rev. edn., New York: New American Library, 1968 [Ballantine, 1978].

Duluth. New York: Random House, 1983 [Ballantine, 1984].

1876: A Novel. New York: Random House, 1976 [Ballantine, 1976].

Empire: A Novel. New York: Random House, 1987 [Ballantine, 1988].

Hollywood: A Novel. New York: Random House, 1990 [Ballantine, 1990].

In a Yellow Wood. New York: E. P. Dutton, 1947.

The Judgment of Paris. New York: E. P. Dutton, 1952. Rev. edn., Boston: Little, Brown, 1965 [Ballantine, 1978].

Julian: A Novel. Boston: Little, Brown, 1964 [Ballantine, 1986].

Kalki: A Novel. New York: Random House, 1978 [Ballantine, 1978].

Lincoln: A Novel. New York: Random House, 1984 [Ballantine, 1985].

Live from Golgotha: The Gospel According to Gore Vidal. New York: Random House, 1992 [Penguin, 1993].

Messiah. New York: E. P. Dutton, 1954. Rev. edn., Boston: Little, Brown, 1965 [Panther, 1973].

Myra Breckinridge. Boston: Little, Brown, 1968 [Vintage, 1986].

Myron: A Novel. New York: Random House, 1974 [Vintage, 1986].

A Search for the King: A Twelfth-Century Legend. New York: E. P. Dutton, 1950 [Ballantine, 1978].

The Season of Comfort. New York: E. P. Dutton, 1949.

Two Sisters: A Memoir in the Form of a Novel. Boston: Little, Brown, 1970 [Bantam, 1971].

Washington, D.C.: A Novel. Boston: Little, Brown, 1967 [Ballantine, 1976].

Williwaw. New York: E. P. Dutton, 1946 [Ballantine, 1978].

Novels by Vidal Writing as Edgar Box

Death Before Bedtime. New York: E. P. Dutton, 1953.

Death in the Fifth Position. New York: E. P. Dutton, 1952.

Death Likes It Hot. New York: E. P. Dutton, 1954.

Short Stories

"Lincoln." *Atlantic*, May 1984: 37–65.

"The Making of the President." *Harper's Magazine*, May 1987: 31–34.

A Thirsty Evil: Seven Short Stories (collection). New York: Zero Press, 1956.

Other Books by Vidal

Armageddon? Essays 1983–1987. London: André Deutsch, 1987 [Grafton, 1989].

At Home: Essays 1982–1988. New York: Random House, 1988 [Vintage, 1990].

The Decline and Fall of the American Empire. Berkeley: Odonian, 1992.

Homage to Daniel Shays: Collected Essays, 1952–1972. New York: Random House, 1972.

Matters of Fact and Fiction (Essays 1973–1976). New York: Random House, 1977.

Palimpsest: A Memoir. New York: Random House, 1995.

Reflections Upon a Sinking Ship. Boston: Little, Brown, 1969.

Rocking the Boat. Boston: Little, Brown, 1962.

Screening History (The William E. Massey Sr. Lectures in the History of American Civilization, 1991). Cambridge, Mass.: Harvard University Press, 1992.

The Second American Revolution and Other Essays (1976–1982). New York: Random House, 1982.

Sex, Death, and Money. New York: Bantam Books, 1968.

United States (Essays 1952–1992). New York: Random House, 1993.

A View From the Diners' Club: Essays 1987–1991. London: Andre Deutsch, 1991.

Views From a Window: Conversations With Gore Vidal. Edited by Robert J. Stanton and Gore Vidal. Secaucus, N.J.: Lyle Stuart, 1980.

Plays

The Best Man: A Play About Politics. Boston: Little, Brown, 1960.

On the March to the Sea: A Southern Tragedy. Evergreen Playscript Series. New York: Grove Press, n.d.

Romulus: A New Comedy, Adapted From a Play by Friedrich Dürrenmatt. New York: Dramatists Play Service, 1962.

Three Plays. London: William Heinemann, 1962.

Visit to a Small Planet: A Comedy Akin to Vaudeville. Boston: Little, Brown, 1957.

Visit to a Small Planet and Other Television Plays. Boston: Little, Brown, 1956.

Articles, Essays, and Reviews Published in Periodicals and Books

"The Agreed-Upon Facts," in William Zinsser, ed. *Paths of Resistance: The Art and Craft of the Political Novel.* Boston: Houghton Mifflin, 1989. 125–152.

"All's Fair: Love, War, and Running for President." *New York Times Book Review,* 18 September 1994: 1.

"The Birds and the Bees." *Nation,* 28 October 1991: 509–511.

"Choking in Holy Smoke." *New Statesman and Society,* 26 June 1992: 12–14.

"Closest Companion: The Unknown Story of the Intimate Friendship Between Franklin Roosevelt and Margaret Suckley." *New York Review of Books,* 11 May 1995: 4–6.

"The Con-Man as Peck's Bad Boy." *Newsweek,* 13 July 1987: 20.

"Cue the Green God, Ted." *Nation,* 7 August 1989: 153–158.

"Dawn Powell, the American Writer." *New York Review of Books,* 5 November 1987: 52–60.

"The Deadly Sins/Pride: The Most Unnerving Sin." *New York Times Book Review,* 4 July 1993: 3.

"The Durrell-Miller Letters 1935–80." *Times Literary Supplement,* 9 September 1988: 979–980.

"E. M. Forster." *Paris Review,* Winter 1987: 211–212.

"The Empire Lovers Strike Back." *Nation,* 22 March 1986: 350–351.

"The Essential Mencken." *Nation,* 26 August 1991: 228–231.

"Every Eckermann Has His Own." *New York Review of Books,* 27 October 1988: 82–83.

"Ford Madox Ford." *Times Literary Supplement,* 22 June 1990: 659–660.

"Founding Father Knows Best: Notes on Our Patriarchal State." *Whole Earth Review*, Spring 1991: 22–27.

"Geopolitical Thoughts: Requiem for the American Empire." *Nation*, 11 January 1986: 1–7.

"Get Gay and Save the Planet." *New Statesman and Society*, 14 August 1992: 12–13.

"Henry James." *New York Review of Books*, 6 November 1986: 7–10.

"How to Take Back Our Country." *Nation*, 4 June 1988: 781–784.

"In the Lair of the Octopus." *Nation*, 5 June 1995: 792–794.

"JFK's War Games." *New Statesman and Society*, 26 November 1993: 24.

"Letter From America." *New Statesman and Society*, 6 May 1994: 11.

"Lincoln Up Close." *New York Review of Books*, 15 August 1991: 21–22.

"Little Wilson and Big God." *New York Review of Books*, 7 May 1987: 3–5.

"Main Street and Babbit." *New York Review of Books*, 8 October 1992: 14–19.

"Making a Mess of the American Empire." *Newsweek*, 11 January 1993: 30–31.

"Monotheism and Its Discontents." *Nation*, 13 July 1992: 37–41.

"Notes on Our Patriarchal State." *Nation*, 27 August 1990: 185–188.

"Remembering Orson Welles." *New York Review of Books*, 1 June 1989: 12–16.

"R.I.P., R.M.N." *Nation*, 16 May 1994: 652–653.

"Scott's Case." *New York Review of Books*, 1 May 1980: 12–20.

"The Sixties: The Last Journal, 1960–1972." *New York Review of Books*, 4 November 1993: 57–59.

"Some Jews and the Gays." *Nation*, 14 November 1981: 489–497.

"State of the Union, 1980." *Esquire*, August 1980: 62.

"Strike Out the State." *New Statesman and Society*, 6 January 1995: 20–21.

"The Thirty Years Wars: Dispatches and Diversions of a Radical Journalist 1965–1994." *Nation*, 12 June 1995: 832–835.

"Time for a People's Convention." *Nation*, 27 January 1992: 73–77.

"The Union of the State: Comes the Devolution." *Nation* 26 December 1994: 789–791.

"Willie: The Life of W. Somerset Maugham." *New York Review of Books*, 1 February 1990: 39–44.

WORKS ABOUT GORE VIDAL

Books

Dick, Bernard F. *The Apostate Angel: A Critical Study of Gore Vidal*. New York: Random House, 1974.

Kiernan, Robert F. *Gore Vidal*. New York: Frederick Ungar, 1982.

Mitzel, John, and Steven Abbot. *Myra & Gore: A New View of Myra Breckinridge and a Candid Interview With Gore Vidal. A Book for Vidalophiles*. Dorchester, Mass.: Manifest Destiny Books, 1974.

Parini, Jay, ed. *Gore Vidal: Writer Against the Grain*. New York: Columbia University Press, 1992.

Stanton, Robert J. *Gore Vidal: A Primary and Secondary Bibliography*. Boston: G. K. Hall, 1978.

White, Ray Lewis. *Gore Vidal*. Boston: Twayne, 1968.

Reviews and Criticism

Barton, David. "Narrative Patterns in the Novels of Gore Vidal." *Notes on Contemporary American Literature*, September 1981: 3–9.

Clemons, Walter. "Gore Vidal's Chronicle of America." *Newsweek*, 9 June 1984: 74–75, 78–79.

Fleming, Thomas. "Inventing Our Probable Past." *New York Times Book Review*, 6 July 1986: 1.

Goodman, Walter. "History as Fiction." *New Leader*, 16 May 1988: 11–12.

Hines, Samuel M., Jr. "Political Change in American Perspectives From the Popular Historical Novels of Michener and Vidal." In *Political Mythology and Popular Fiction*. Ernest J. Yanarella and Lee Sigelman, eds. Westport, Conn.: Greenwood, 1988. 81–89.

Osteen, Mark. "Paths of Resistance: The Art and Craft of the Political Novel." *Modern Fiction Studies*, Summer 1991: 357–358.

Pease, Donald E. "Citizen Vidal and Mailer's America." *Raritan: A Quarterly Review*, Spring 1992: 72–98.

Shatsky, Joel. "Gore Vidal (1925–)." In *Contemporary Gay American Novelists: A Bio-Bibliographical Critical Sourcebook*. Emmanuel S. Nelson, ed. Westport, Conn.: Greenwood, 1993. 375–80.

Tatum, James. "The 'Romanitas' of Gore Vidal." *Raritan: A Quarterly Review*, Spring 1992: 99–122.

REVIEWS AND CRITICISM OF THE NOVELS

Untitled items are book reviews.

Williwaw

Daniels, Jonathan. "Dirty Weather." *Saturday Review of Literature*, 6 July 1946: 27–28.

Fields, Arthur C. "Turbulence of the Sea." New York *Herald Tribune Weekly Book Review*, 23 June 1946: 17.

Prescott, Orville. "Books of the Times." *New York Times*, 17 June 1946: 19.

S[tevens], A[ustin]. "Aleutian Twister." *New York Times Book Review*, 23 June 1946: 4.

In a Yellow Wood

Aldridge, John W. "The New Generation of Writers: With Some Reflections on the Older Ones." *Harper's Magazine*, November 1947: 423–432.

Anon. *Kirkus*, 15 January 1947: 43.

Anon. *New Yorker*, 22 March 1947: 103.

Barr, Donald. "The Veteran's Choice." *New York Times Book Review*, 16 March 1947: 10.

The City and the Pillar

McLaughlin, Richard. "Precarious Status." *Saturday Review of Literature*, 10 January 1948: 14–15.

Summers, Claude J. " 'The Cabin and the River,' Gore Vidal's *The City and the Pillar*." *Gay Fictions: Wilde to Stonewall: Studies in a Male Homosexual Literary Tradition*. New York: Continuum, 1990. 112–129.

Woods, Gregory. "The City and the Pillar: Complete and Revised, With a Preface by the Author." *Times Literary Supplement*, 29 July 1994: 19.

The Season of Comfort

Aldridge, John W. "A Boy and His Mom." *Saturday Review of Literature*, 15 January 1949: 19–20.

Broderick, John. "Strong Start, Weak Finish." *New Yorker*, 15 January 1949: 67–68.

Rolo, Charles J. "Life With Mother." *Atlantic*, February 1949: 86.

Dark Green, Bright Red

Barr, Donald. "From Patio and Jungle." *New York Times Book Review*, 8 October 1950: 4, 28.

Kingery, Robert E. *Library Journal*, 1 October 1950: 1662.

Rolo, Charles J. "The Office; the Revolution." *Atlantic*, November 1950: 99–101.

Shrapnel, Norman. "New Novels." *Manchester Guardian*, 11 August 1950: 4.

A Search for the King

Langbaum, Robert E. "The Questing Hero." *Nation*, 15 April 1950: 352.

Lerman, Leo. "The Legend of Richard." *New York Times Book Review*, 15 January 1950: 4, 16.

Putnam, Samuel. "Animated Tapestry." *Saturday Review of Literature*, 14 January 1950: 10.

The Judgment of Paris

Aldridge, John W[atson]. "Three Tempted Him." *New York Times Book Review*, 9 March 1952: 4, 29.

Crane, Milton. "Plundered Myth." *Saturday Review*, 22 March 1952: 18.

[Warren, Robert Penn]. *New Republic*, 21 April 1952: 22.

Messiah

Davenport, John. "An East African Tragedy." *Observer*, 10 July 1955: 12.

Geismar, Maxwell. "Deadly Altar." *New York Times Book Review*, 25 April 1954: 4.

Knight, Damon. *In Search of Wonder: Essays on Modern Science Fiction*, rev. edn. Chicago: Advent Publishers, 1967. 175–176.

Stone, Jerome. "Frightening Future." *Saturday Review*, 22 May 1954: 34–35.

Ziolkowski, Theodore. *Fictional Transfigurations of Jesus*. Princeton: Princeton University Press, 1972. 250–257 and *passim*.

Julian

Allen, Walter. "The Last Pagan." *New York Review of Books*, 30 July 1964: 20–21.

Armstrong, David. "A Pagan Modern?" *Arion*, Winter 1964: 137–146.

Auchincloss, Louis. "The Best Man, Vintage 361 A.D." *Life*, 12 June 1964: 19, 21.

Barrett, William. "Death of the Gods." *Atlantic*, July 1964: 134–135.

Burgess, Anthony. "A Touch of the Apostasies." *Spectator*, 16 October 1964: 518.

Creation

Amiel, Barbara. *Maclean's*, 13 April 1981: 56.

Clemons, Walter. *Newsweek*, 20 April 1981: 90–91.

Duvall, Elizabeth. *Atlantic*, April 1981: 120–121.

Gray, Paul. *Time*, 30 March 1981: 83–84.

Holleran, Andrew. *New York*, 30 March 1981: 42.

La Salle, Peter. *America*, 23 May 1981: 429.

Murry, Oswyn. "Whoring After Strange Gods." *Times Literary Supplement*, 29 May 1981: 595.

Talmey, Allene. *Vogue*, May 1981: 42–43.

Burr

Ackroyd, Peter. "Blood, Thunder, and Gore." *Spectator*, 27 March 1976: 20.

Bardacke, Frances L. "The American Dream as Nightmare." *San Diego Magazine*, June 1976: 37–38.

Conrad, Peter. "Look at Us." *New Review*, July 1975: 63–66.

Dangerfield, George. "Less Than History and Less Than Fiction." *New York Times Book Review*, 28 October 1973: 2.

Dworkin, Ronald. "Ghost of America's Future." London *Sunday Times*, 24 March 1974: 40.

French, Philip. "Vice President." *New Statesman*, 22 March 1974: 415.

Hogarty, Ken. "Burr." *English Journal*, January 1989: 86.

Leonard, John. "Vidal—Another Opinion." *New York Times Book Review*, 28 October 1973: 55.

Maloff, Saul. "A Fiction of History." *New Republic*, 10 November 1973: 23–24.

Poirier, Richard. "The Heart Has Its Treasons." *Book World*, 28 October 1973: 3.

Lincoln

Clemons, Walter. "Gore Vidal's Chronicles of America: In 'Lincoln,' the Legendary Honest Abe Is Seen as a Tough and Shrewd Politician." *Newsweek*, 11 June 1984: 74–77.

Edwards, Owen Dudley. *History Today*, December 1984: 55.

———. "Fiction as History: On an Earlier President." *Encounter*, January 1985: 33–42.

Gray, Paul. *Time*, 21 May 1984: 87–88.

Holzer, Harold, Richard N. Current, and Gore Vidal. "Vidal's 'Lincoln': An Exchange." *New York Review of Books*, 18 August 1988: 66–69.

Howard, Maureen. *Yale Review*, Winter 1985: xvi.

Keneally, Thomas. *New Republic*, 2 July 1984: 32–34.

Koenig, Rhoda. *New York*, 18 June 1984: 74.

Milford, Nancy. *Vogue*, June 1984: 151.

Robertson, Heather. *Maclean's*, 2 July 1984: 54.

von Hoffman, Nicholas. *Nation*, 16 June 1984: 744–745.

Ward, Geoffrey C. *American Heritage*, August-September 1984: 18–19.

Woodward, C. Vann, and Gore Vidal. "Gore Vidal's 'Lincoln'?: An Exchange." *New York Review of Books*, 28 April 1988: 56–58.

1876

Ackroyd, Peter. "Blood, Thunder, and Gore." *Spectator*, 27 March 1976: 20.

Amiel, Barbara. "My Country, Wrong or Wrong." *Maclean's*, 5 April 1976: 72, 74.

Bardacke, Frances L. "The American Dream as Nightmare." *San Diego Magazine*, June 1976: 37–38.

Bradbury, Malcolm. "A Modern Mugwump." *Observer*, 21 March 1976: 31.

Breslin, Jimmy. "The Rule of Sentence." *Harper's Magazine*, March 1976: 106, 110–111.

Conrad, Peter. "Re-inventing America." *Times Literary Supplement*, 26 March 1976: 347–348.

Flower, Dean. "Fiction Chronicle." *Hudson Review*, Summer 1976: 270–282.

French, Philip. "Us and Them." *New Statesman*, 19 March 1976: 376.

Kaplan, Justin. "Halfway to the Bicentennial." *Saturday Review/World*, 6 March 1976: 24–25.

Lehmann-Haupt, Christopher. "Books of the Times." *New York Times*, 30 July 1976: 19C.

Empire

Baker, Brock. "*Empire*, the Novel." *New Criterion*, April 1988: 86–88.

Delbanco, Andrew. *New Republic*, 14 September 1987: 49–54.

Gates, David. *Newsweek*, 15 June 1987: 70.

Geeslin, Campbell. *People Weekly*, 22 June 1987: 17–18.

Gray, Paul. *Time*, 22 June 1987: 73–74.

Hemesath, James B. *Library Journal*, July 1987: 99.

Kaplan, Justin. *New York Times Book Review*, 14 June 1987: 1.

Kellman, Steven G. *USA Today* (Magazine), November 1987: 94–95.

Koenig, Rhoda. *New York*, 8 June 1987: 72–73.

Leader, Zachary. "Myra Breckinridge and Myron." *Times Literary Supplement*, 20 November 1989: 1272.

Poirier, Richard. *New York Review of Books*, 24 September 1987: 31–33.

Waldman, Steven. *Washington Monthly*, September 1987: 45–48.

Hollywood

Auchincloss, Louis. *New York Review of Books*, 29 March 1990: 20–22.

Conarroe, Joel. *New York Times Book Review*, 21 January 1990: 1.

Davis, Clive. *New Statesman & Society*, 3 November 1989: 35–36.

Gabler, Neal. *Vogue*, February 1990: 212–214.

Pritchard, William H. *Hudson Review*, Autumn 1990: 489–497.

Skow, John. *Time*, 12 February 1990: 66.

Snider, Norman. *Maclean's*, 5 March 1990: 63.

Steinberg, Sybil. *Publishers Weekly*, 15 December 1989: 56.

Wood, Michael. *Times Literary Supplement*, 10 November 1989: 1243.

Washington, D.C.

Ackroyd, Peter. "Blood, Thunder, and Gore." *Spectator*, 27 March 1976: 20.

Bardacke, Frances L. "The American Dream as Nightmare." *San Diego Magazine*, June 1976: 37–38.

Greenfield, Josh. "A Skeleton in Every Closet." *New York Times Book Review*, 30 April 1967: 4, 45.

Lehan, Richard. "Fiction, 1967." *Contemporary Literature*, Autumn 1968: 538–553.

Sheed, Wilfred. "Affairs of State." *Commentary*, September 1967: 93–94.

Weeks, Edward. "Inside 'Inside Washington.' " *Atlantic*, August 1967: 98–99.

Two Sisters

Enright, D. J. "A Mirror in the Form of a Book." *Listener*, 24 September 1970: 416.

Epstein, Joseph. "A Scandalmonger's Oversight." *Book World*, 5 July 1970: 1, 3.

Gold, Herbert. "Why 'I'?" *Saturday Review/World*, 8 February 1975: 18–21.

Myra Breckinridge

Edel, Leon. "Books I Liked Best in 1968." *Book World*, 1 December 1968: 4.

Fremont-Smith, Eliot. "Like Fay Wray If the Light Is Right." *New York Times*, 3 February 1968: 27.

Hentoff, Margot. "Growing Up Androgynous." *New York Review of Books*, 9 May 1968: 32–33.

Leader, Zachary. "Myra Breckinridge and Myron." *Times Literary Supplement*, 20 November 1989: 1272.

Nichols, Lewis. "Underground." *New York Times Book Review*, 28 January 1968: 32.

Stimpson, Catharine R. "My O My O Myra." *New England Review*, Fall 1991: 102–13. Rpt. In Parini, pp. 183–198.

Myron

Conrad, Peter. "Look at Us." *New Review*, July 1975: 63–66.

Leader, Zachary. "Myra Breckinridge and Myron." *Times Literary Supplement*, 20 November 1989: 1272.

Pritchard, William H. "Novel Sex and Violence." *Hudson Review*, Spring 1975: 147–160.

Stimpson, Catharine R. "My O My O Myra." *New England Review*, Fall 1991: 102–13. Rpt. In Parini, pp. 183–198.

Kalki

Berryman, Charles. "Satire in Vidal's *Kalki*." *Critique: Studies in Modern Fiction*, 1980: 88–96.

King, Francis. *Spectator*, 22 April 1978: 23.

Staley, Thomas F. *Southern Review*, Summer 1979: 702.

Williams, David. *Punch*, 29 August 1979: 338.

Duluth

Beatty, Jack. *New Republic*, 30 May 1983: 37–38.

Crowley, John W. "A Winter in Duluth: Gore Vidal and W. D. Howells." *Notes on Contemporary Literature*, September 1988: 4–5.

Fletcher, M. D. "Vidal's *Duluth* as 'Post-Modern' Political Satire." *Ihalia: Studies in Literary Humor*, Spring-Summer 1986: 10–21.

Koenig, Rhoda. *New York*, 6 June 1983: 55.

Prescott, Peter S. *Newsweek*, 23 May 1983: 77–78.

Sheppard, R. Z. *Time*, 13 June 1983: 76.

Live from Golgotha

Clifford, Andrew. *New Scientist*, 2 January 1993: 42.

Davis, Robert Gorham. *Free Inquiry*, Spring 1993: 55–57.

Dawidoff, Robert. *Advocate*, 25 August 1992: 81.

Disch, Thomas M. *Nation*, 16 November 1992: 606–608.

Drake, Robert. *Lambda Book Report*, January-February 1993: 35–37.

Gates, David. *Newsweek*, 31 August 1992: 69.

Johnson, Diane. *New York Review of Books*, 8 April 1993: 24–26.

Kazin, Alfred. *New Republic*, 5 October 1992: 36–37.

Kennedy, Douglas. *New Statesman & Society*, 6 November 1992: 50.

Klinghoffer, David. *National Review*, 30 November 1992: 50–52.

Korn, Eric. *Times Literary Supplement*, 2 October 1992: 20.

Krist, Gary. *Hudson Review*, Spring 1993: 240–246.

Malin, Irving. *Commonweal*, 6 November 1992: 38–39.

Neilson, Heather. "*Live from Golgotha*: Gore Vidal's Second 'Fifth Gospel.' " *LiNQ*, October 1995: 79–91.

Samway, Patrick H. *America*, 16 January 1993: 18–19.

Sheed, Wilfrid. *New Yorker*, 26 October 1992: 130–34.

Thomas, D. M. *New York Times Book Review*, 4 October 1992: 13.

Weales, Gerald. "Jesus Who?" *Gettysburg Review*, Autumn 1993: 688–696.

OTHER SECONDARY SOURCES

Ashley, Bob. *The Study of Popular Fiction: A Source Book*. London: Pinter, 1989.

Bair, Deidre. *Anaïs Nin: A Biography*. New York: G. P. Putnam's Sons, 1995.

Bakhtin, M. M. *The Dialogic Imagination: Four Essays*. Ed., Michael Holquist, trans. Caryl Emerson and Michael Holquist. Austin: University of Texas Press, 1981.

Bender, Bert. *Sea-Brothers: The Tradition of American Sea Fiction from "Moby Dick" to the Present*. Philadelphia: University of Pennsylvania Press, 1988.

Bourgeau, Art. *The Mystery Lover's Companion*. New York: Crown, 1986.

Cawelti, John G. "The Concept of Formula in the Study of Popular Literature." Excerpted in Bob Ashley, *The Study of Popular Fiction: A Source Book*. London: Pinter, 1989.

Dekker, George. *The American Historical Romance*. Cambridge: Cambridge University Press, 1987.

Donald, David Herbert. *Lincoln*. New York: Simon & Schuster, 1995.

Fitch, Noël Riley. *Anaïs: The Erotic Life of Anaïs Nin*. New York: Little, Brown, 1993.

Fleishman, Avrom. *The English Historical Novel: Walter Scott to Virginia Woolf*. Baltimore: Johns Hopkins University Press, 1971.

Foucault, Michel. "What Is an Author?" In Josue V. Harari, ed. and trans., *Textual Strategies: Perspectives in Post-Structuralist Criticism*. Ithaca: Cornell University Press, 1979: 141–60.

Freud, Sigmund. *A General Introduction to Psychoanalysis*. New York: Pocket Books, 1952.

———. *The Interpretation of Dreams*. New York: Avon, 1965.

Grun, Bernard. *The Timetables of History: A Horizontal Linkage of People and Events*, rev. edn. New York: Simon and Schuster, 1982.

Hanchett, William. *The Lincoln Murder Conspiracies*. Urbana: University of Illinois Press, 1986.

Henderson, Harry B. *Versions of the Past: The Historical Imagination in American Fiction*. New York: Oxford University Press, 1974.

Hunt, Lynn, ed. *The New Cultural History*. Berkeley and Los Angeles: University of California Press, 1989.

Mizruchi, Susan L. *The Power of Historical Knowledge: Narrating the Past in Hawthorne, James, and Dreiser*. Princeton: Princeton University Press, 1988.

Orel, Harold. *The Historical Novel from Scott to Sabatini: Changing Attitudes Toward a Literary Genre, 1814–1920*. New York: St. Martin's, 1995.

Peterson, Merrill D. *Lincoln in American Memory*. Oxford: Oxford University Press, 1994.

Radway, Janice A. *Reading the Romance: Women, Patriarchy, and Popular Literature*. Chapel Hill: University of North Carolina Press, 1984.

Scholes, Robert. *Fabulation and Metafiction*. Urbana: University of Illinois Press, 1979.

Trager, James. *The People's Chronology: A Year-by-Year Account of Human Events from Prehistory to the Present*, rev. edn. New York: Henry Holt, 1992.

Veeser, H. Aram. *The New Historicism*. London: Routledge, 1989.

———. *The New Historicism Reader*. London: Routledge, 1994.

White, Hayden. *Metahistory: The Historical Imagination in Nineteenth-Century Europe*. Baltimore: Johns Hopkins University Press, 1973.

———. *Tropics of Discourse: Essays in Cultural Criticism*. Baltimore: Johns Hopkins University Press, 1978.

Index

About the Authors

SUSAN BAKER is Professor of English at the University of Nevada in Reno. She is coeditor (with Dorothea Kehler) of *In Another Country: Feminist Perspectives on Renaissance Drama* (1991) and is completing a book-length study of Shakespeare in detective fiction.

CURTIS S. GIBSON, her husband, is a nonacademic enthusiast of Gore Vidal's work. Both Baker and Gibson have essays forthcoming in *St. James Guide to Crime and Mystery Writers* (4th Edition).

Recent Titles in
Critical Companions to Popular Contemporary Writers
Kathleen Gregory Klein, Series Editor